TABLE OF CONTENTS

IN+R⊕DUC+I⊕N

Here's what has come before. Jackie Estacado, better known as The Darkness, took over the Central American country of Sierra Muñoz. Jackie aligned himself with Professor Kirchner, whom he allowed to live in order for the Professor to study him to learn more about the Darkness. He became the reigning drug lord over the country by peddling a highly addictive drug known as Nightfall that was chemically engineered from the Darkness power itself. Professor Kirchner's plans unfolded when Jackie's manufactured love slave becomes pregnant. Jackie then began to lose control of his darklings as well as his absolute reign over the Darkness power. In a weakened state, he fell into the hands of a resistance force that had vowed to kill him. Jackie then helped the resistance in fulfilling the promise to end the cartel. The child that was growing inside of his love slave quickly cut himself away from her and faced his father. Jackie had to battle his fully grown and cocky son born of pure Darkness. Jackie, however, was too smart for his offspring and he killed his foolish, hybrid-born son. With much of his control over the Darkness gone, and his darklings turned against him, Jackie was left to figure out how to gain control of his Darkness once again.

Jackie, abandoned by the Darkness, found himself in a town controlled by two witches: a mother and a daughter that fed off people's dreams. The mother, known as the witch of the wall, tried to steal Jackie's dreams and quickly discovered she bit off more than she could chew. On his way back to New York, Jackie stumbled into a losing battle against Aphrodite IV. She transported him to the Sovereign, and it's there that Jackie made the deal with the Sovereign to do his bidding in exchange for getting the full powers of the Darkness back, which he discovers to be a lie. After that, Jackie paid a fortune teller and saw a disturbing glimpse of his death in the future at the hands of the Magdalena.

In this volume you hold in your hands, we catch up with Jackie following a mysterious woman with a red scarf who leads him into an encounter with an ageless former wielder of the Darkness known only as the Foreigner. The man convinces Jackie that he's always been in control of his power, and that it's only Jackie who can restore the powers of the Darkness and not the Sovereign. Now a confident Jackie at full strength pays a visit to the Sovereign. Taking out many of his men, the Sovereign is no match for the Darkness. Forcing the Sovereign to flee with the promise of another meeting, Jackie now decides it's time to enlist his own organization to counter the Sovereign's next move. With all of his pieces in place, Jackie is back in his comfort zone as a modern mobster...back to doing what he does best.

My love for *The Darkness* began when I first took notice of it at a comic book store in Illinois a few years back. I was searching the rack for something new and unique. I saw the cover and what seemed at the time to be a *Witchblade* vs. *The Darkness* crossover. While I recognized *Witchblade* from the work with Image Comics years before, I didn't recognize *The Darkness*. I was curious to find out who this Darkness character was. I also saw another cover featuring *The Darkness* and *Tomb Raider* Lara Croft. After reading these two comics with the Darkness, I had found another character to follow. I fell in love with the storyline and became a diehard fan but didn't become a true fan-for-life until after I saw *The Darkness/Superman* crossover covers. Jackie is a character I can relate to because he has to juggle countless problems and he isn't perfect. I hope you'll discover the same appreciation for *The Darkness* in this volume.

--**Lance Briggs**
March 20010

Lance Briggs has been with the Chicago Bears since the 2003 NFL draft. He is a five times Pro Bowl selected player. He has been an avid comic fan long before becoming a NFL superstar .

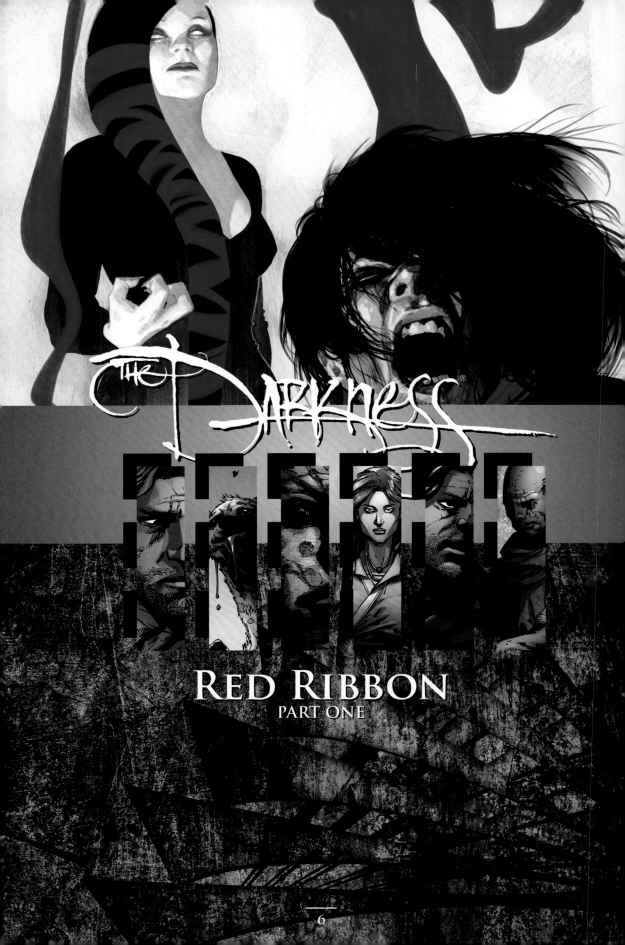

THE DARKNESS

RED RIBBON
PART ONE

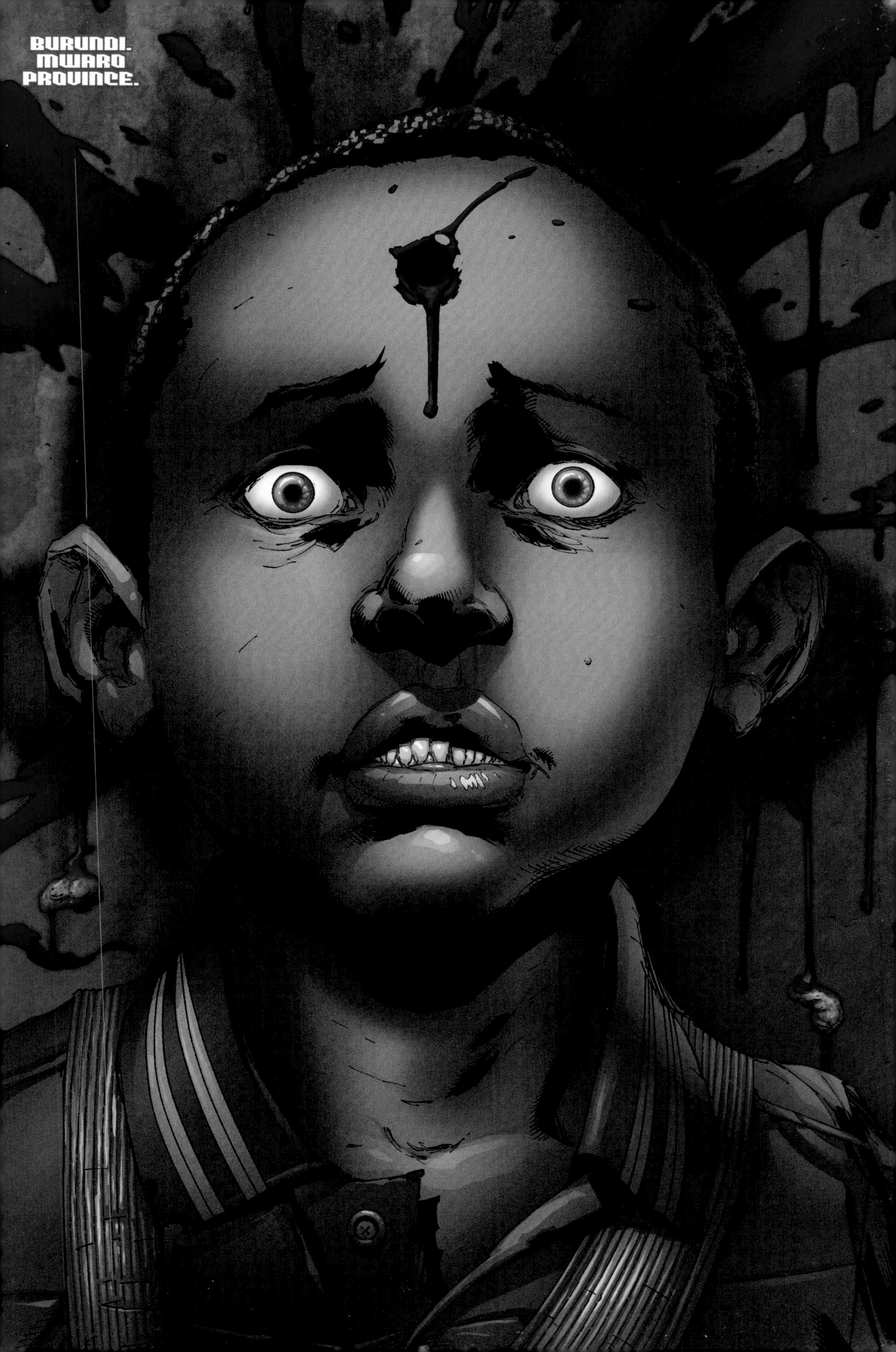
BURUNDI.
MWARO
PROVINCE.

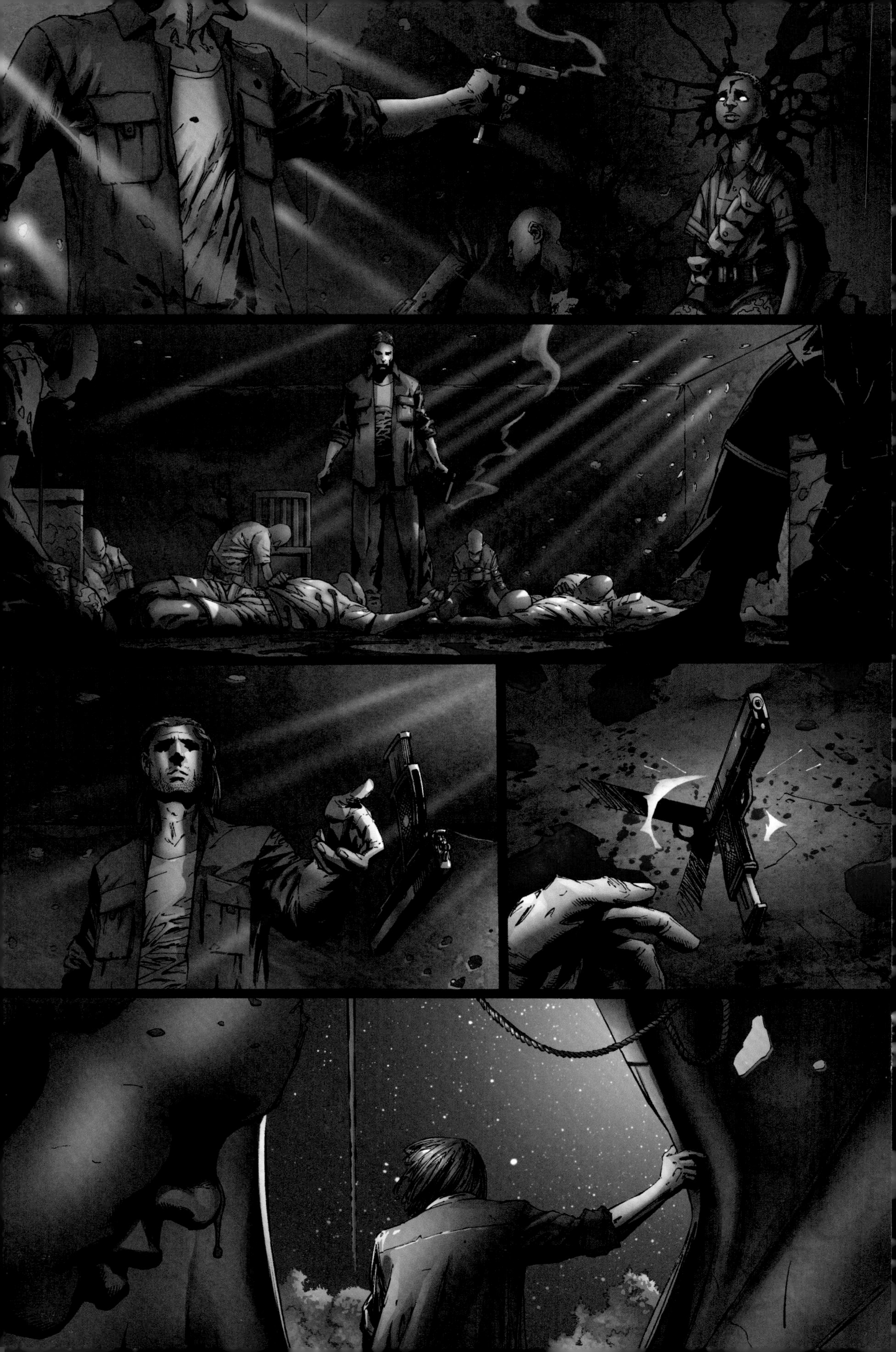

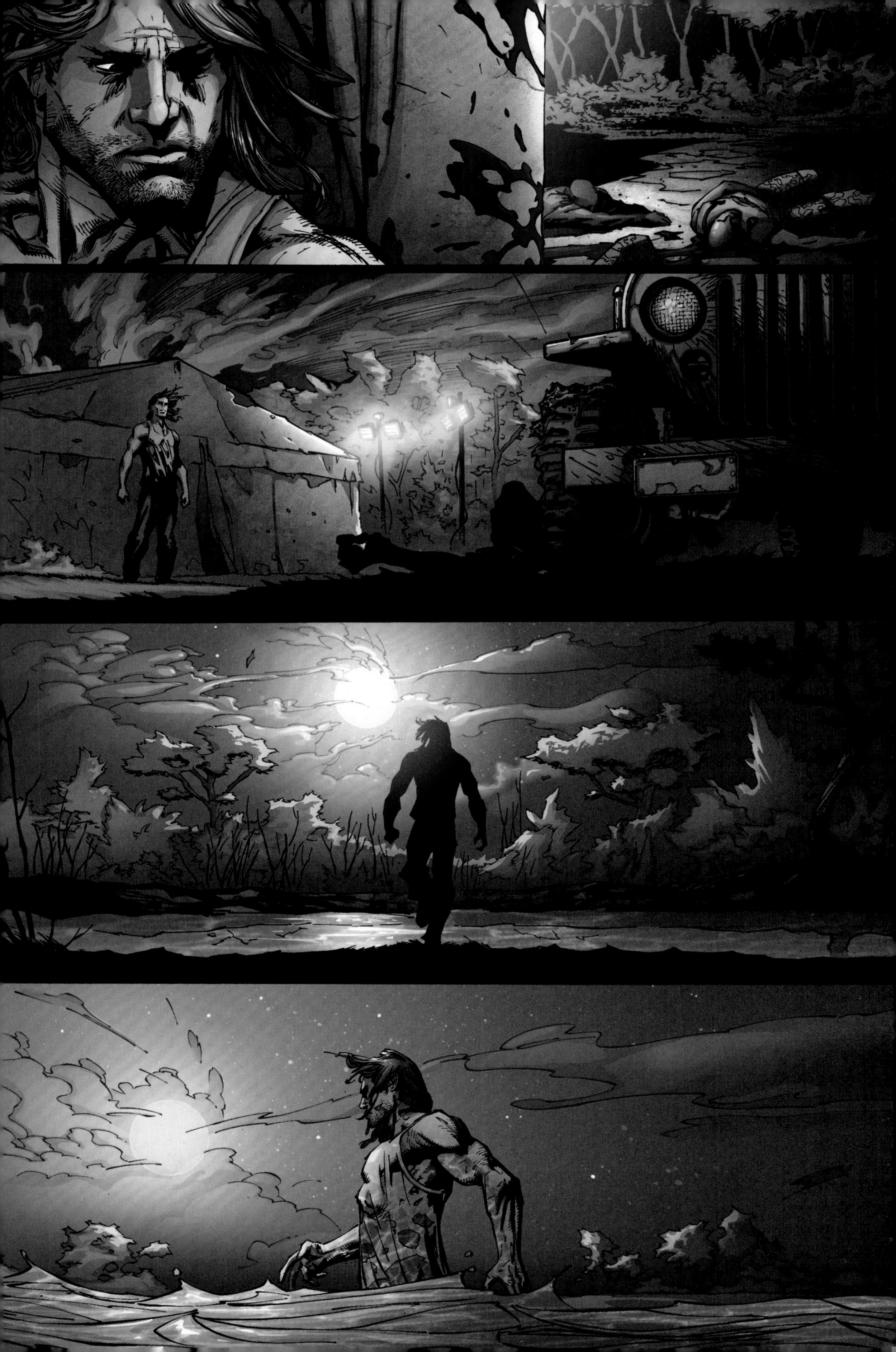

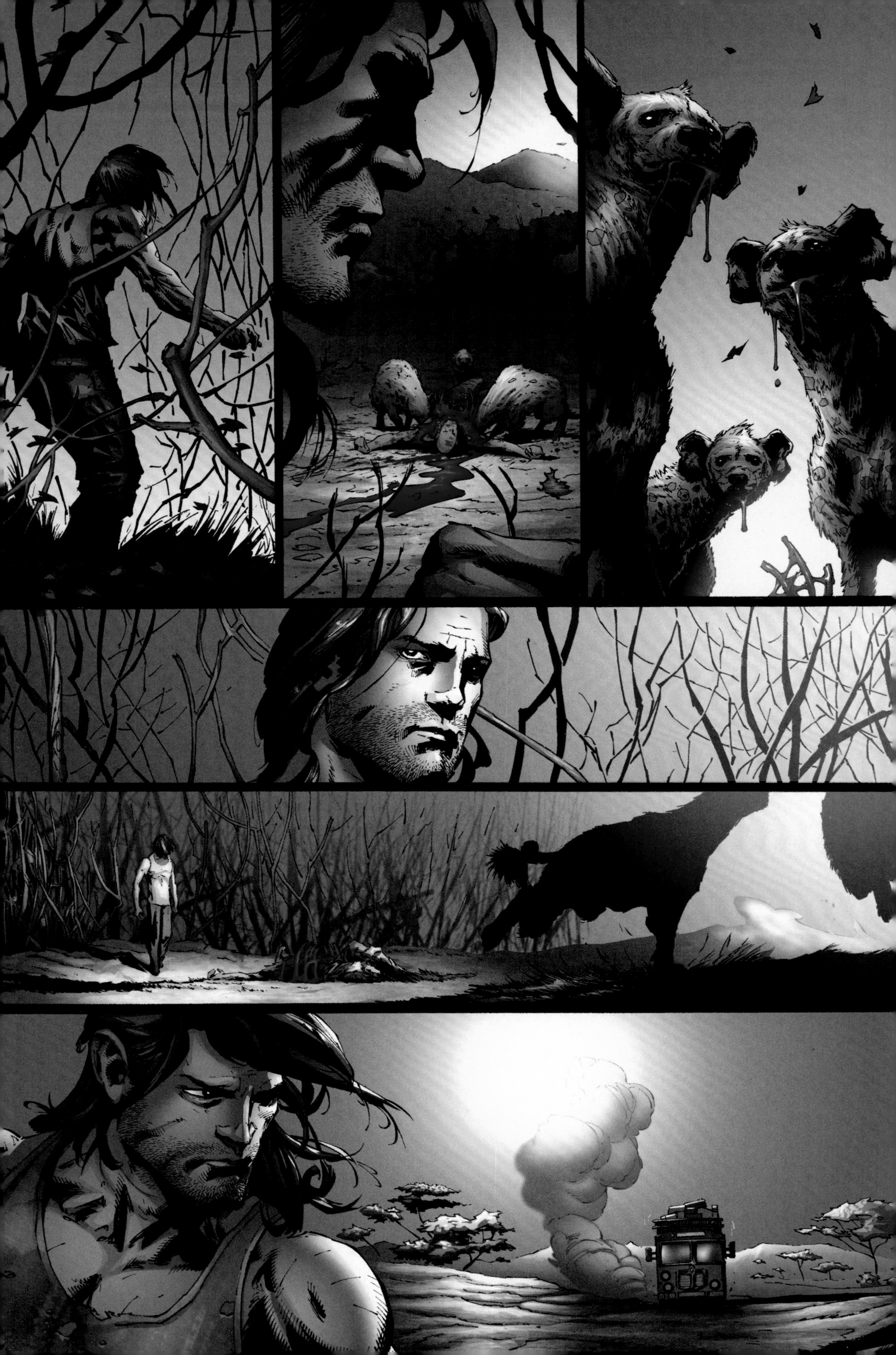

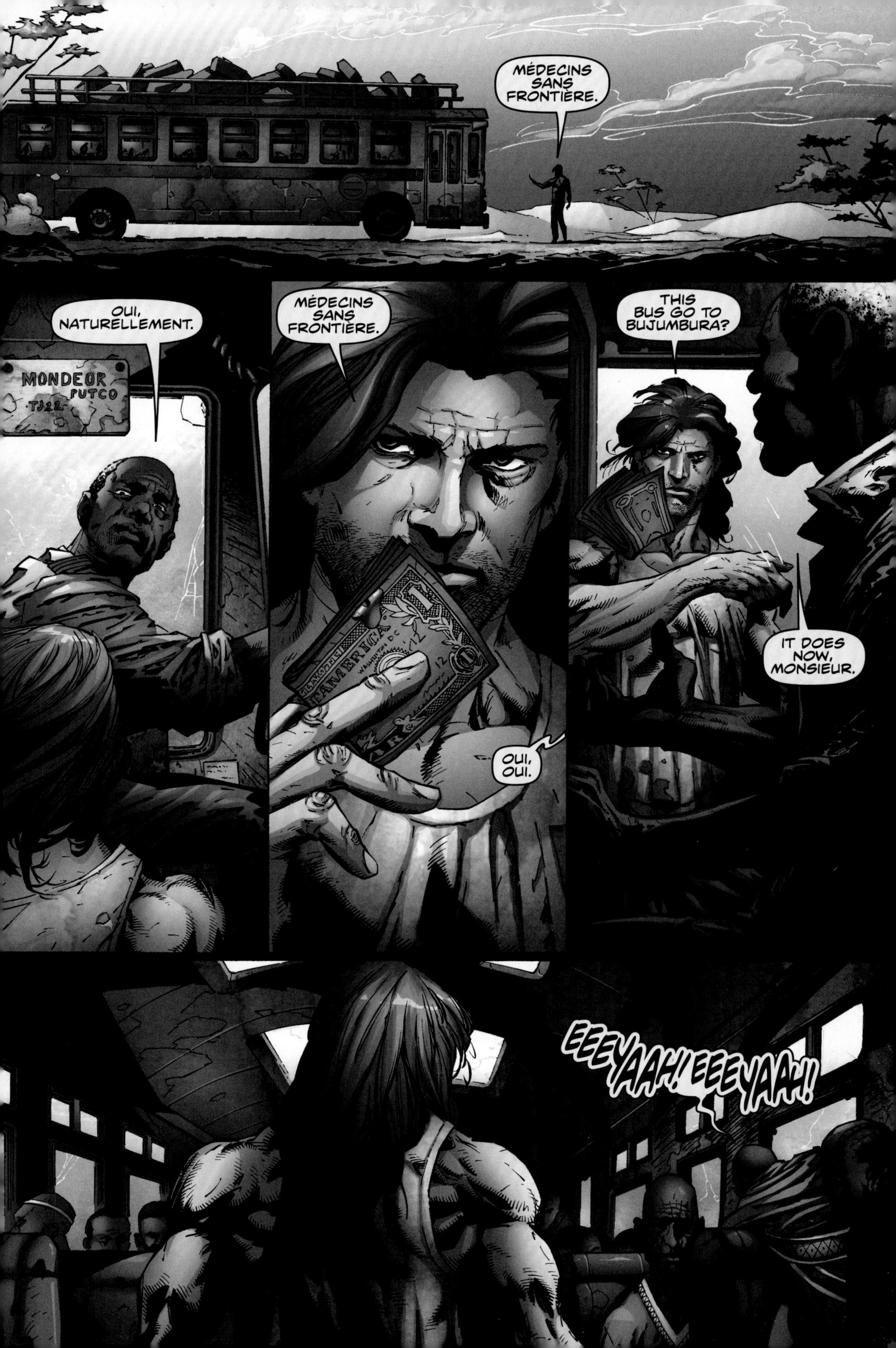
MÉDECINS SANS FRONTIÈRE.
MONDEOR PUTCO TJ22
OUI, NATURELLEMENT.
MÉDECINS SANS FRONTIÈRE.
OUI, OUI.
THIS BUS GO TO BUJUMBURA?
IT DOES NOW, MONSIEUR.
EEEYAAH! EEEYAAH!

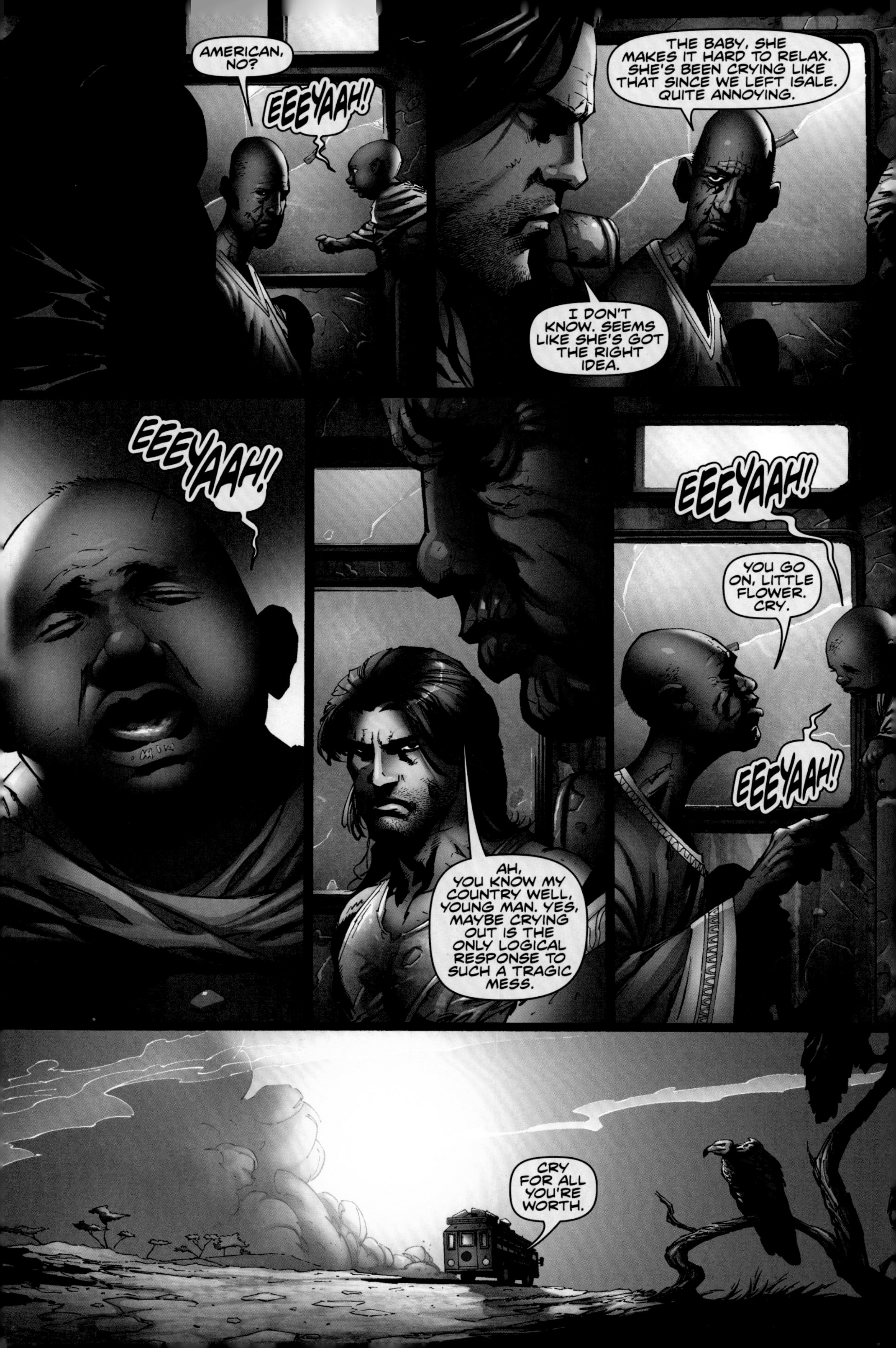
AMERICAN, NO?
EEEYAAH!
THE BABY, SHE MAKES IT HARD TO RELAX. SHE'S BEEN CRYING LIKE THAT SINCE WE LEFT ISALE. QUITE ANNOYING.
I DON'T KNOW. SEEMS LIKE SHE'S GOT THE RIGHT IDEA.
EEEYAAH!
AH, YOU KNOW MY COUNTRY WELL, YOUNG MAN. YES, MAYBE CRYING OUT IS THE ONLY LOGICAL RESPONSE TO SUCH A TRAGIC MESS.
EEEYAAH!
YOU GO ON, LITTLE FLOWER. CRY.
EEEYAAH!
CRY FOR ALL YOU'RE WORTH.

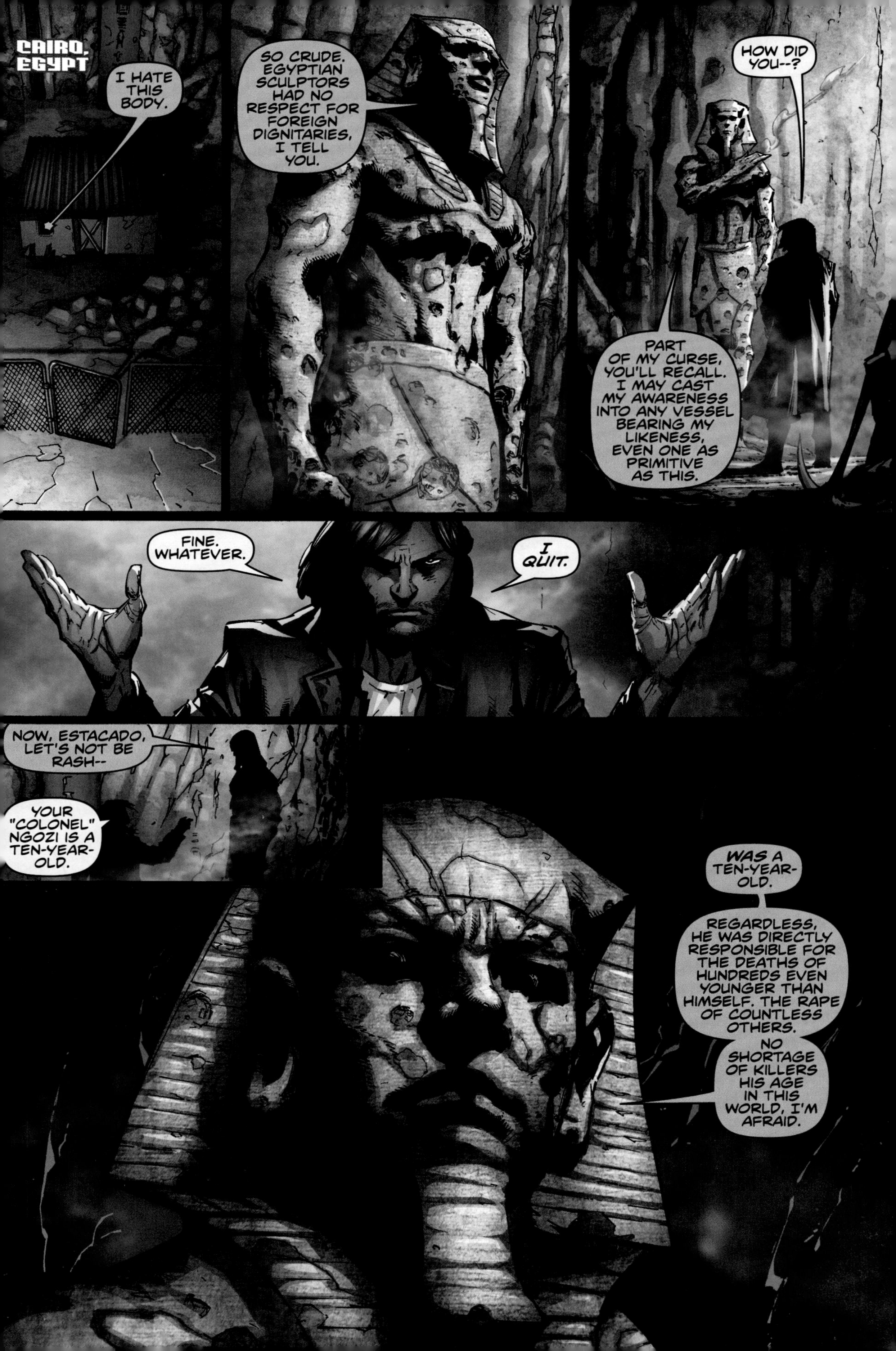
CAIRO, EGYPT
I HATE THIS BODY.
SO CRUDE. EGYPTIAN SCULPTORS HAD NO RESPECT FOR FOREIGN DIGNITARIES, I TELL YOU.
HOW DID YOU--?
PART OF MY CURSE, YOU'LL RECALL. I MAY CAST MY AWARENESS INTO ANY VESSEL BEARING MY LIKENESS, EVEN ONE AS PRIMITIVE AS THIS.
FINE. WHATEVER.
I QUIT.
NOW, ESTACADO, LET'S NOT BE RASH--
YOUR "COLONEL" NGOZI IS A TEN-YEAR-OLD.
WAS A TEN-YEAR-OLD.
REGARDLESS, HE WAS DIRECTLY RESPONSIBLE FOR THE DEATHS OF HUNDREDS EVEN YOUNGER THAN HIMSELF. THE RAPE OF COUNTLESS OTHERS.
NO SHORTAGE OF KILLERS HIS AGE IN THIS WORLD, I'M AFRAID.

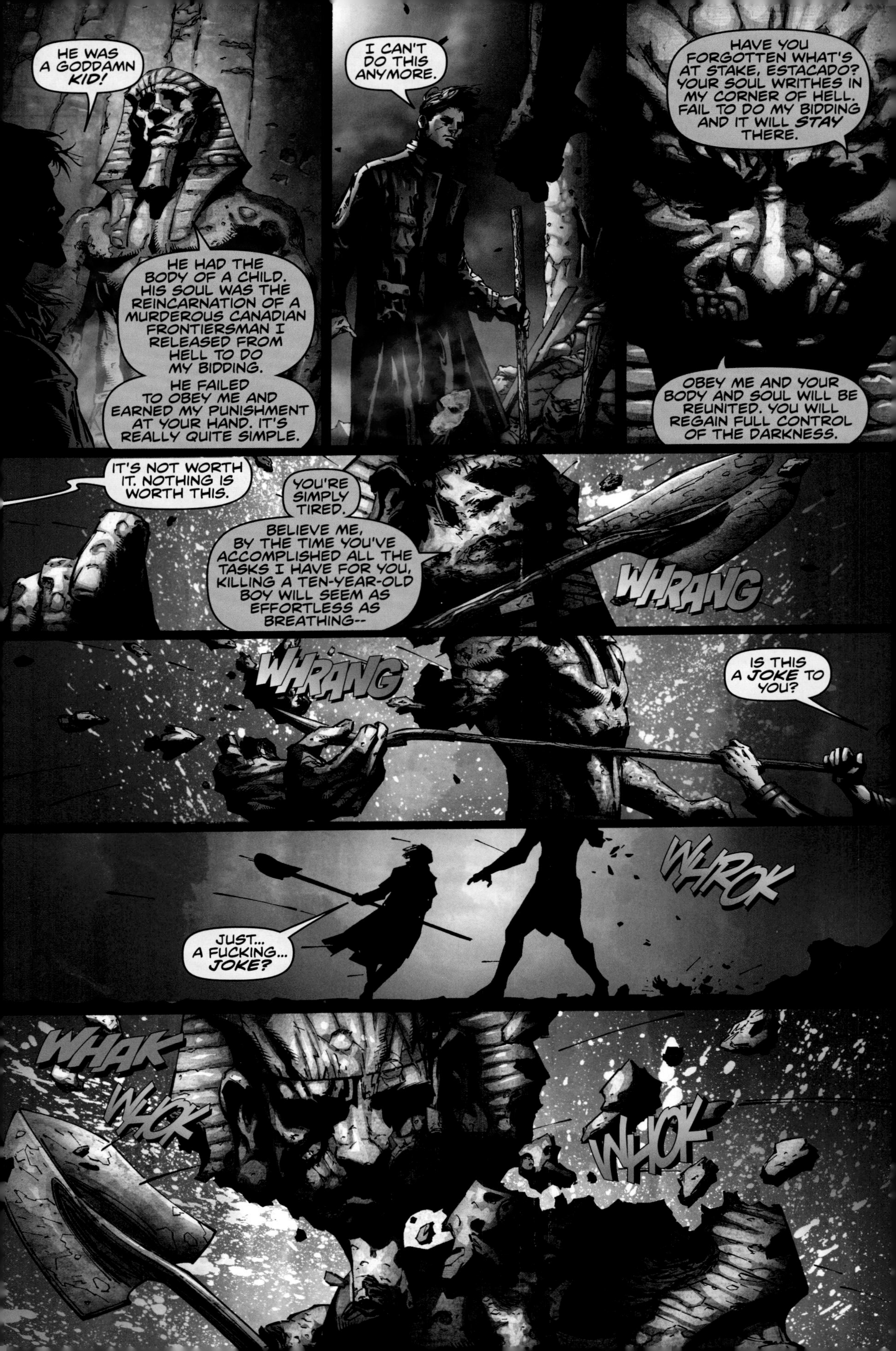
HE WAS A GODDAMN *KID!*
HE HAD THE BODY OF A CHILD. HIS SOUL WAS THE REINCARNATION OF A MURDEROUS CANADIAN FRONTIERSMAN I RELEASED FROM HELL TO DO MY BIDDING.
HE FAILED TO OBEY ME AND EARNED MY PUNISHMENT AT YOUR HAND. IT'S REALLY QUITE SIMPLE.
I CAN'T DO THIS ANYMORE.
HAVE YOU FORGOTTEN WHAT'S AT STAKE, ESTACADO? YOUR SOUL WRITHES IN MY CORNER OF HELL. FAIL TO DO MY BIDDING AND IT WILL *STAY* THERE.
OBEY ME AND YOUR BODY AND SOUL WILL BE REUNITED. YOU WILL REGAIN FULL CONTROL OF THE DARKNESS.
IT'S NOT WORTH IT. NOTHING IS WORTH THIS.
YOU'RE SIMPLY TIRED.
BELIEVE ME, BY THE TIME YOU'VE ACCOMPLISHED ALL THE TASKS I HAVE FOR YOU, KILLING A TEN-YEAR-OLD BOY WILL SEEM AS EFFORTLESS AS BREATHING--
WHRANG
WHRANG
IS THIS A *JOKE* TO YOU?
WHROK
JUST... A FUCKING... *JOKE?*
WHAK
WHOK
WHOK

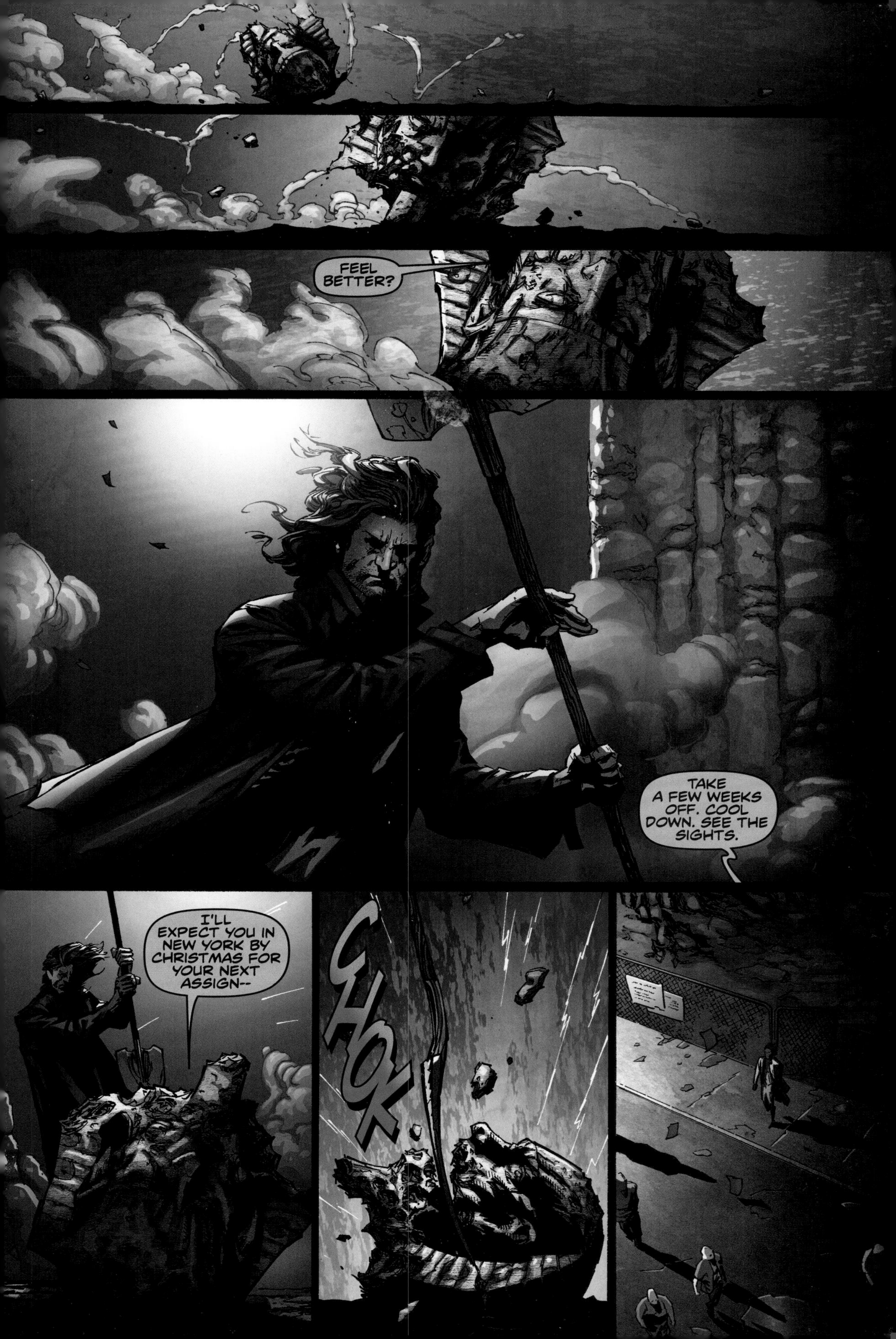
FEEL BETTER?
TAKE A FEW WEEKS OFF. COOL DOWN. SEE THE SIGHTS.
I'LL EXPECT YOU IN NEW YORK BY CHRISTMAS FOR YOUR NEXT ASSIGN--
CHOK

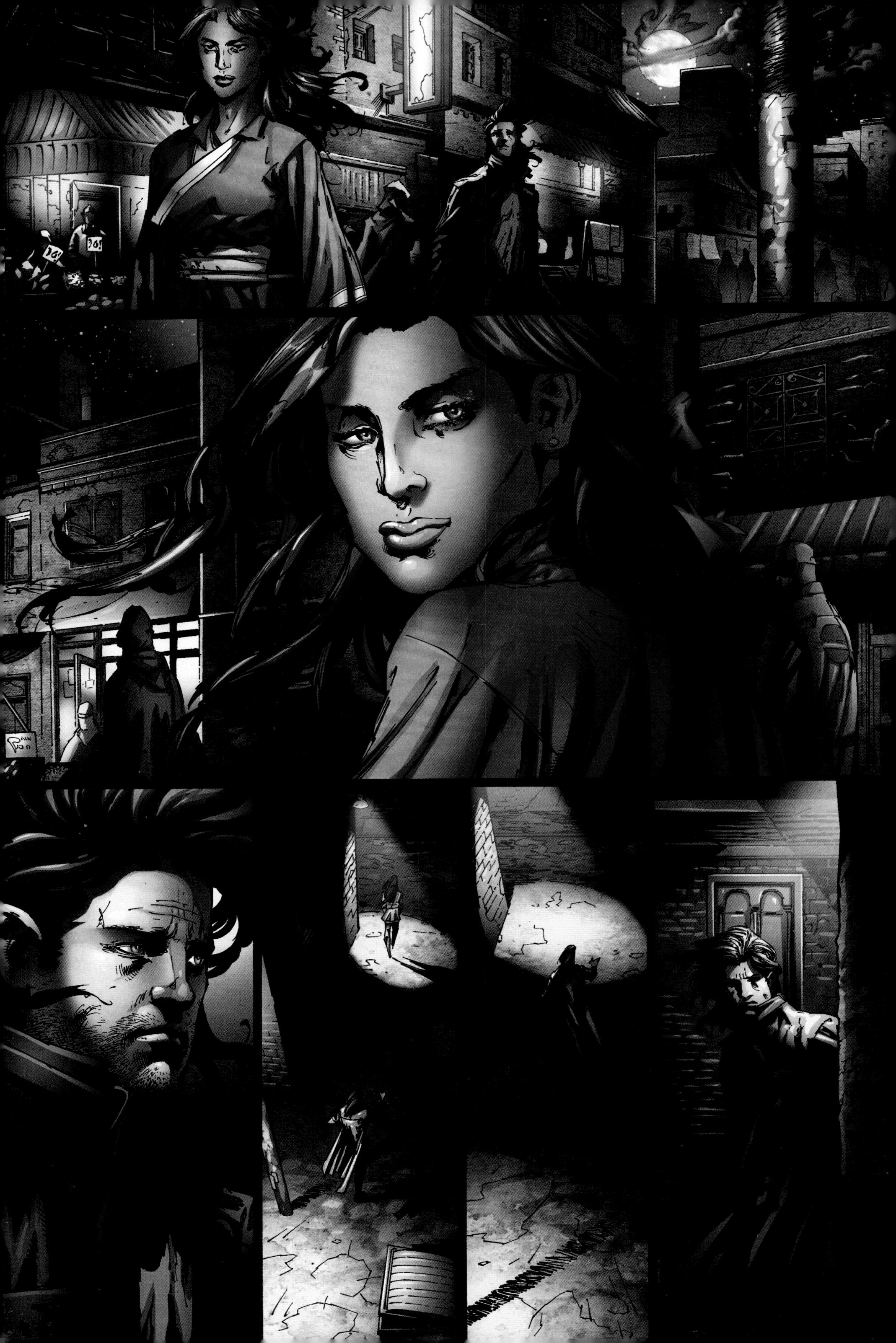

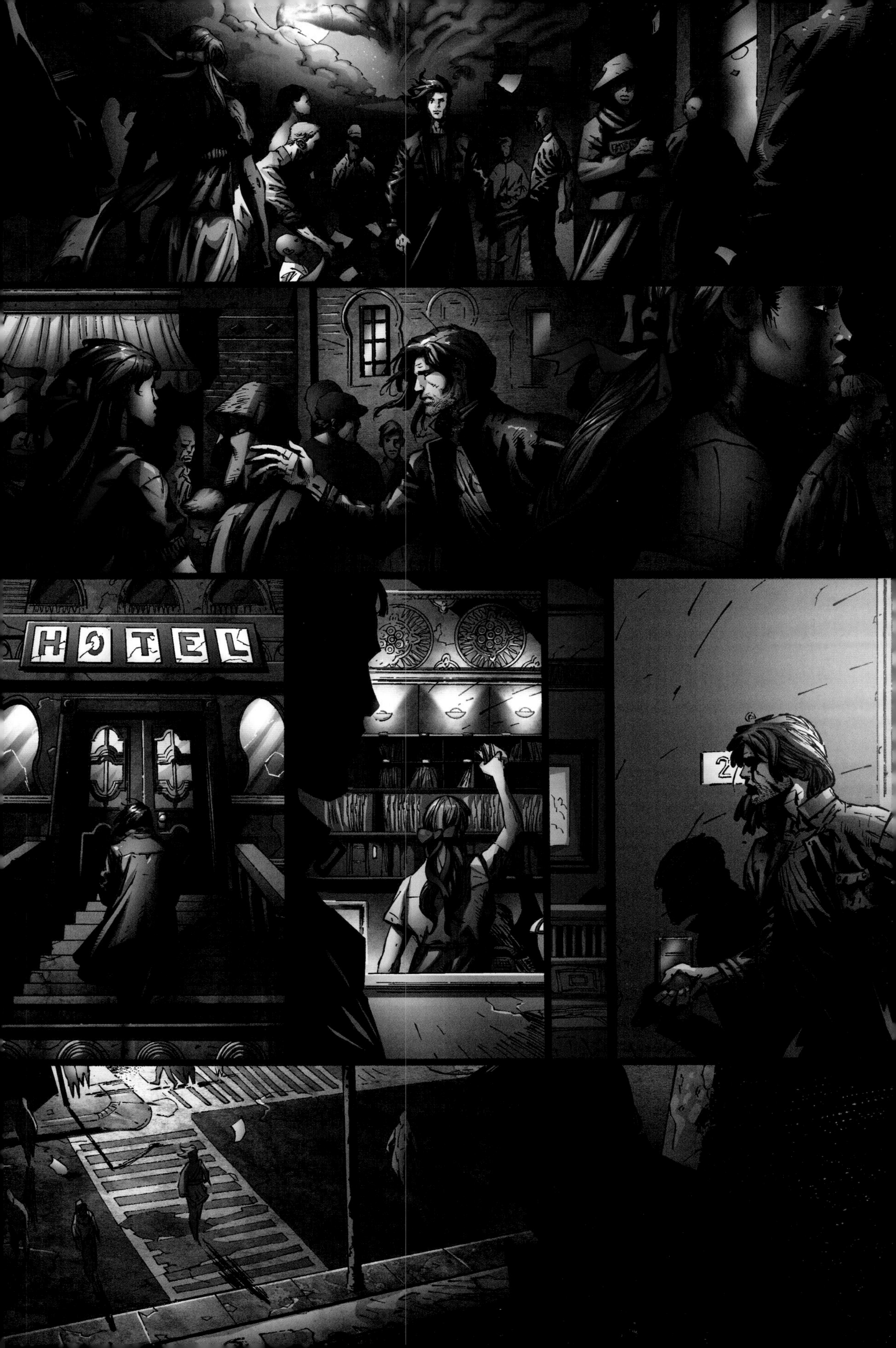
HOTEL

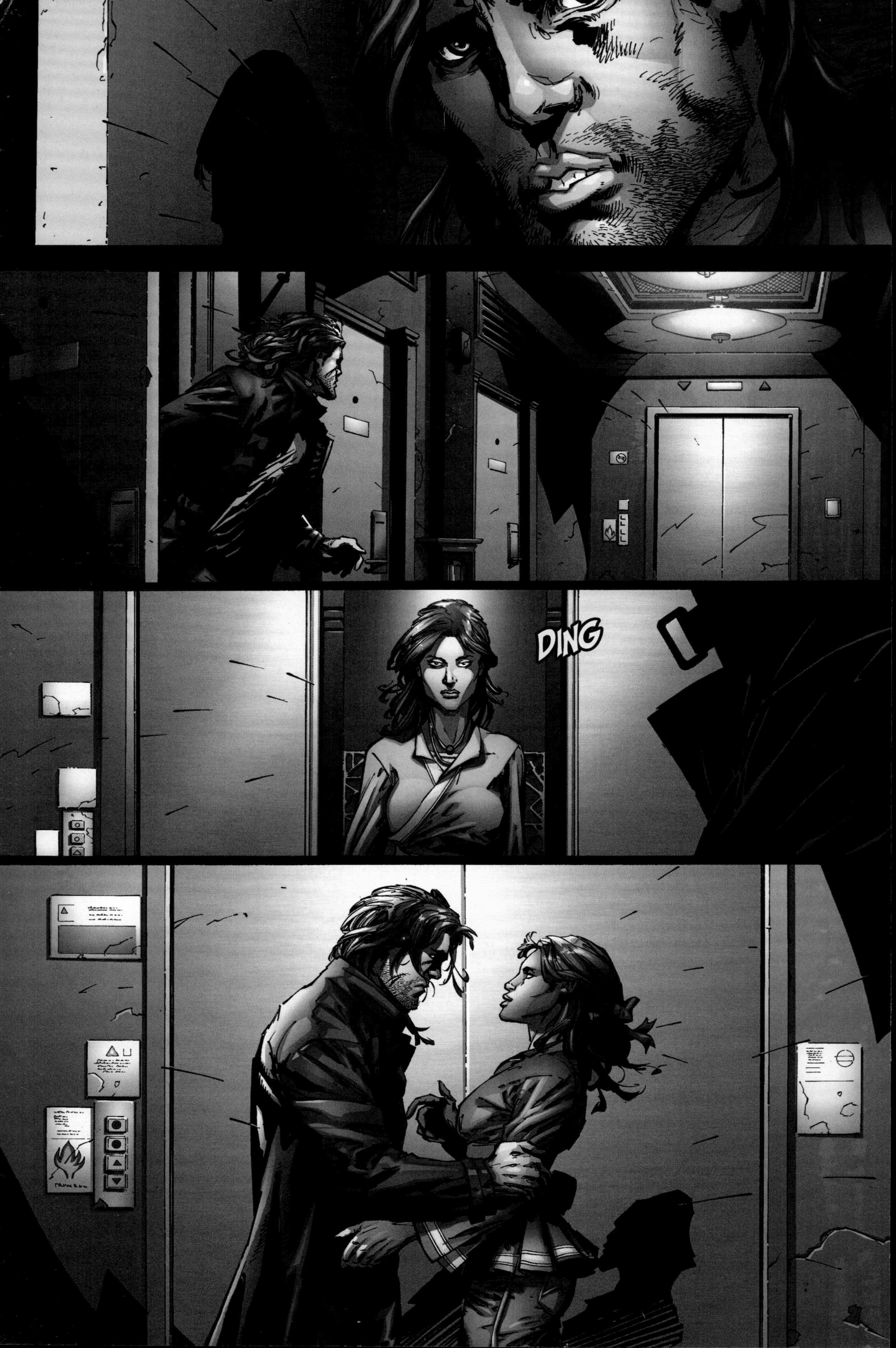
DING

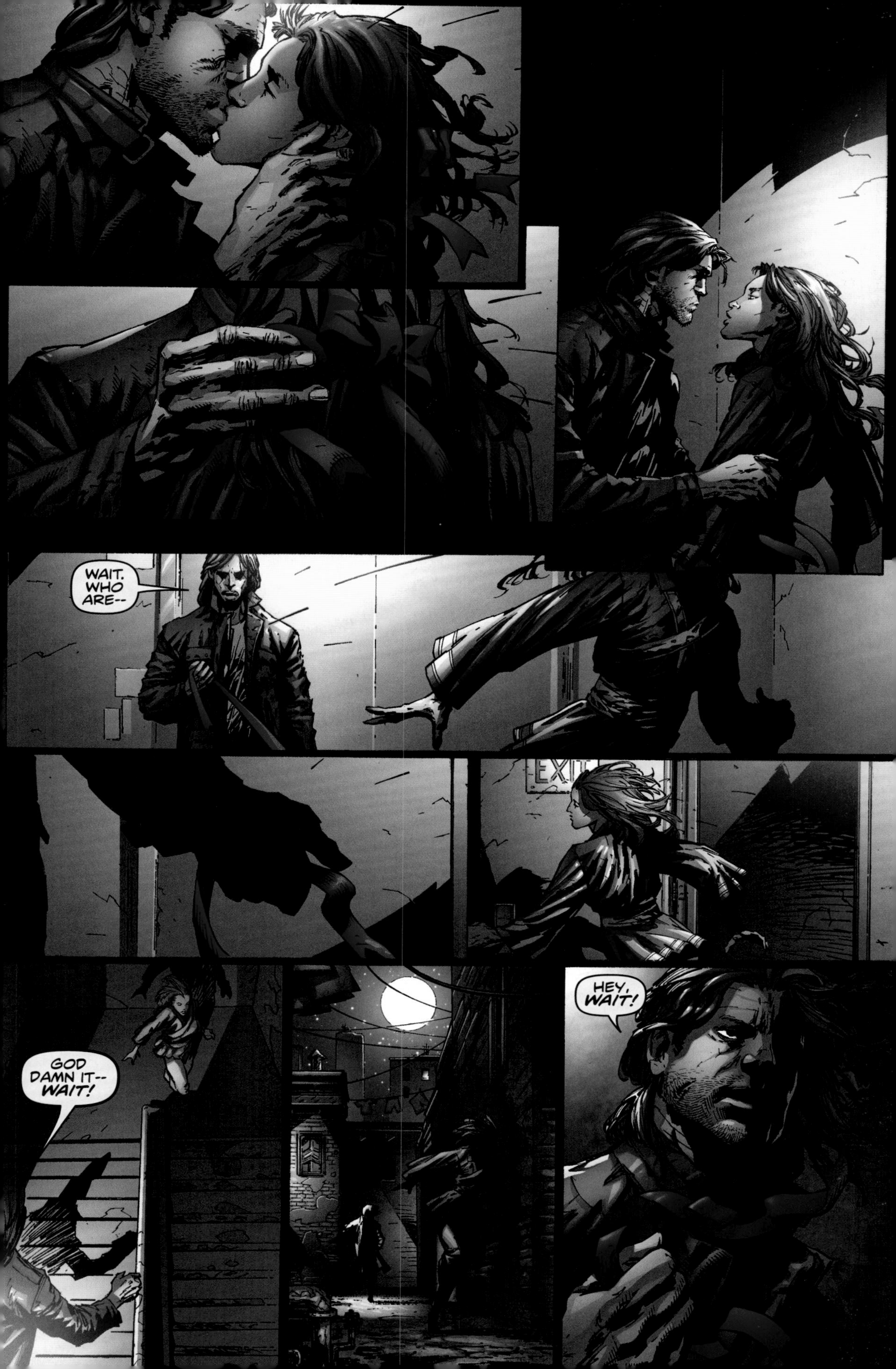
WAIT. WHO ARE--
HEY, WAIT!
GOD DAMN IT-- WAIT!

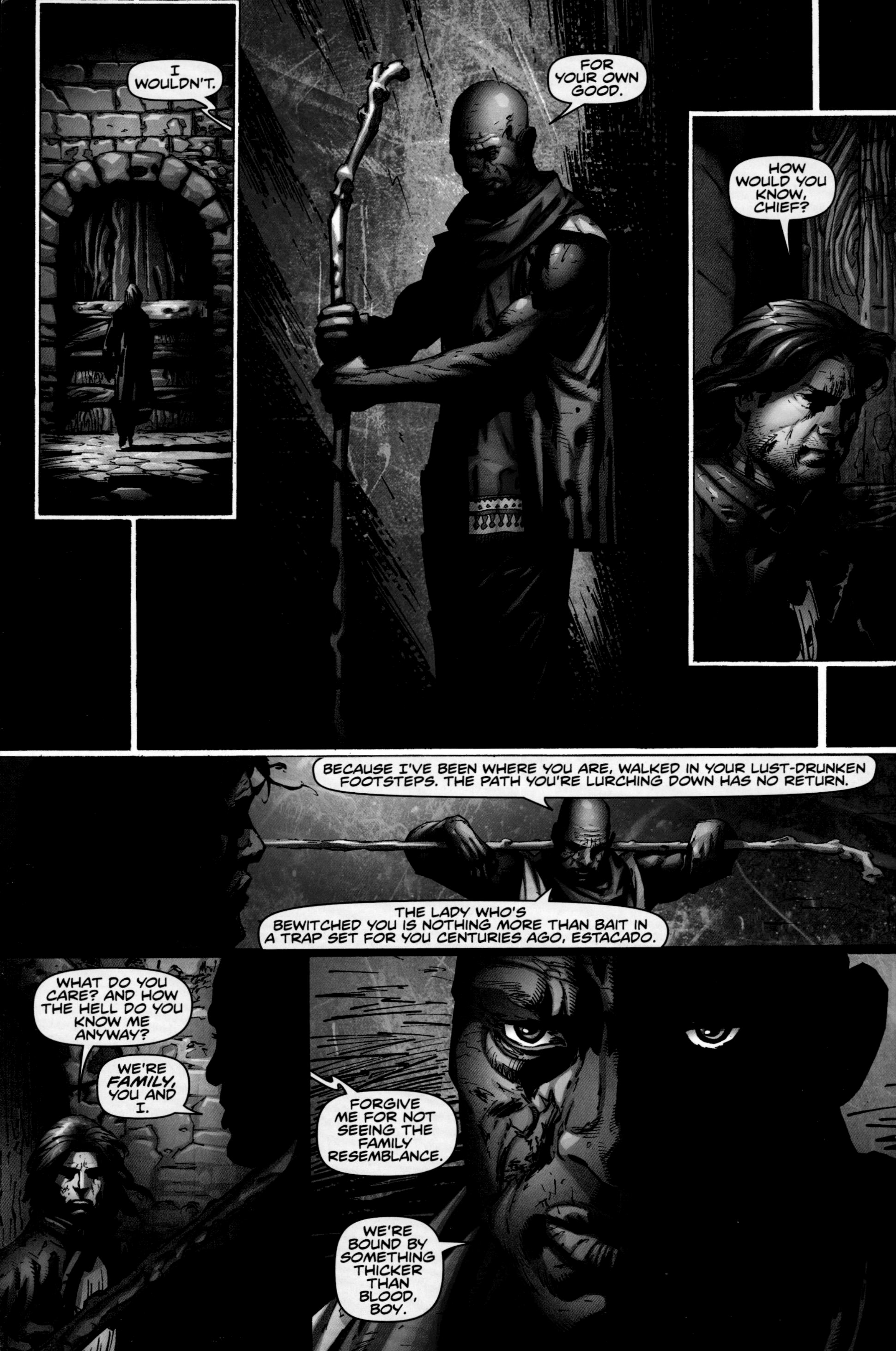
I WOULDN'T.
FOR YOUR OWN GOOD.
HOW WOULD YOU KNOW, CHIEF?
BECAUSE I'VE BEEN WHERE YOU ARE, WALKED IN YOUR LUST-DRUNKEN FOOTSTEPS. THE PATH YOU'RE LURCHING DOWN HAS NO RETURN.
THE LADY WHO'S BEWITCHED YOU IS NOTHING MORE THAN BAIT IN A TRAP SET FOR YOU CENTURIES AGO, ESTACADO.
WHAT DO YOU CARE? AND HOW THE HELL DO YOU KNOW ME ANYWAY?
WE'RE *FAMILY*, YOU AND I.
FORGIVE ME FOR NOT SEEING THE FAMILY RESEMBLANCE.
WE'RE BOUND BY SOMETHING THICKER THAN BLOOD, BOY.

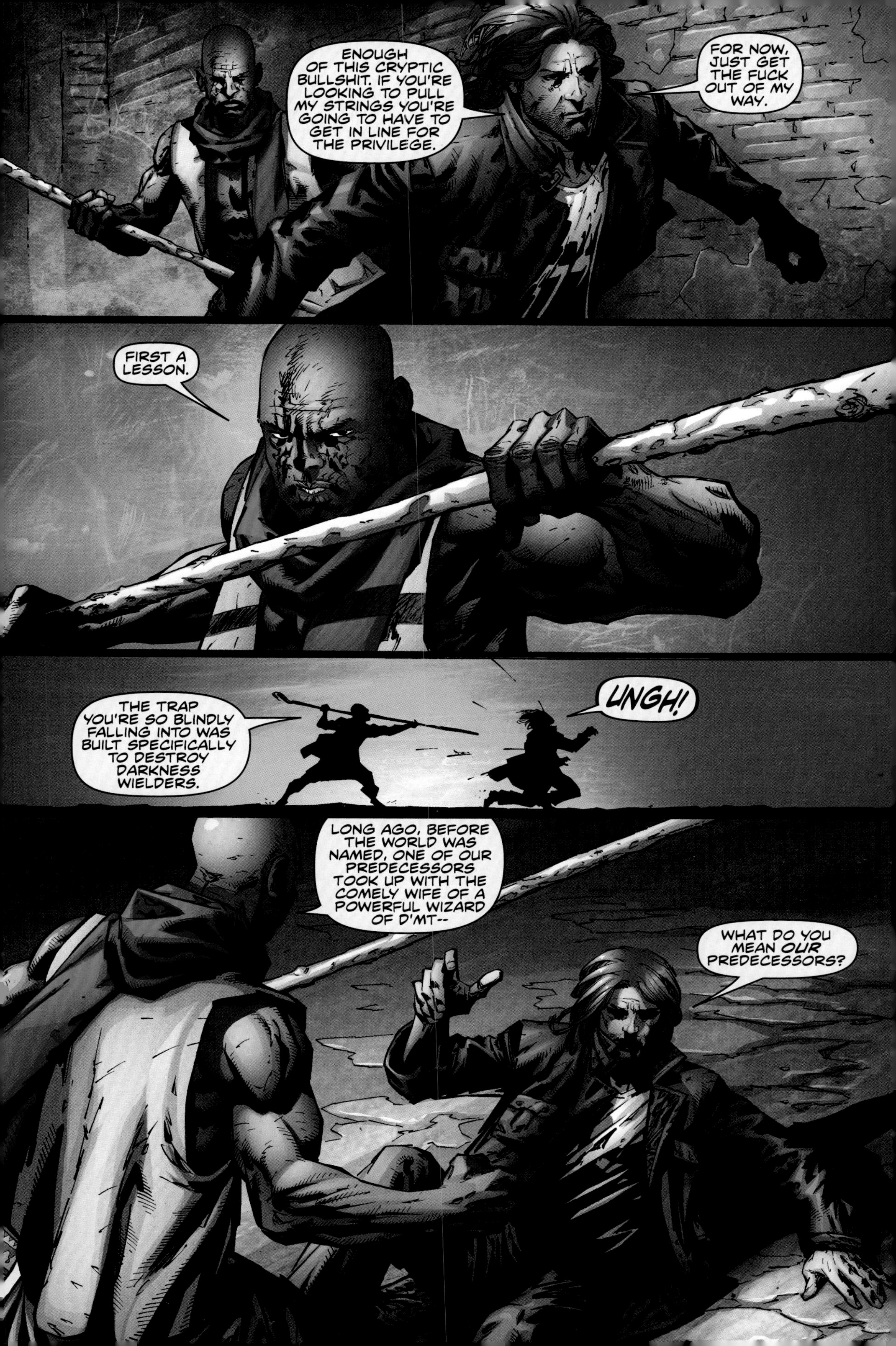
ENOUGH OF THIS CRYPTIC BULLSHIT. IF YOU'RE LOOKING TO PULL MY STRINGS YOU'RE GOING TO HAVE TO GET IN LINE FOR THE PRIVILEGE.
FOR NOW, JUST GET THE FUCK OUT OF MY WAY.
FIRST A LESSON.
THE TRAP YOU'RE SO BLINDLY FALLING INTO WAS BUILT SPECIFICALLY TO DESTROY DARKNESS WIELDERS.
UNGH!
LONG AGO, BEFORE THE WORLD WAS NAMED, ONE OF OUR PREDECESSORS TOOK UP WITH THE COMELY WIFE OF A POWERFUL WIZARD OF D'MT--
WHAT DO YOU MEAN *OUR* PREDECESSORS?

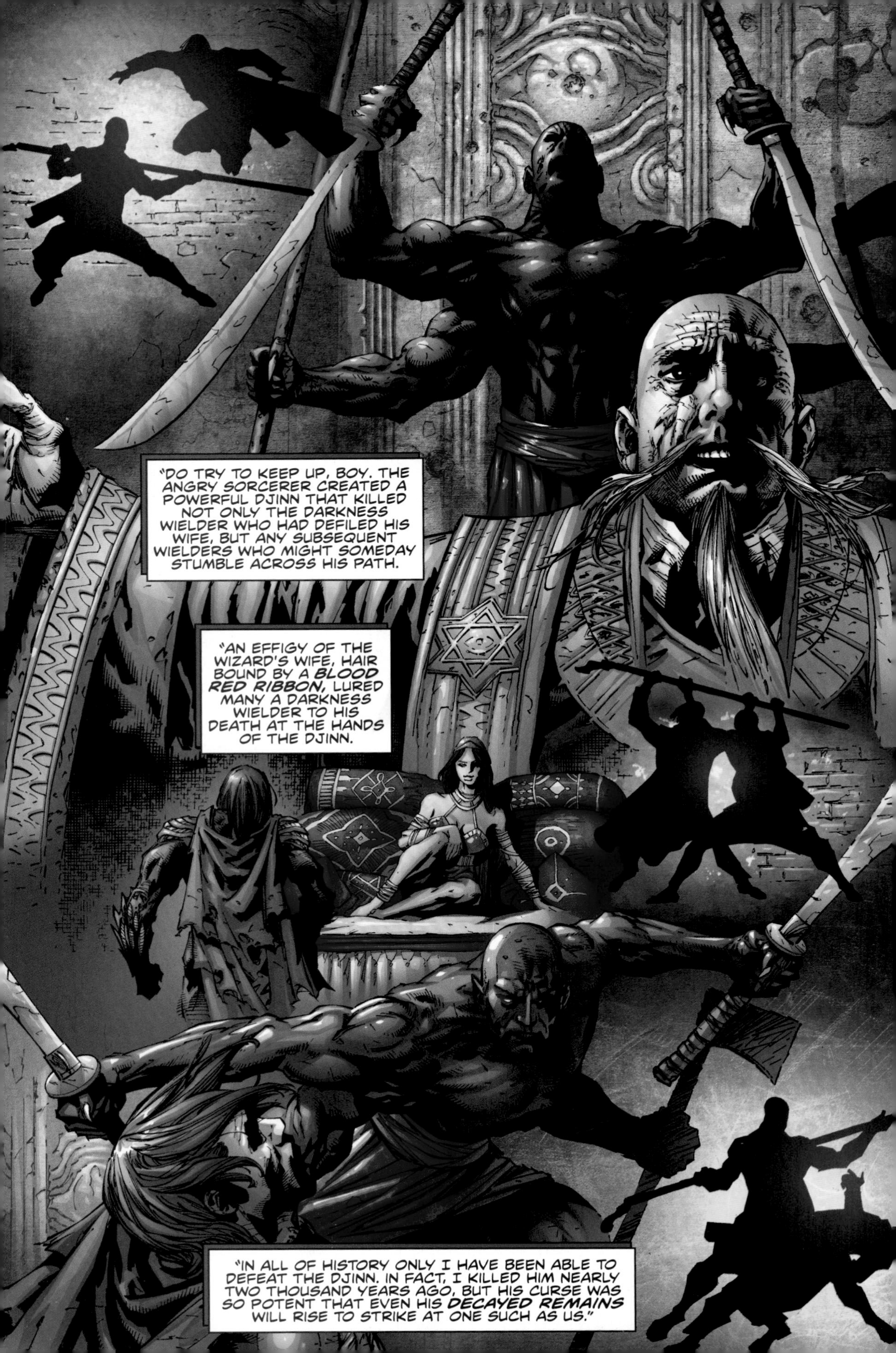
"DO TRY TO KEEP UP, BOY. THE ANGRY SORCERER CREATED A POWERFUL DJINN THAT KILLED NOT ONLY THE DARKNESS WIELDER WHO HAD DEFILED HIS WIFE, BUT ANY SUBSEQUENT WIELDERS WHO MIGHT SOMEDAY STUMBLE ACROSS HIS PATH.
"AN EFFIGY OF THE WIZARD'S WIFE, HAIR BOUND BY A BLOOD RED RIBBON, LURED MANY A DARKNESS WIELDER TO HIS DEATH AT THE HANDS OF THE DJINN.
"IN ALL OF HISTORY ONLY I HAVE BEEN ABLE TO DEFEAT THE DJINN. IN FACT, I KILLED HIM NEARLY TWO THOUSAND YEARS AGO, BUT HIS CURSE WAS SO POTENT THAT EVEN HIS DECAYED REMAINS WILL RISE TO STRIKE AT ONE SUCH AS US."

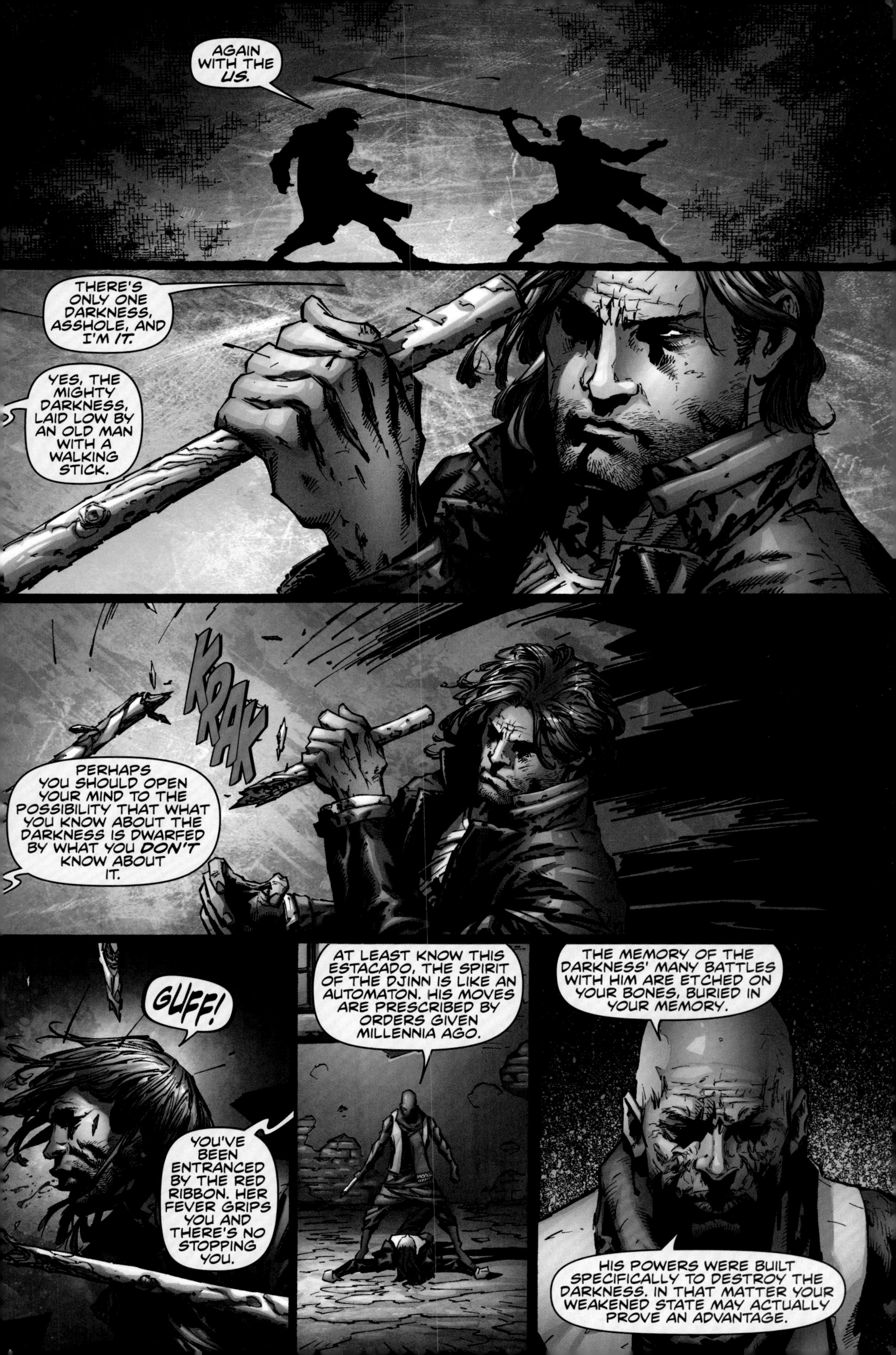
AGAIN WITH THE US.
THERE'S ONLY ONE DARKNESS, ASSHOLE, AND I'M IT.
YES, THE MIGHTY DARKNESS, LAID LOW BY AN OLD MAN WITH A WALKING STICK.
KRAK
PERHAPS YOU SHOULD OPEN YOUR MIND TO THE POSSIBILITY THAT WHAT YOU KNOW ABOUT THE DARKNESS IS DWARFED BY WHAT YOU DON'T KNOW ABOUT IT.
GUFF!
YOU'VE BEEN ENTRANCED BY THE RED RIBBON. HER FEVER GRIPS YOU AND THERE'S NO STOPPING YOU.
AT LEAST KNOW THIS ESTACADO, THE SPIRIT OF THE DJINN IS LIKE AN AUTOMATON. HIS MOVES ARE PRESCRIBED BY ORDERS GIVEN MILLENNIA AGO.
THE MEMORY OF THE DARKNESS' MANY BATTLES WITH HIM ARE ETCHED ON YOUR BONES, BURIED IN YOUR MEMORY.
HIS POWERS WERE BUILT SPECIFICALLY TO DESTROY THE DARKNESS. IN THAT MATTER YOUR WEAKENED STATE MAY ACTUALLY PROVE AN ADVANTAGE.

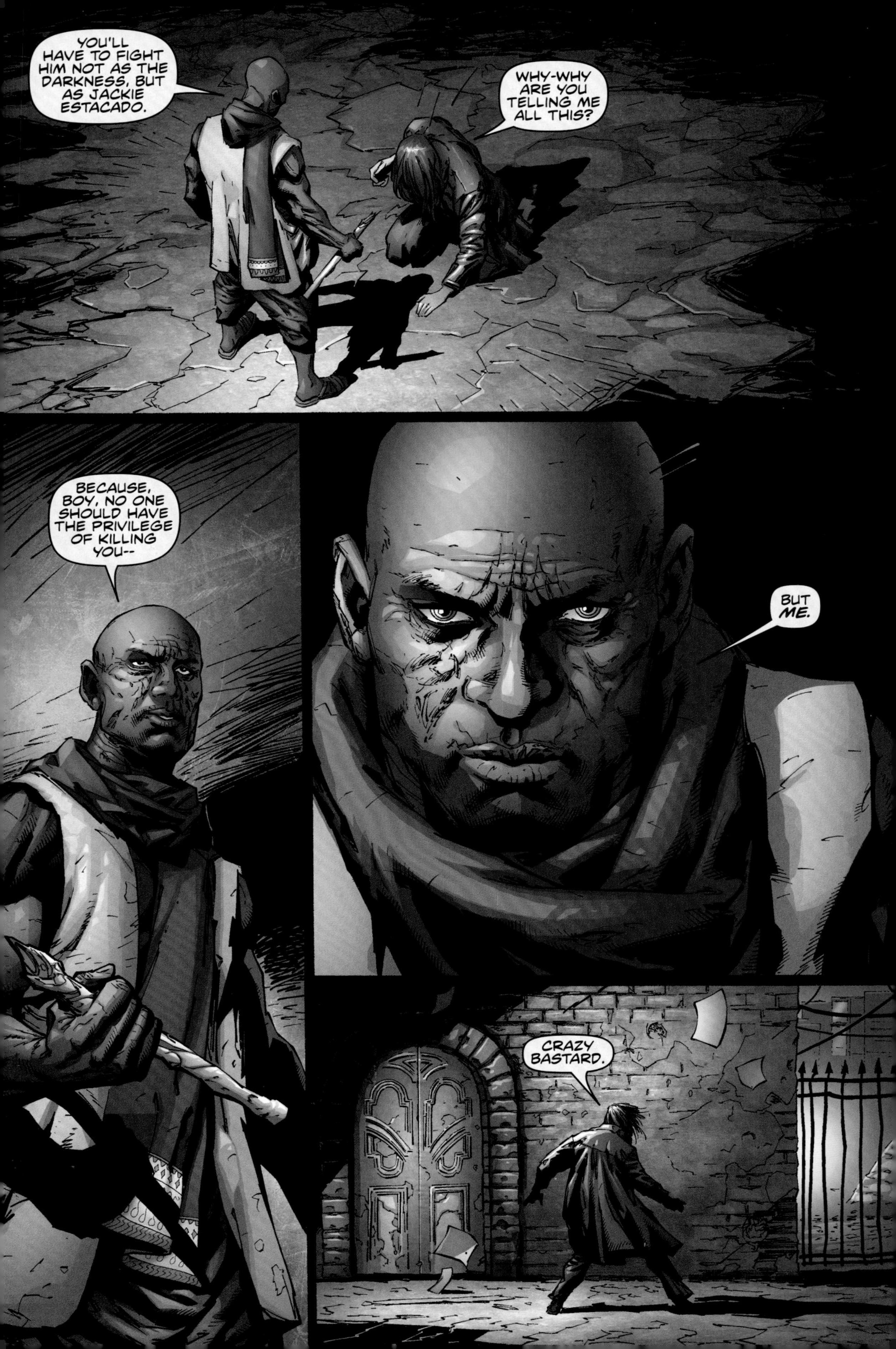
YOU'LL HAVE TO FIGHT HIM NOT AS THE DARKNESS, BUT AS JACKIE ESTACADO.
WHY-WHY ARE YOU TELLING ME ALL THIS?
BECAUSE, BOY, NO ONE SHOULD HAVE THE PRIVILEGE OF KILLING YOU--
BUT *ME*.
CRAZY BASTARD.

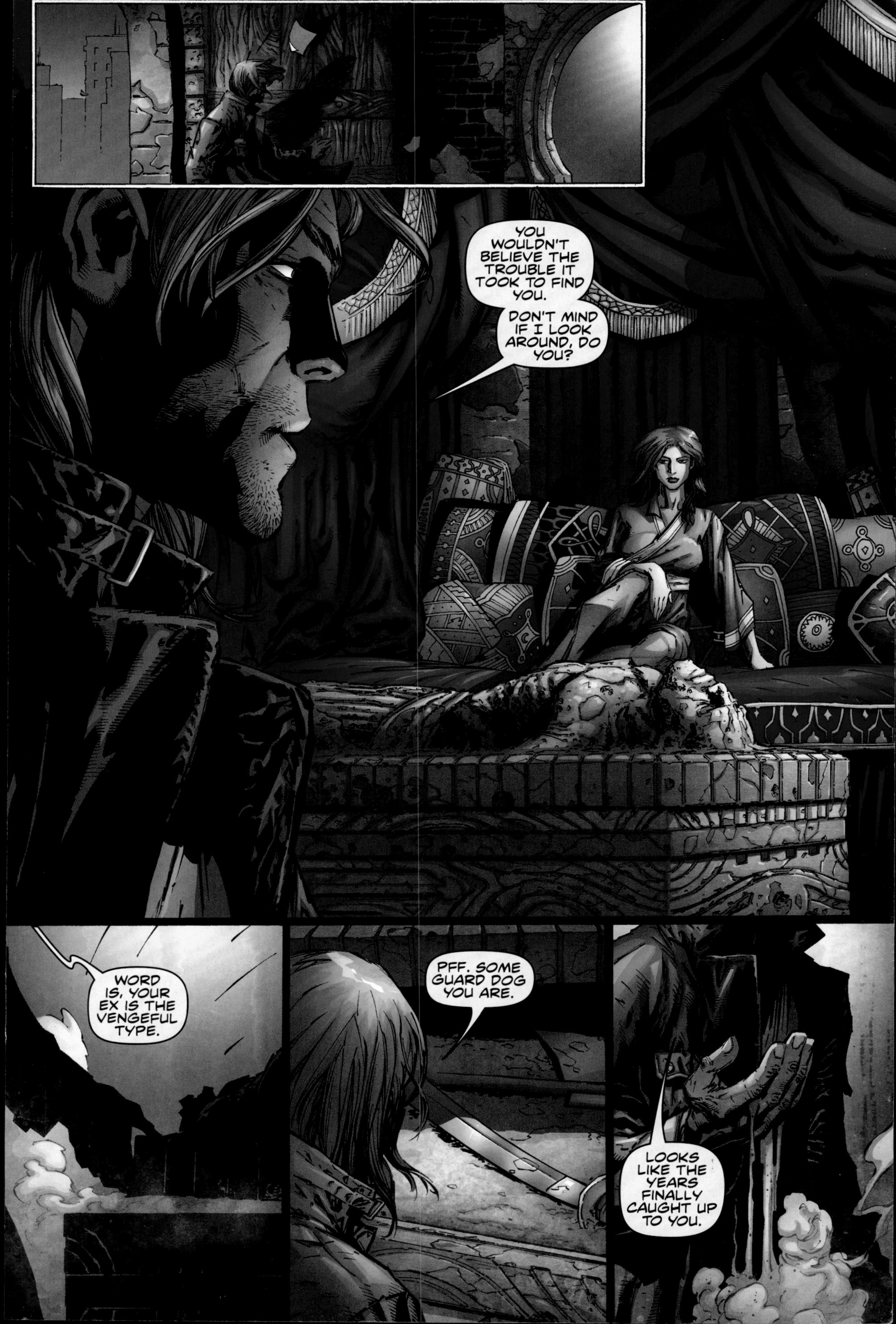
YOU WOULDN'T BELIEVE THE TROUBLE IT TOOK TO FIND YOU.
DON'T MIND IF I LOOK AROUND, DO YOU?
WORD IS, YOUR EX IS THE VENGEFUL TYPE.
PFF. SOME GUARD DOG YOU ARE.
LOOKS LIKE THE YEARS FINALLY CAUGHT UP TO YOU.

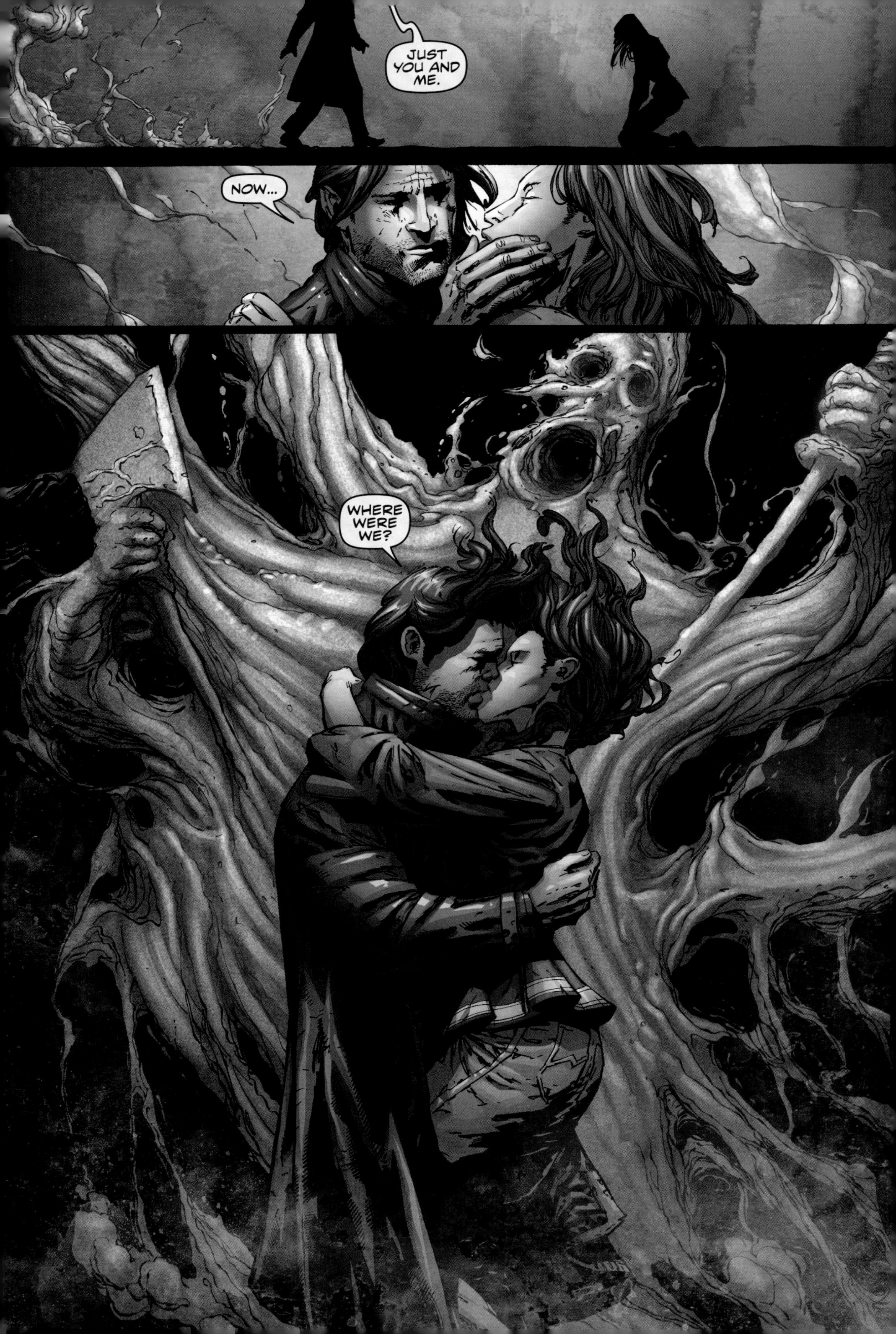
JUST YOU AND ME.
NOW...
WHERE WERE WE?

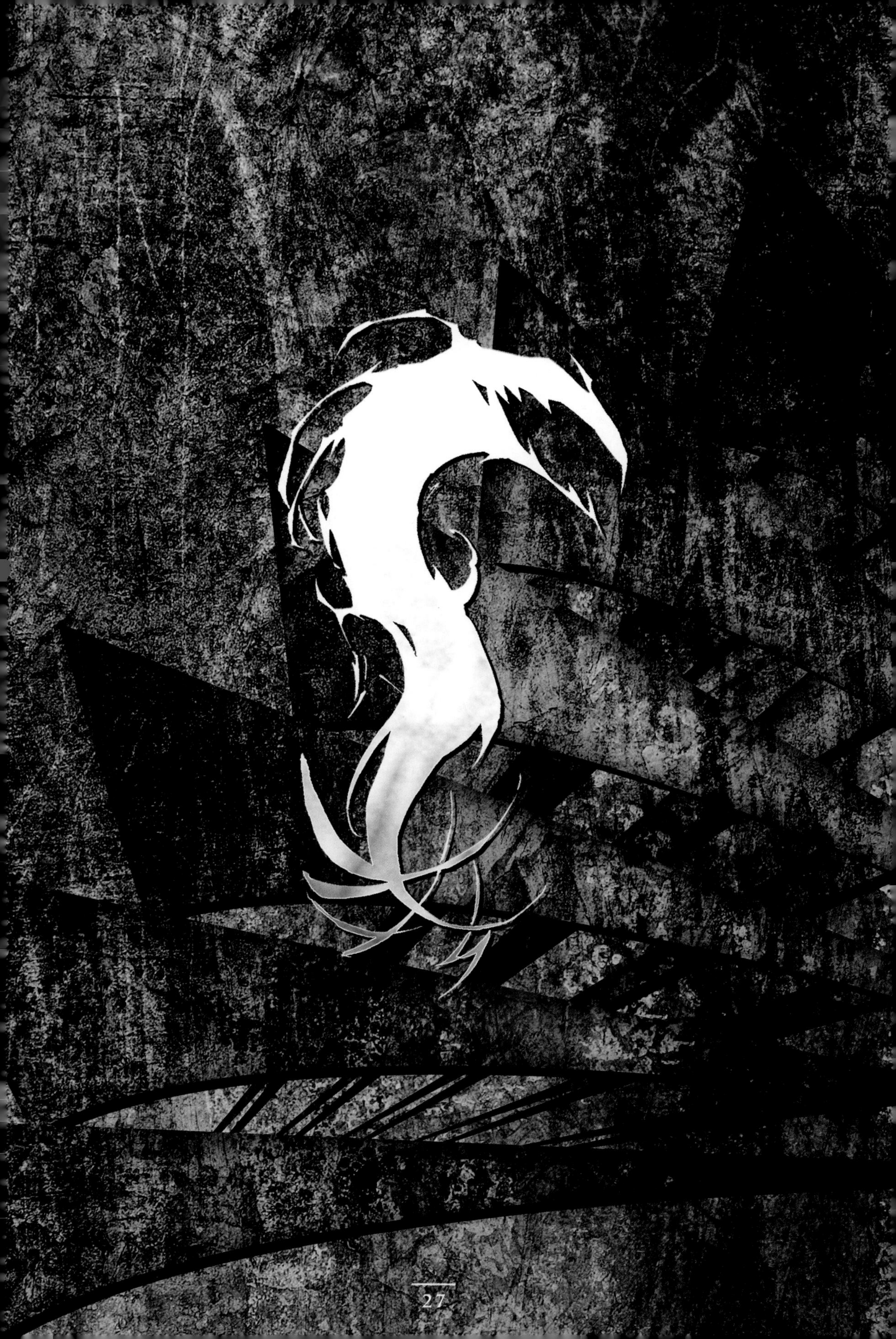

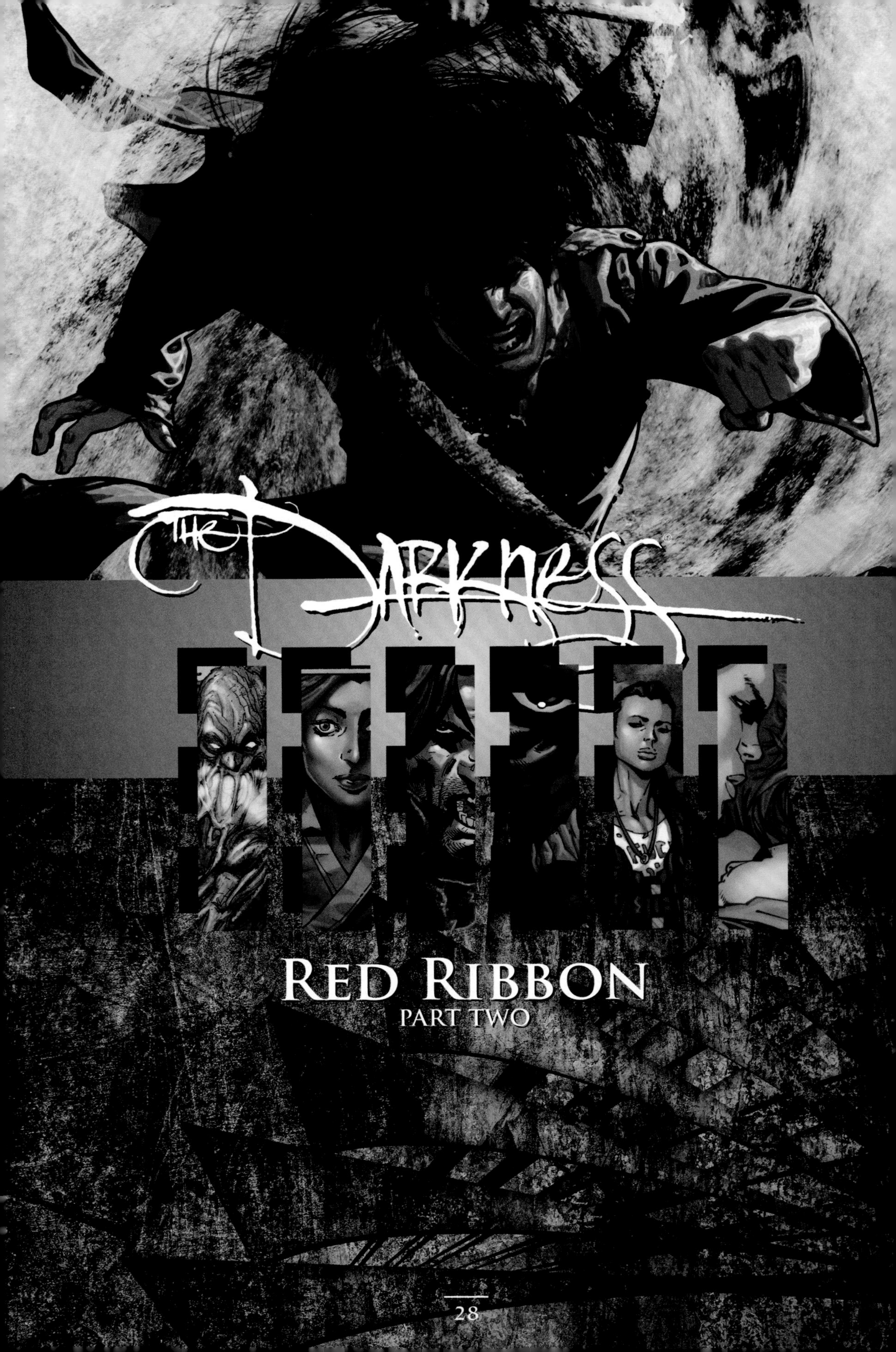
THE DARKNESS
RED RIBBON
PART TWO

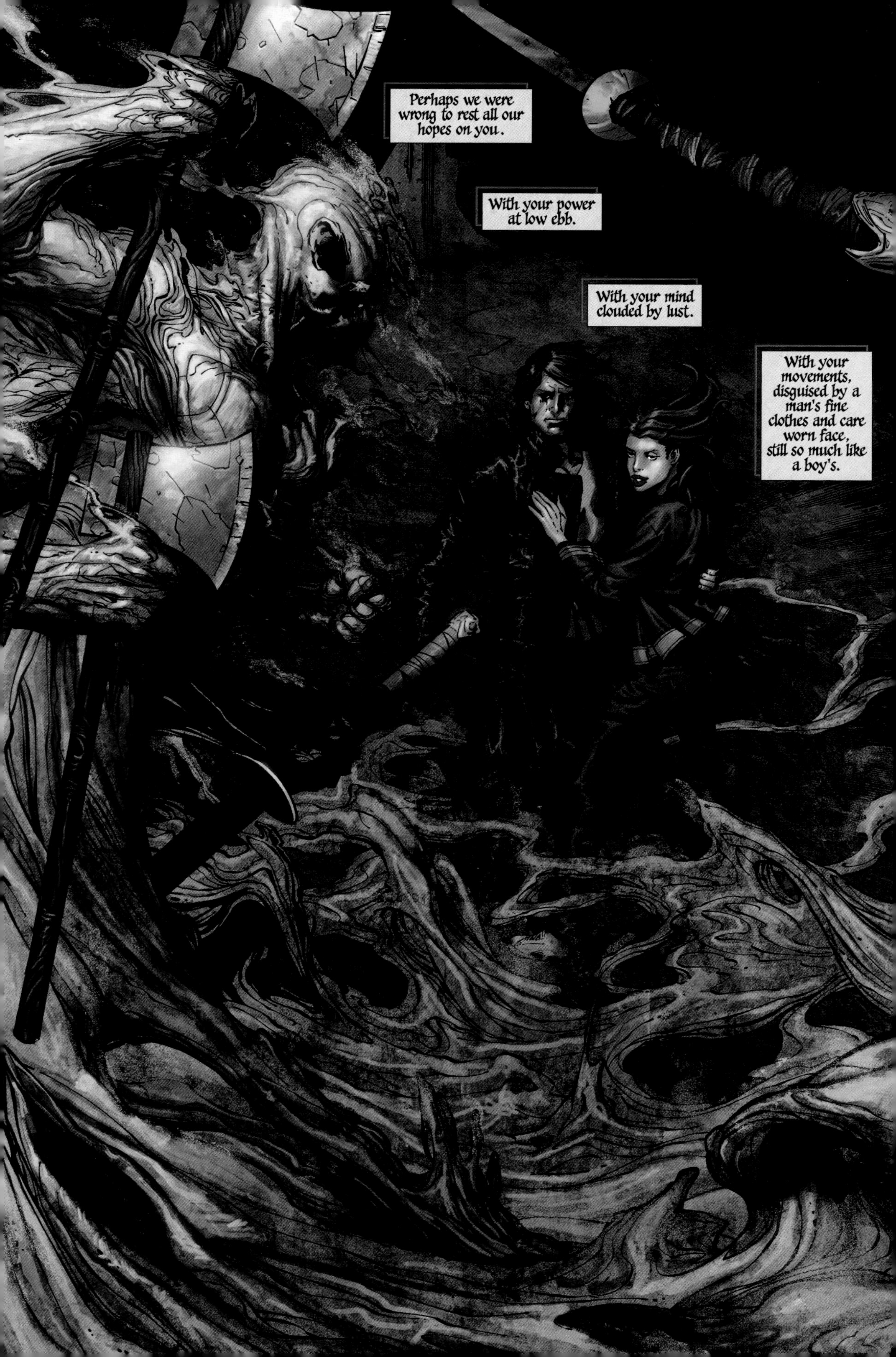
Perhaps we were wrong to rest all our hopes on you.
With your power at low ebb.
With your mind clouded by lust.
With your movements, disguised by a man's fine clothes and care worn face, still so much like a boy's.

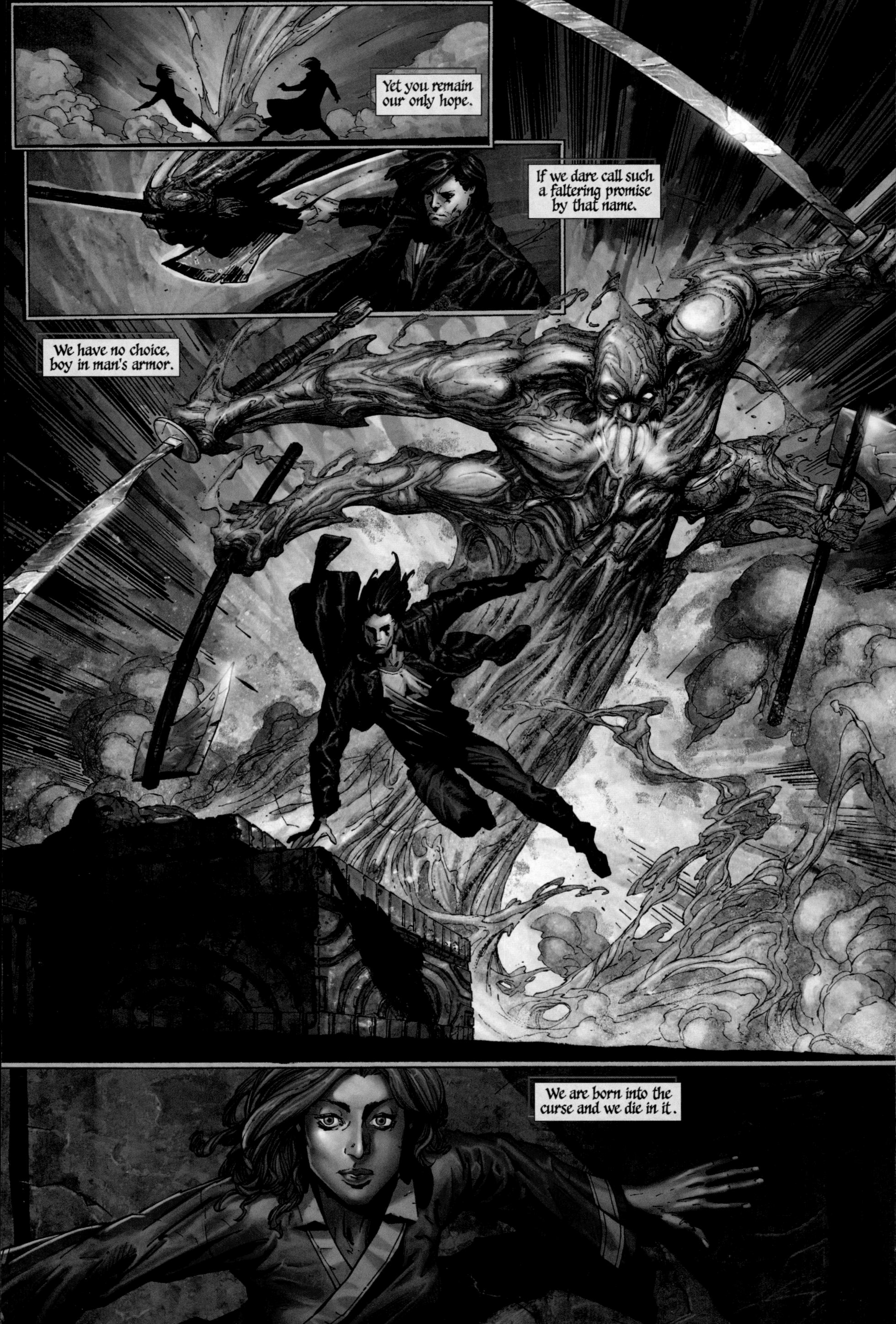
Yet you remain our only hope.
If we dare call such a faltering promise by that name.
We have no choice, boy in man's armor.
We are born into the curse and we die in it.

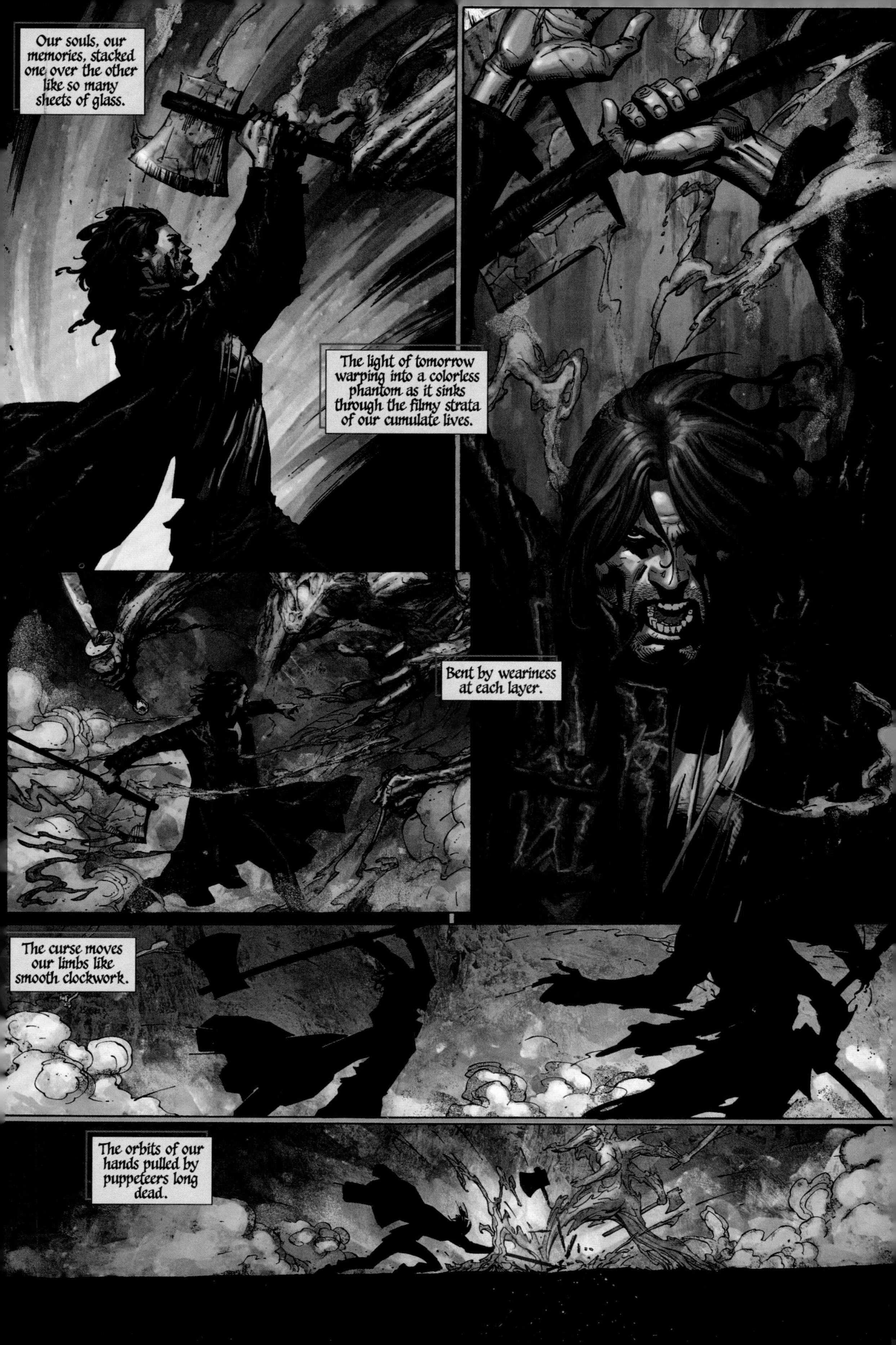

Our souls, our memories, stacked one over the other like so many sheets of glass.
The light of tomorrow warping into a colorless phantom as it sinks through the filmy strata of our cumulate lives.
Bent by weariness at each layer.
The curse moves our limbs like smooth clockwork.
The orbits of our hands pulled by puppeteers long dead.

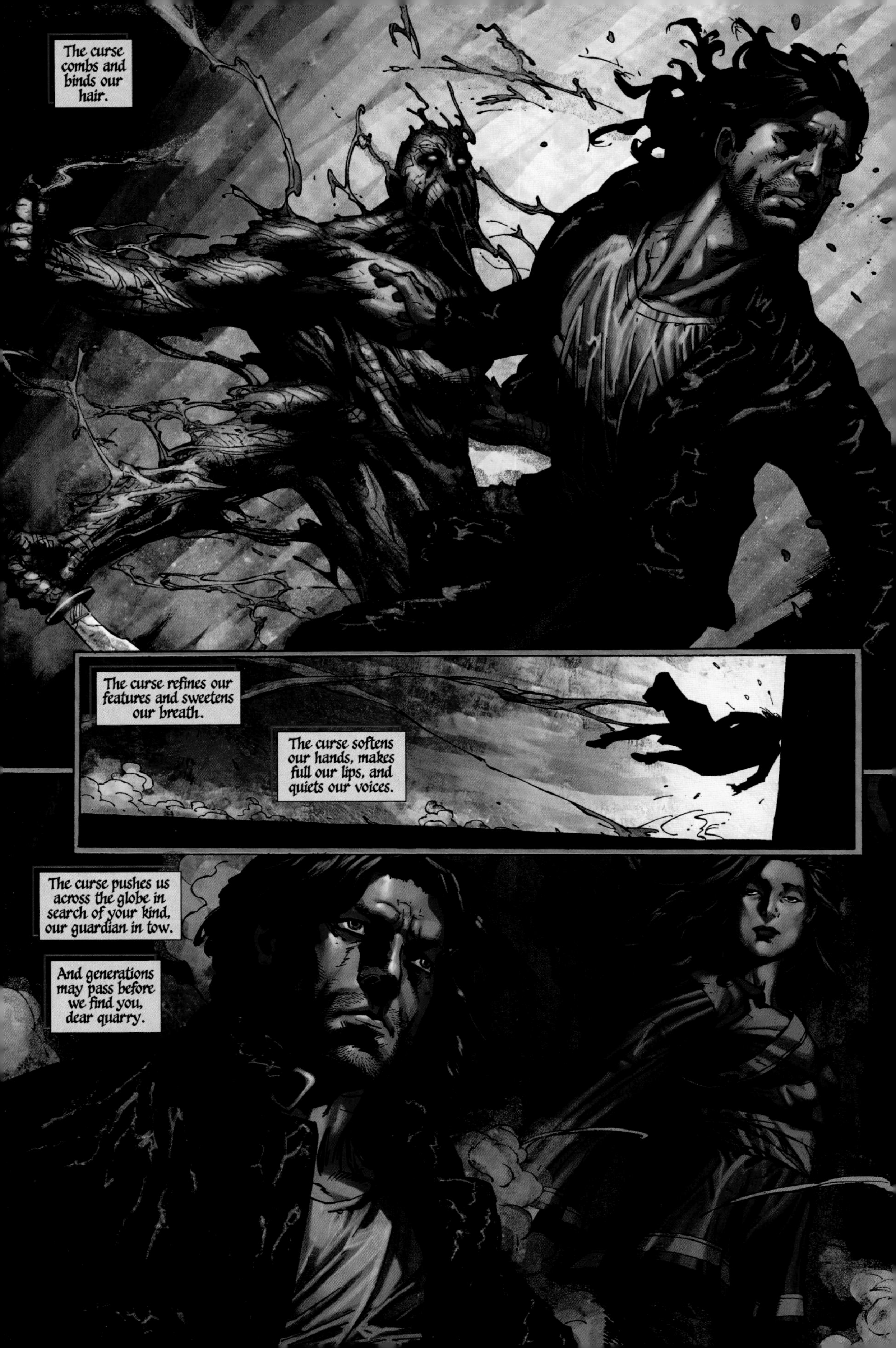

The curse combs and binds our hair.
The curse refines our features and sweetens our breath.
The curse softens our hands, makes full our lips, and quiets our voices.
The curse pushes us across the globe in search of your kind, our guardian in tow.
And generations may pass before we find you, dear quarry.

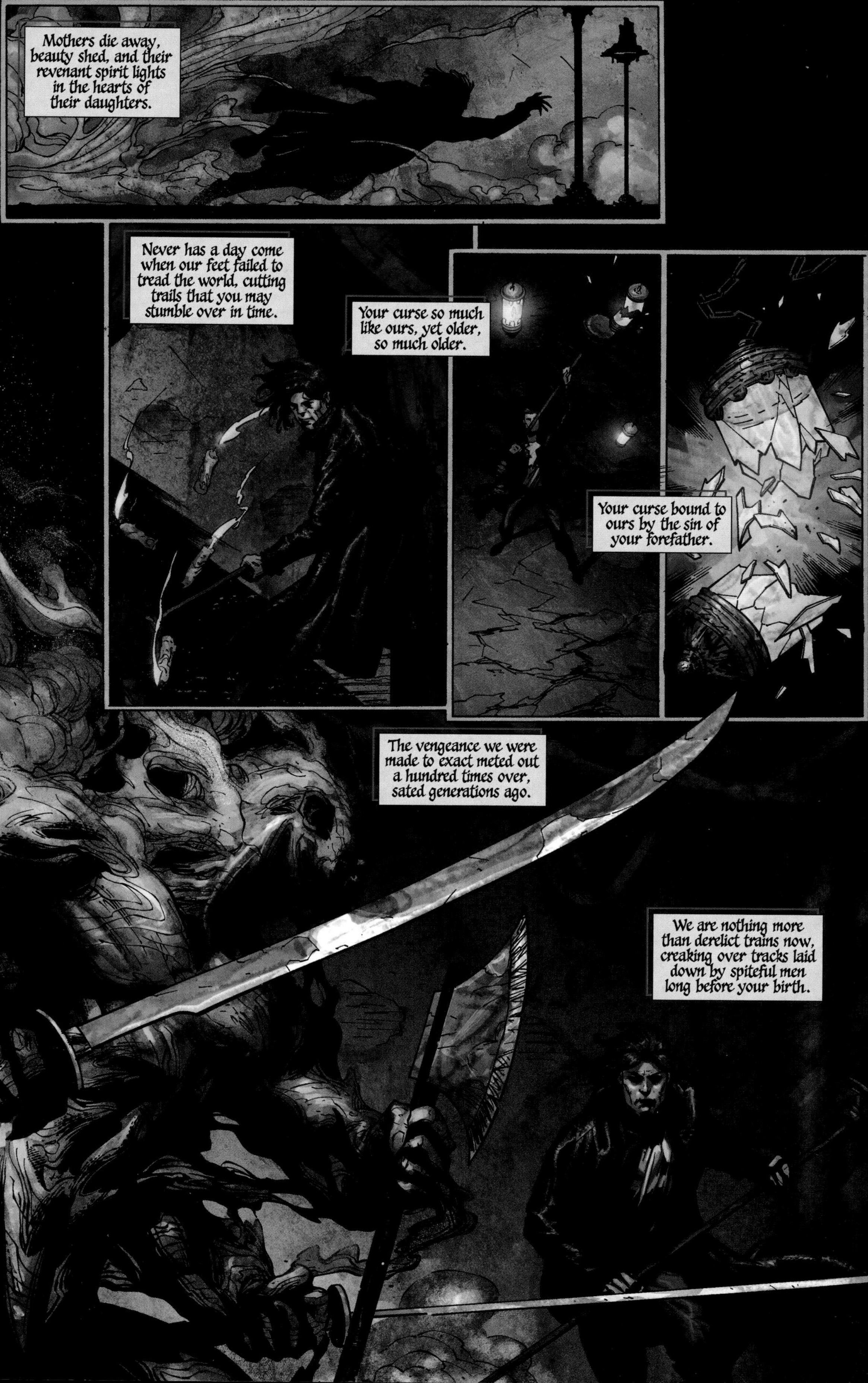
Mothers die away, beauty shed, and their revenant spirit lights in the hearts of their daughters.
Never has a day come when our feet failed to tread the world, cutting trails that you may stumble over in time.
Your curse so much like ours, yet older, so much older.
Your curse bound to ours by the sin of your forefather.
The vengeance we were made to exact meted out a hundred times over, sated generations ago.
We are nothing more than derelict trains now, creaking over tracks laid down by spiteful men long before your birth.

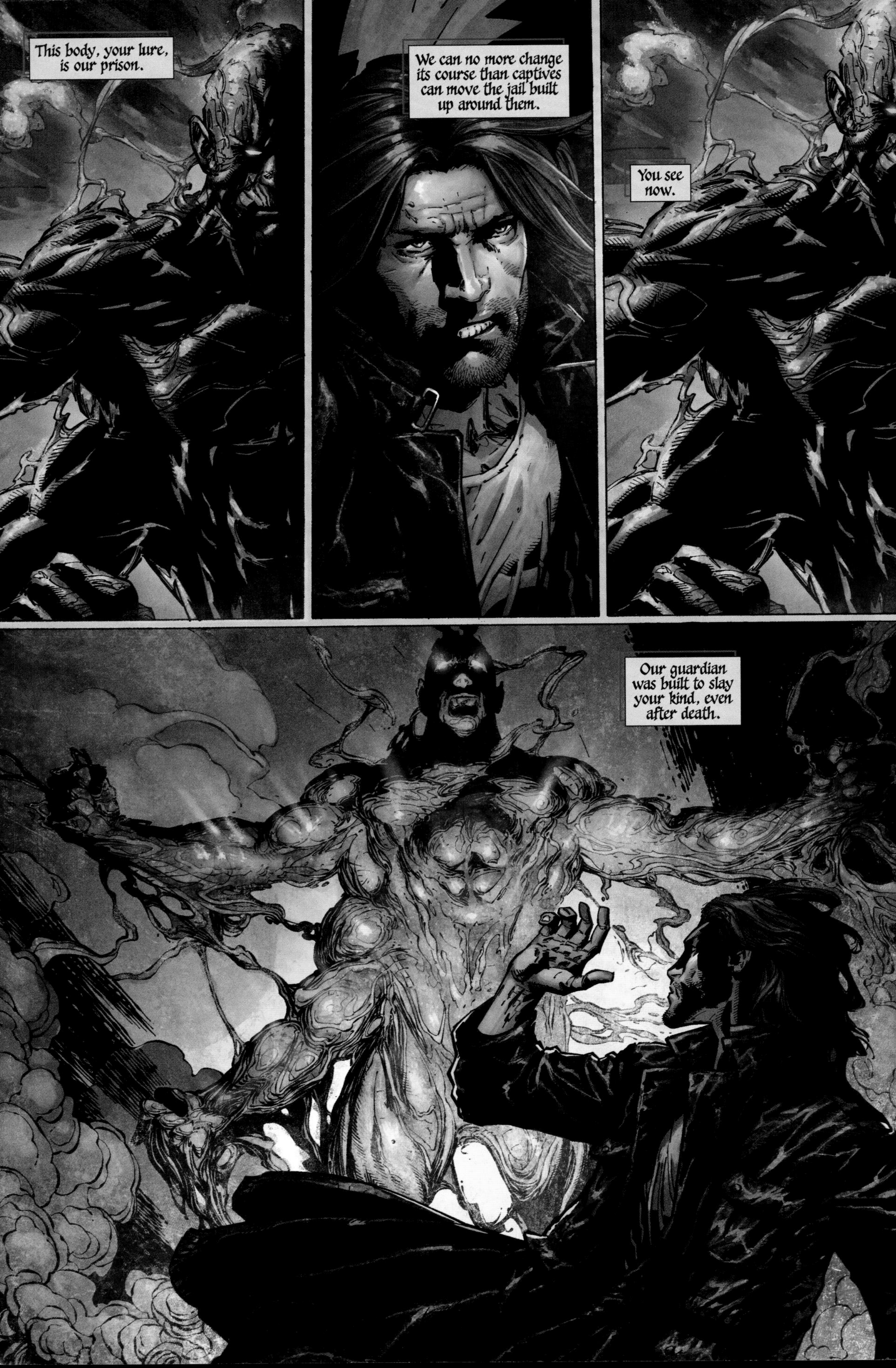
This body, your lure, is our prison.
We can no more change its course than captives can move the jail built up around them.
You see now.
Our guardian was built to slay your kind, even after death.

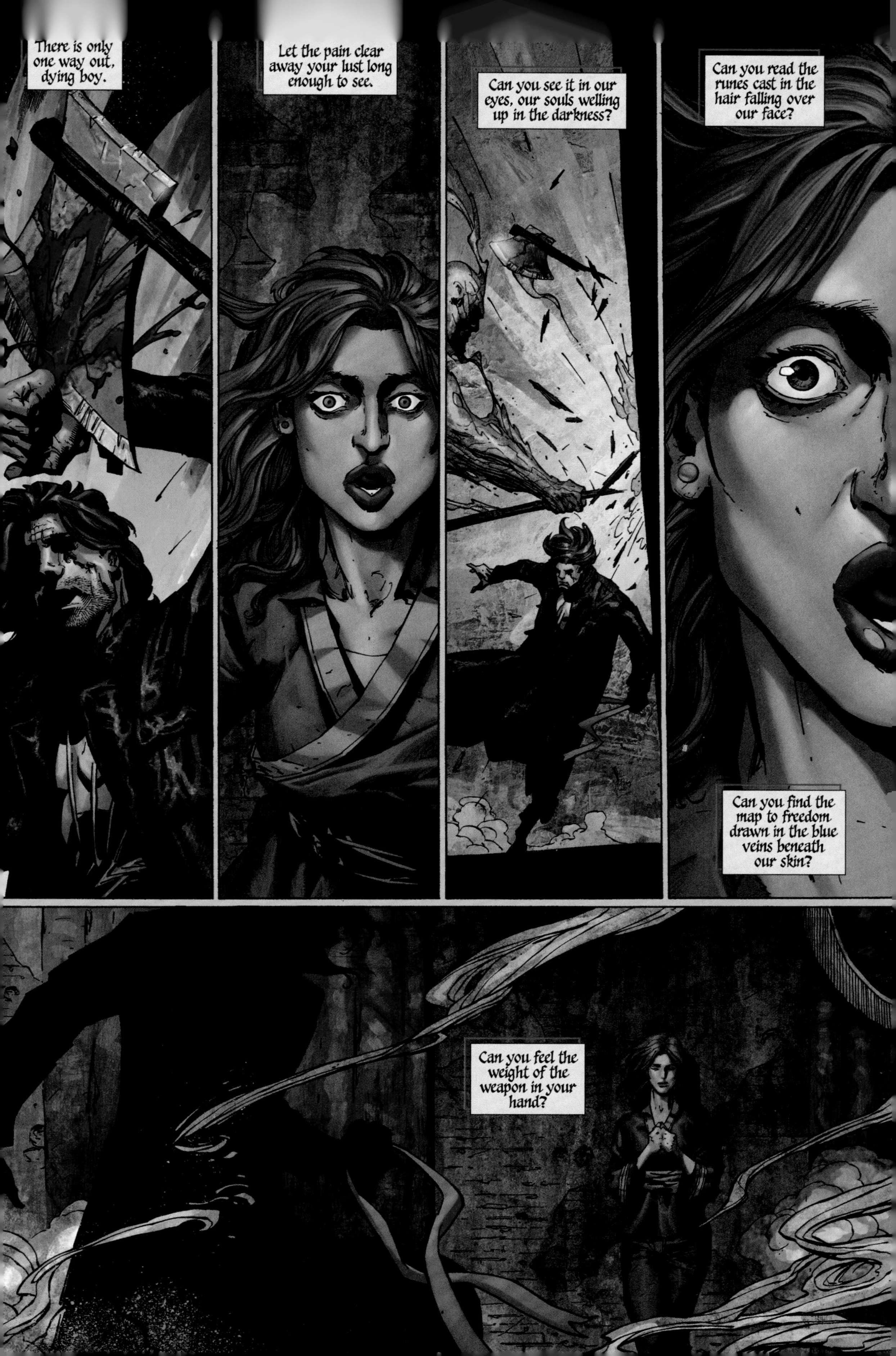
There is only one way out, dying boy.
Let the pain clear away your lust long enough to see.
Can you see it in our eyes, our souls welling up in the darkness?
Can you read the runes cast in the hair falling over our face?
Can you find the map to freedom drawn in the blue veins beneath our skin?
Can you feel the weight of the weapon in your hand?

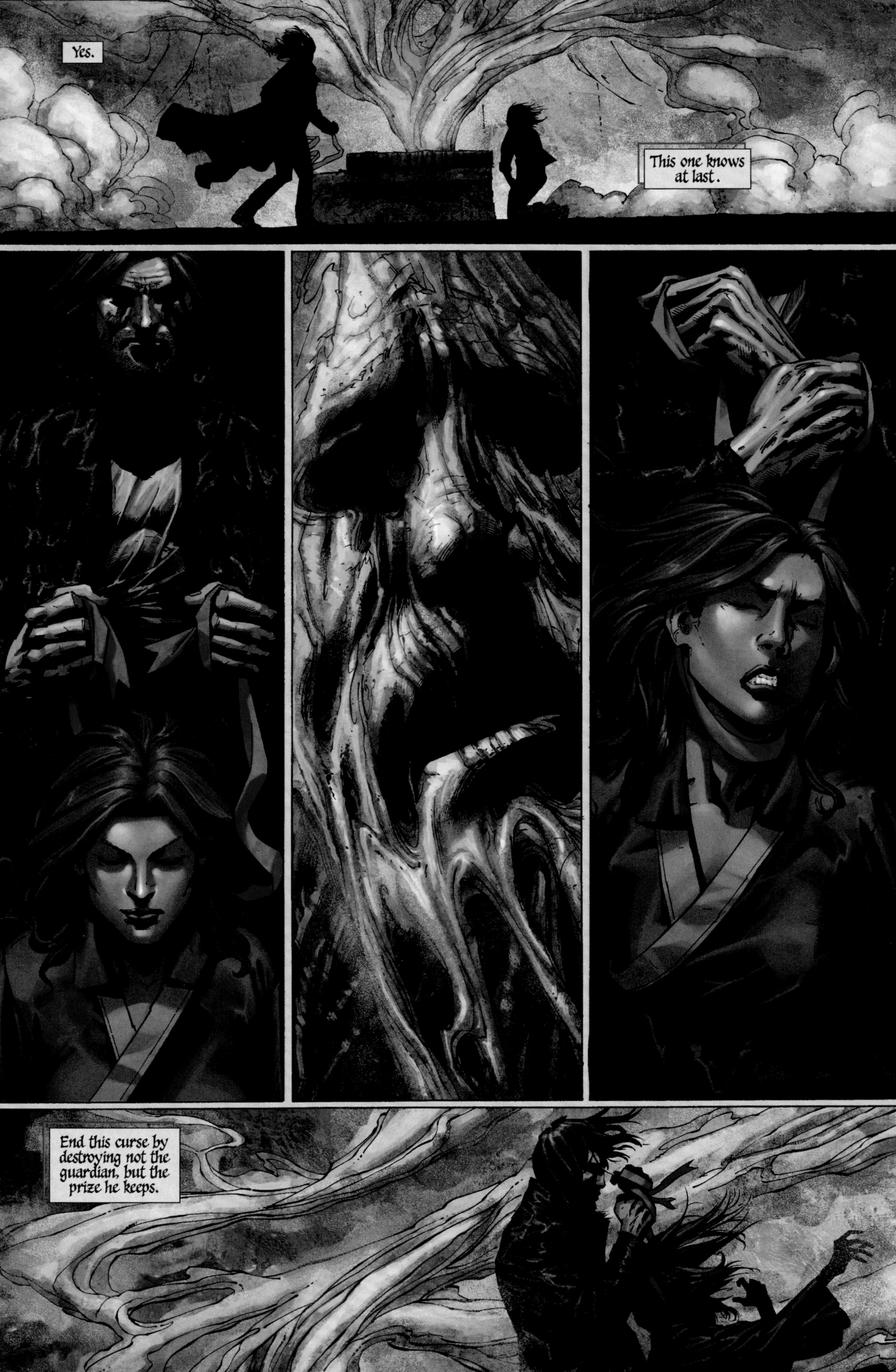
Yes.
This one knows at last.
End this curse by destroying not the guardian, but the prize he keeps.

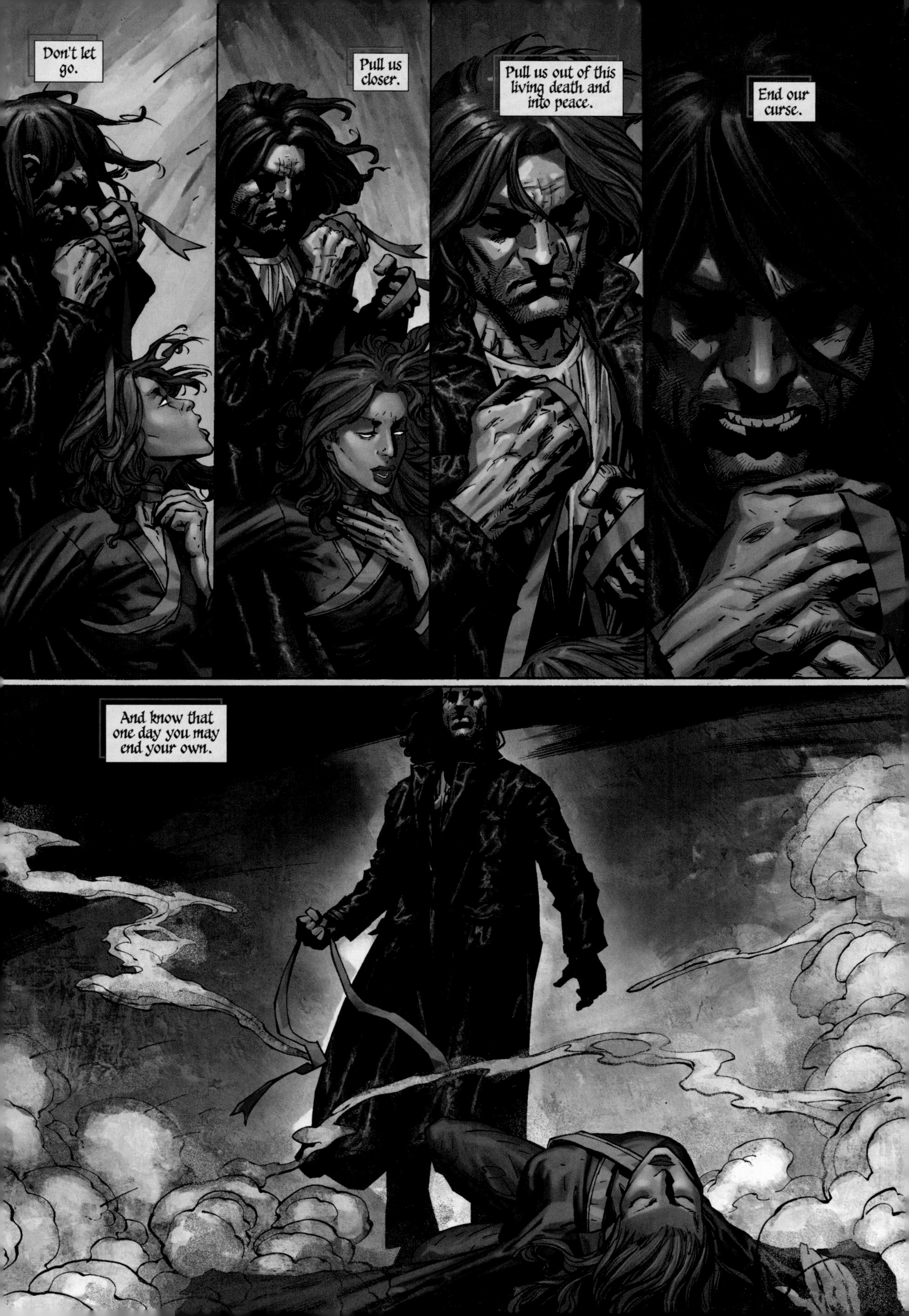

Don't let go.
Pull us closer.
Pull us out of this living death and into peace.
End our curse.
And know that one day you may end your own.

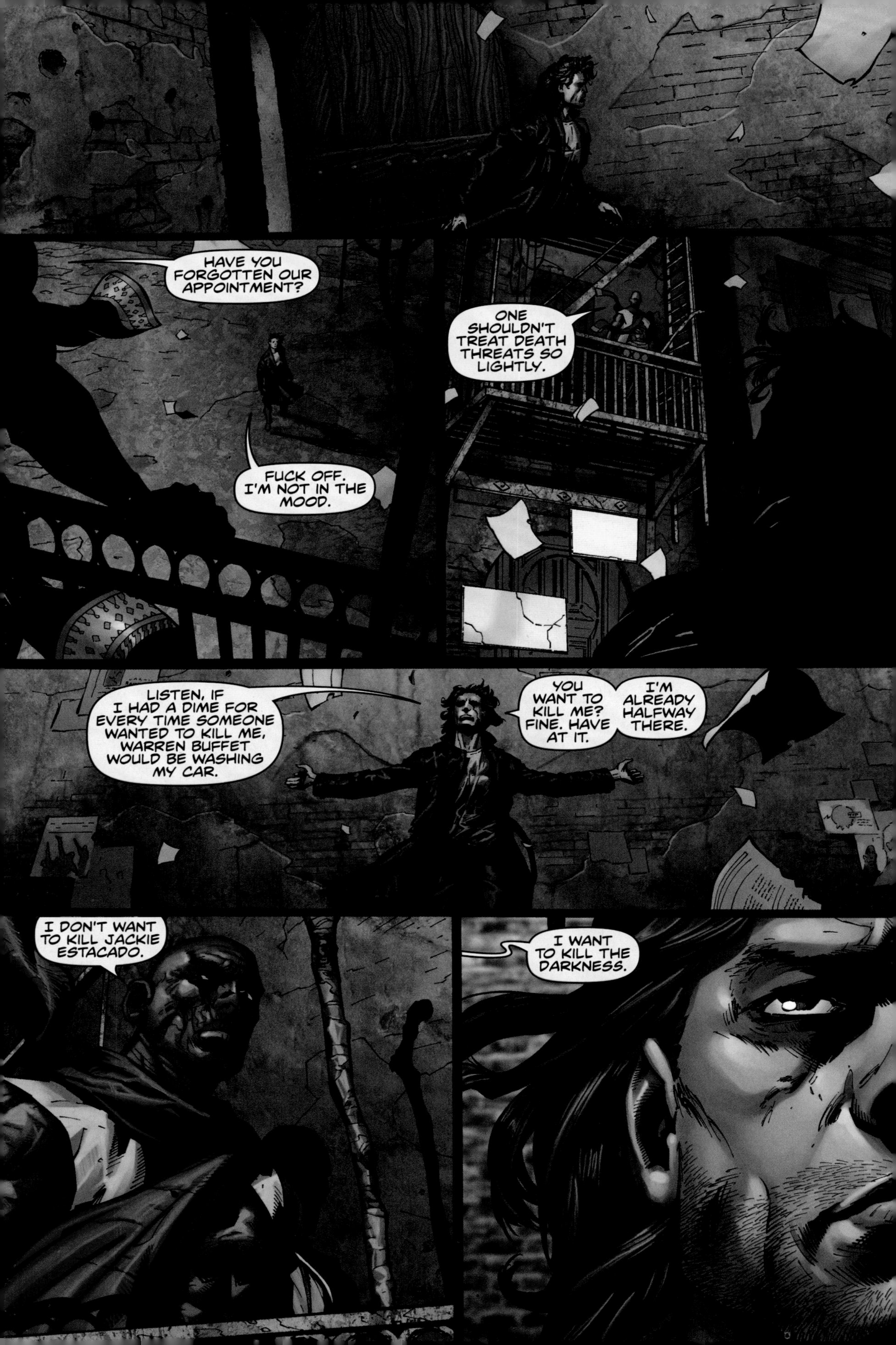
HAVE YOU FORGOTTEN OUR APPOINTMENT?
FUCK OFF. I'M NOT IN THE MOOD.
ONE SHOULDN'T TREAT DEATH THREATS SO LIGHTLY.
LISTEN, IF I HAD A DIME FOR EVERY TIME SOMEONE WANTED TO KILL ME, WARREN BUFFET WOULD BE WASHING MY CAR.
YOU WANT TO KILL ME? FINE. HAVE AT IT.
I'M ALREADY HALFWAY THERE.
I DON'T WANT TO KILL JACKIE ESTACADO.
I WANT TO KILL THE DARKNESS.

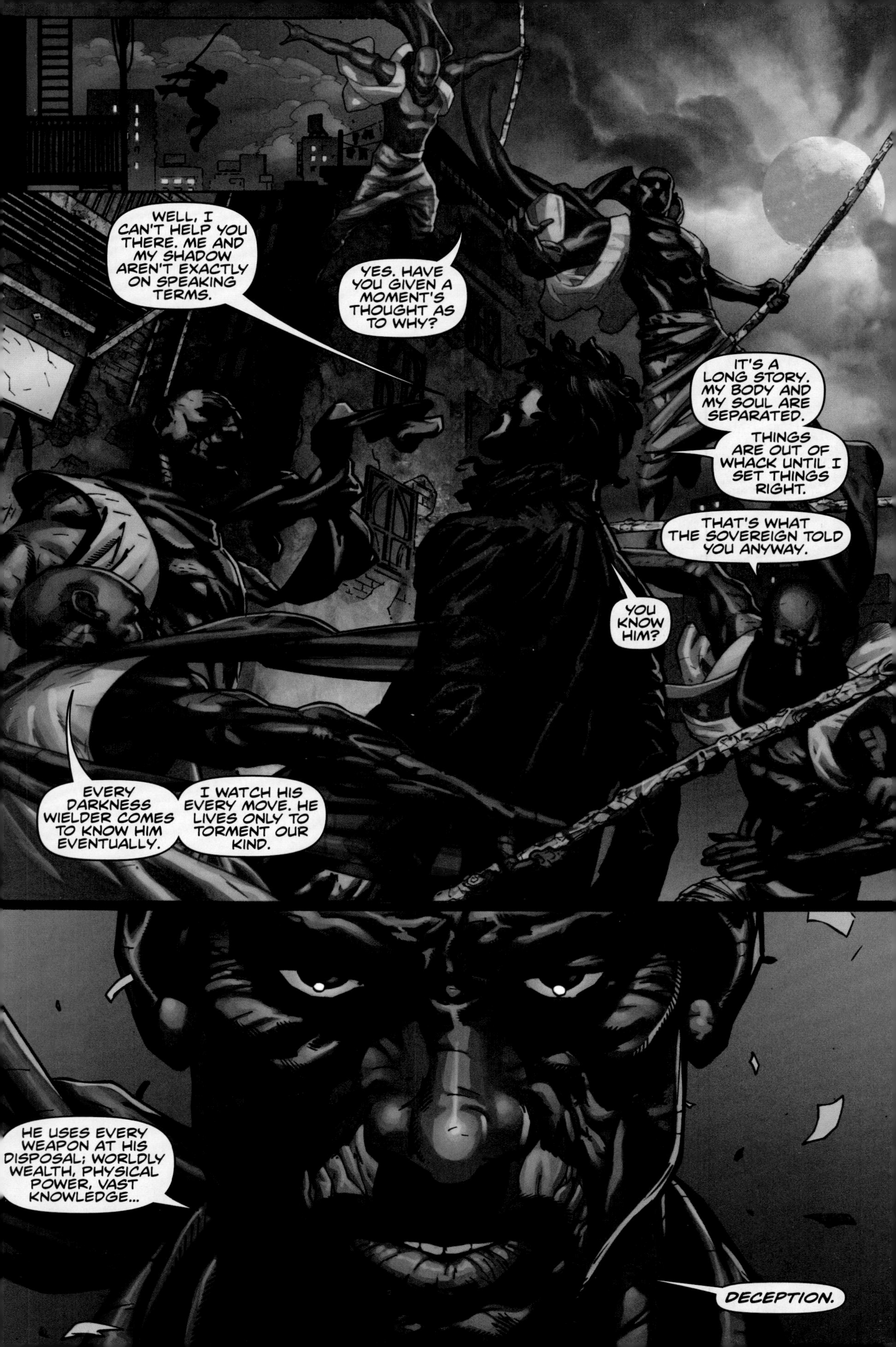
WELL, I CAN'T HELP YOU THERE. ME AND MY SHADOW AREN'T EXACTLY ON SPEAKING TERMS.
YES. HAVE YOU GIVEN A MOMENT'S THOUGHT AS TO WHY?
IT'S A LONG STORY. MY BODY AND MY SOUL ARE SEPARATED.
THINGS ARE OUT OF WHACK UNTIL I SET THINGS RIGHT.
THAT'S WHAT THE SOVEREIGN TOLD YOU ANYWAY.
YOU KNOW HIM?
EVERY DARKNESS WIELDER COMES TO KNOW HIM EVENTUALLY.
I WATCH HIS EVERY MOVE. HE LIVES ONLY TO TORMENT OUR KIND.
HE USES EVERY WEAPON AT HIS DISPOSAL; WORLDLY WEALTH, PHYSICAL POWER, VAST KNOWLEDGE...
DECEPTION.

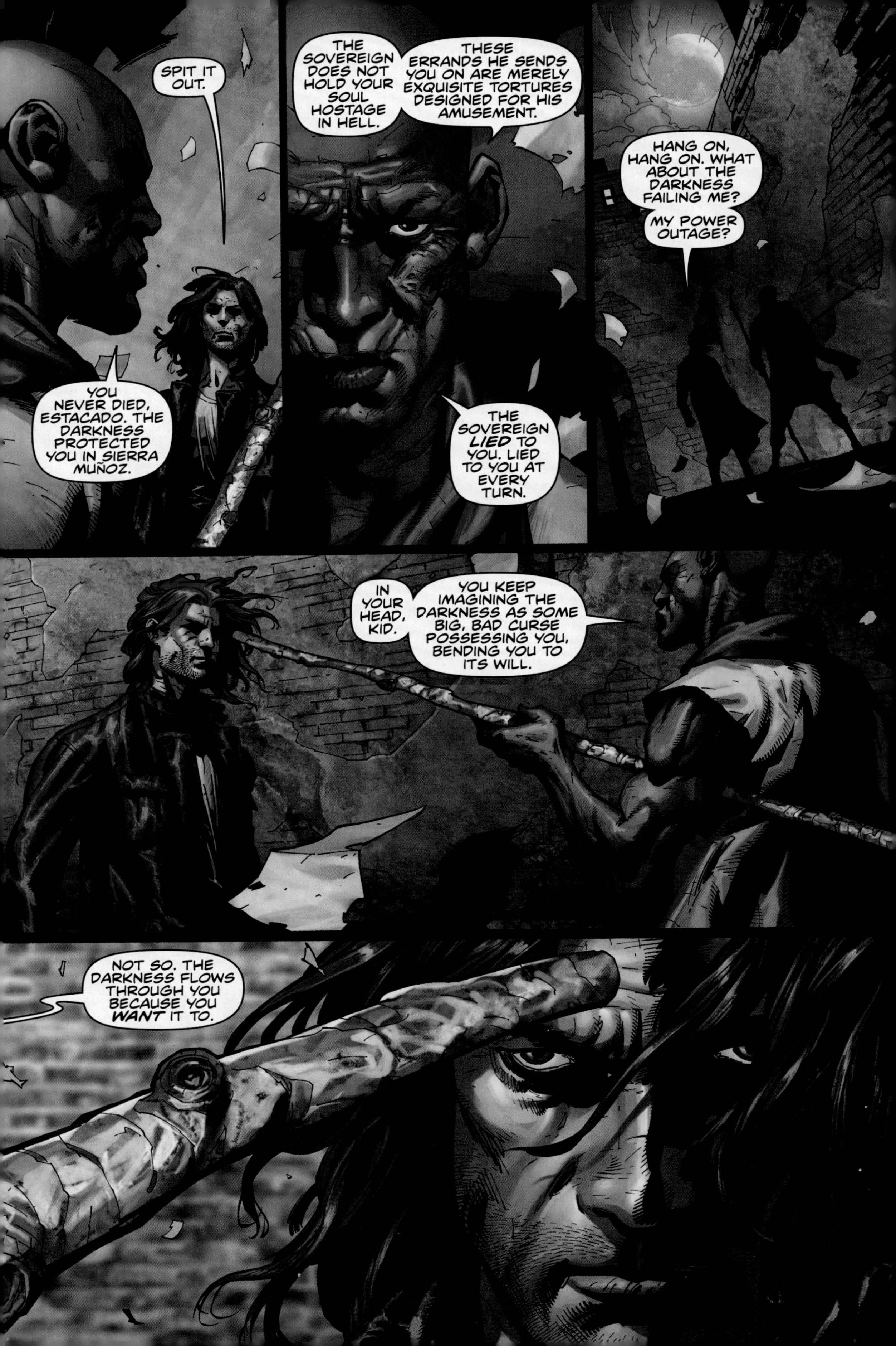
SPIT IT OUT.
YOU NEVER DIED, ESTACADO. THE DARKNESS PROTECTED YOU IN SIERRA MUÑOZ.
THE SOVEREIGN DOES NOT HOLD YOUR SOUL HOSTAGE IN HELL.
THESE ERRANDS HE SENDS YOU ON ARE MERELY EXQUISITE TORTURES DESIGNED FOR HIS AMUSEMENT.
THE SOVEREIGN LIED TO YOU. LIED TO YOU AT EVERY TURN.
HANG ON, HANG ON. WHAT ABOUT THE DARKNESS FAILING ME?
MY POWER OUTAGE?
IN YOUR HEAD, KID.
YOU KEEP IMAGINING THE DARKNESS AS SOME BIG, BAD CURSE POSSESSING YOU, BENDING YOU TO ITS WILL.
NOT SO. THE DARKNESS FLOWS THROUGH YOU BECAUSE YOU WANT IT TO.

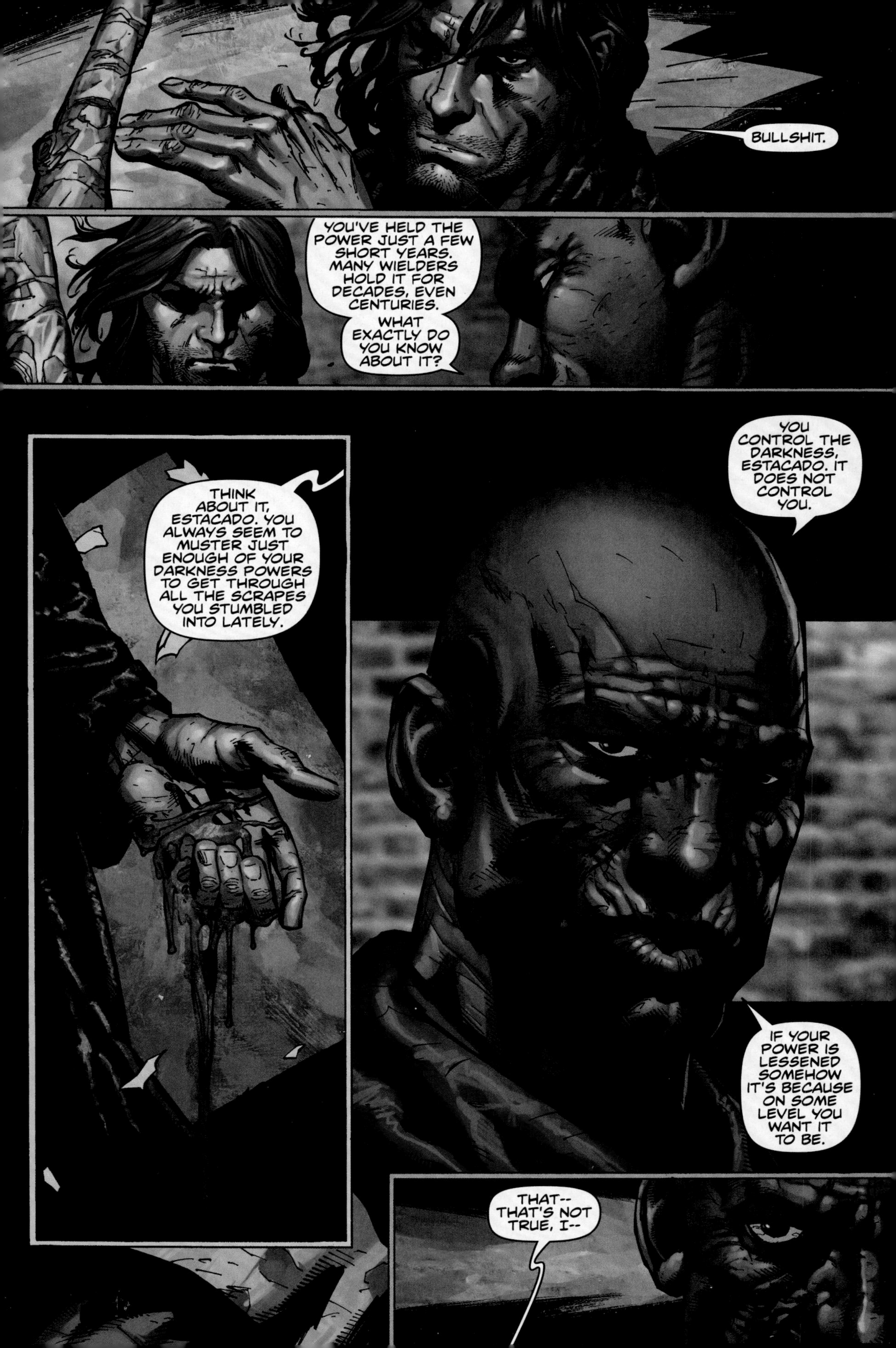
BULLSHIT.
YOU'VE HELD THE POWER JUST A FEW SHORT YEARS. MANY WIELDERS HOLD IT FOR DECADES, EVEN CENTURIES.
WHAT EXACTLY DO YOU KNOW ABOUT IT?
YOU CONTROL THE DARKNESS, ESTACADO. IT DOES NOT CONTROL YOU.
THINK ABOUT IT, ESTACADO. YOU ALWAYS SEEM TO MUSTER JUST ENOUGH OF YOUR DARKNESS POWERS TO GET THROUGH ALL THE SCRAPES YOU STUMBLED INTO LATELY.
IF YOUR POWER IS LESSENED SOMEHOW IT'S BECAUSE ON SOME LEVEL YOU WANT IT TO BE.
THAT-- THAT'S NOT TRUE, I--

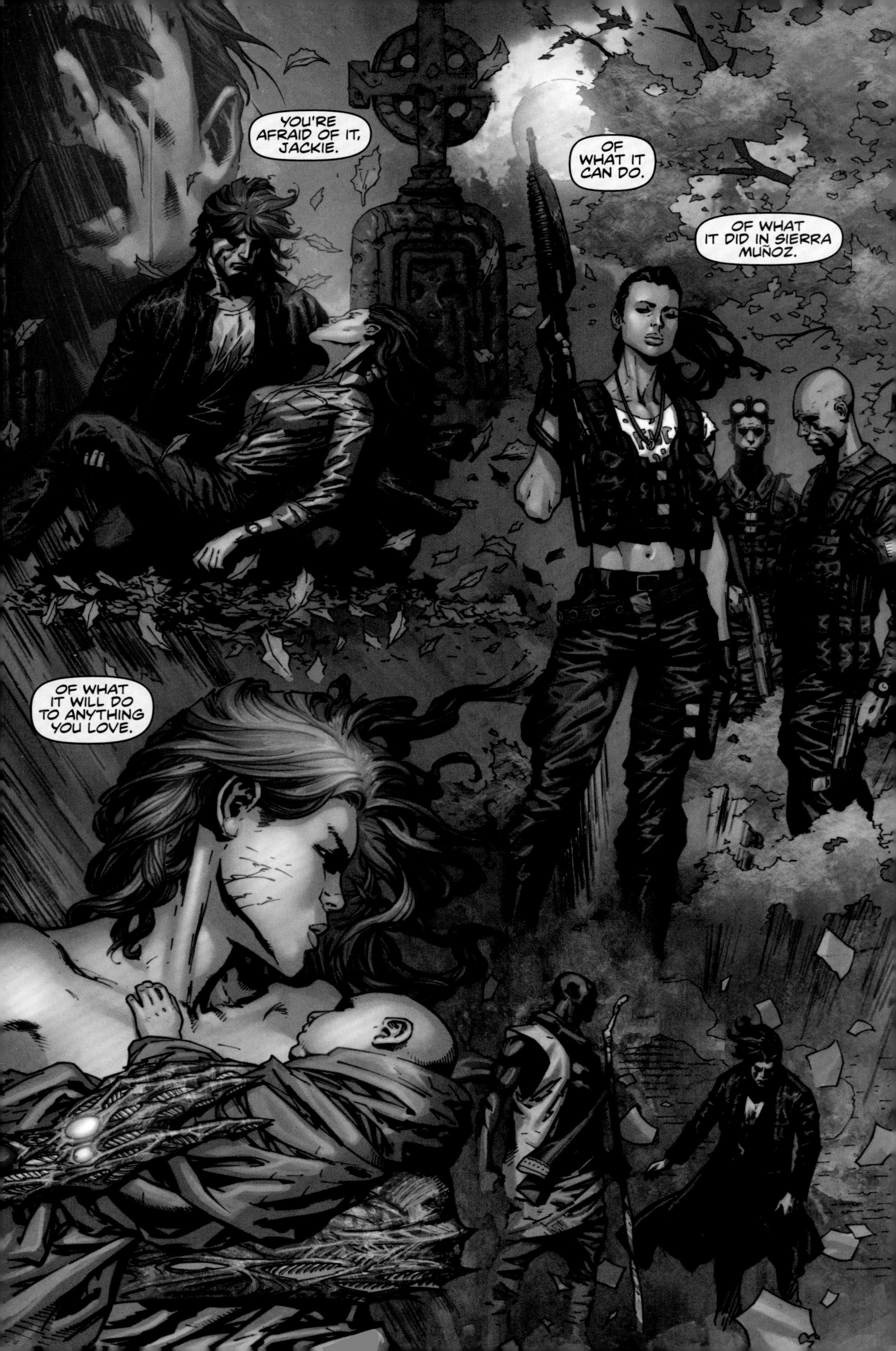
YOU'RE AFRAID OF IT, JACKIE.
OF WHAT IT CAN DO.
OF WHAT IT DID IN SIERRA MUÑOZ.
OF WHAT IT WILL DO TO ANYTHING YOU LOVE.

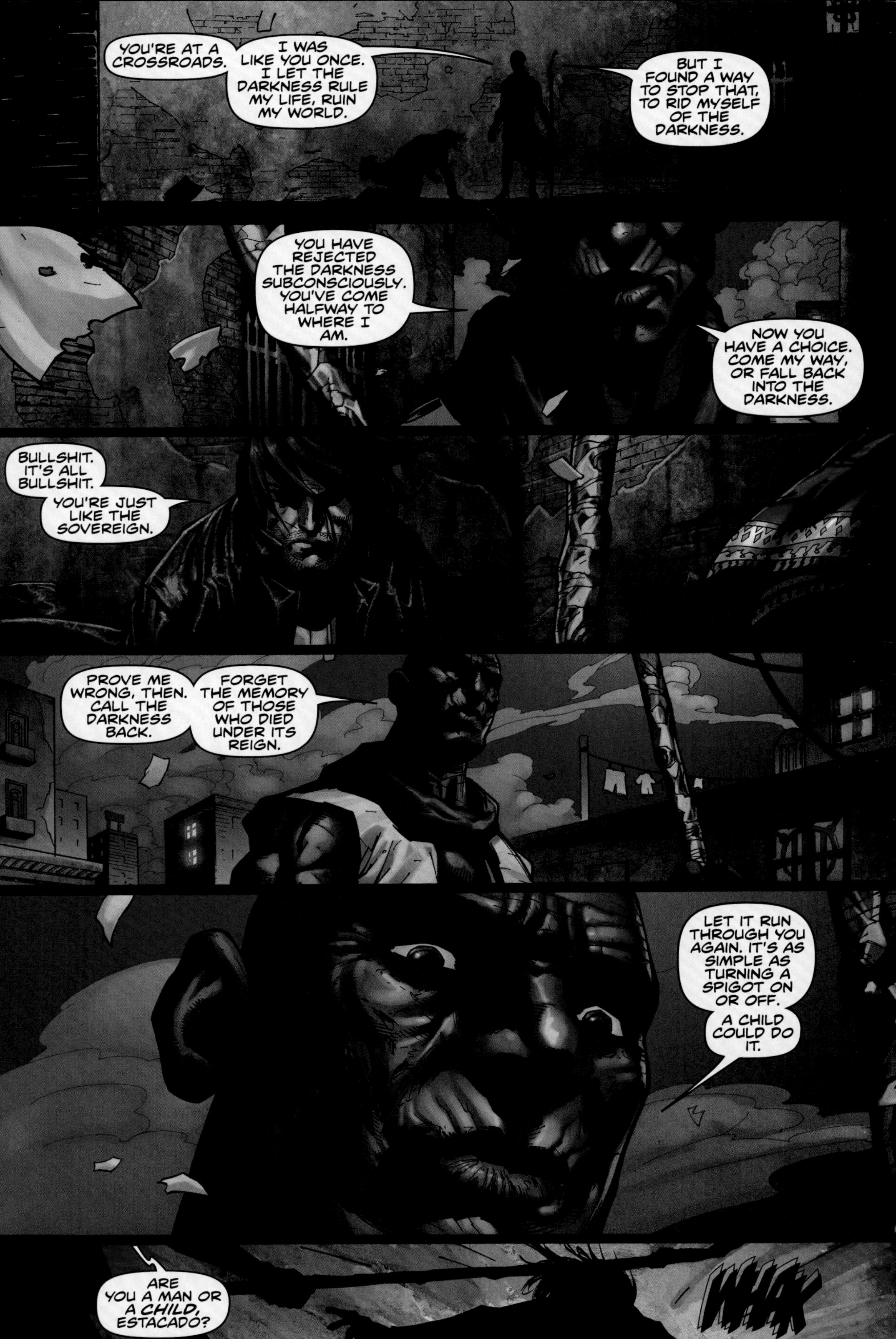

YOU'RE AT A CROSSROADS.
I WAS LIKE YOU ONCE. I LET THE DARKNESS RULE MY LIFE, RUIN MY WORLD.
BUT I FOUND A WAY TO STOP THAT, TO RID MYSELF OF THE DARKNESS.
YOU HAVE REJECTED THE DARKNESS SUBCONSCIOUSLY. YOU'VE COME HALFWAY TO WHERE I AM.
NOW YOU HAVE A CHOICE. COME MY WAY, OR FALL BACK INTO THE DARKNESS.
BULLSHIT. IT'S ALL BULLSHIT.
YOU'RE JUST LIKE THE SOVEREIGN.
PROVE ME WRONG, THEN. CALL THE DARKNESS BACK.
FORGET THE MEMORY OF THOSE WHO DIED UNDER ITS REIGN.
LET IT RUN THROUGH YOU AGAIN. IT'S AS SIMPLE AS TURNING A SPIGOT ON OR OFF.
A CHILD COULD DO IT.
ARE YOU A MAN OR A CHILD, ESTACADO?
WHAK

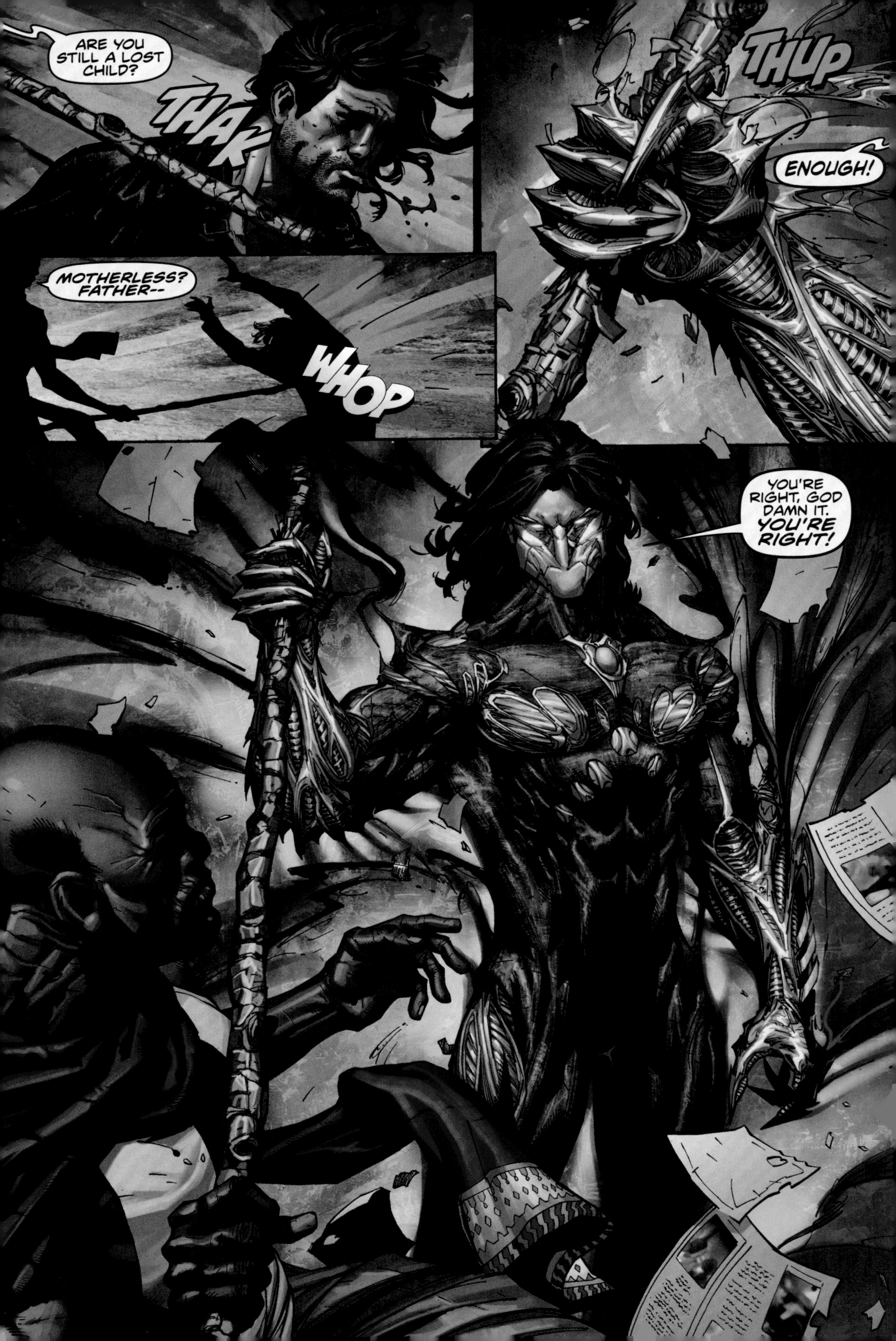
ARE YOU STILL A LOST CHILD?
THAK
THUP
ENOUGH!
MOTHERLESS? FATHER--
WHOP
YOU'RE RIGHT, GOD DAMN IT. YOU'RE RIGHT!

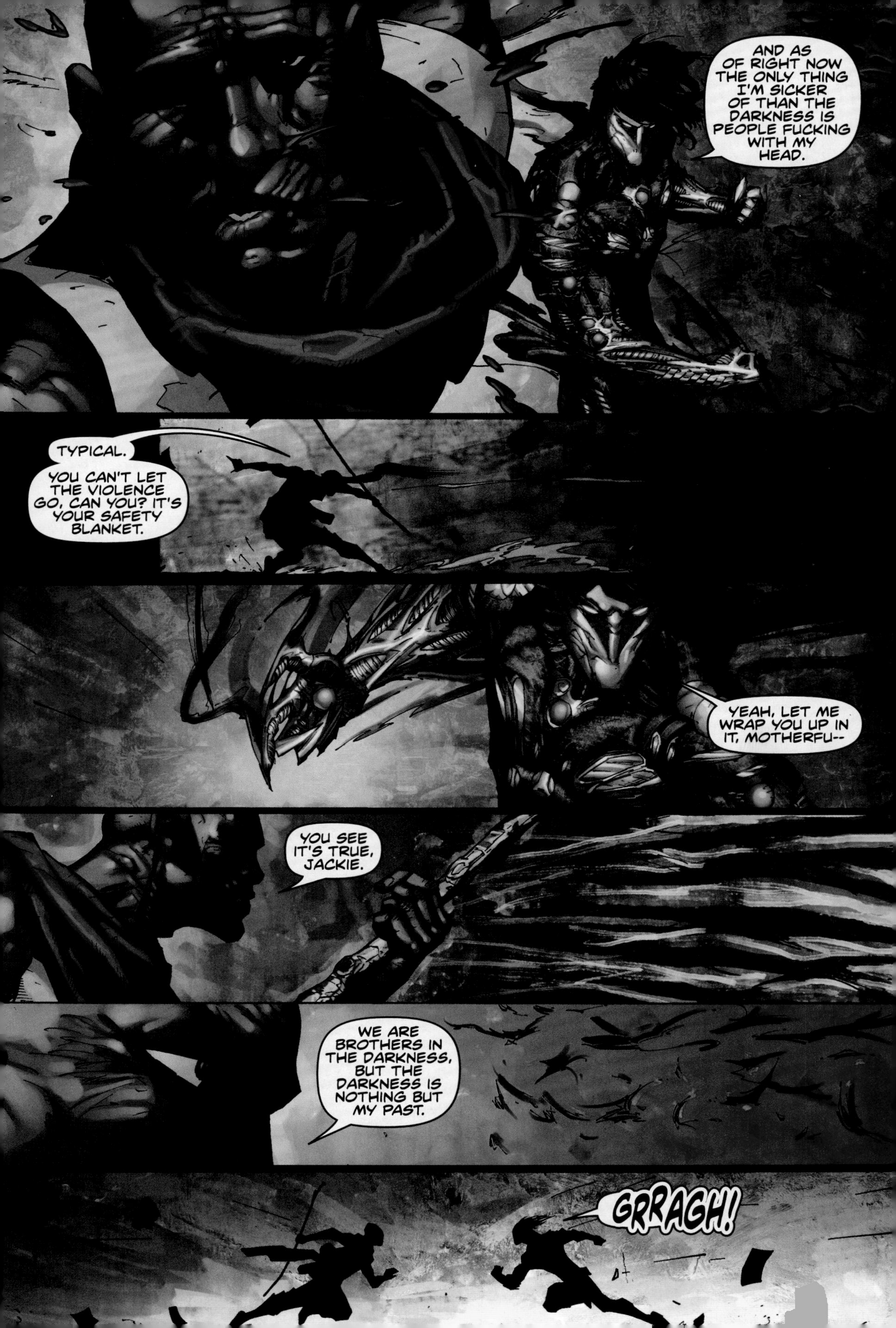
AND AS OF RIGHT NOW THE ONLY THING I'M SICKER OF THAN THE DARKNESS IS PEOPLE FUCKING WITH MY HEAD.
TYPICAL.
YOU CAN'T LET THE VIOLENCE GO, CAN YOU? IT'S YOUR SAFETY BLANKET.
YEAH, LET ME WRAP YOU UP IN IT, MOTHERFU--
YOU SEE IT'S TRUE, JACKIE.
WE ARE BROTHERS IN THE DARKNESS, BUT THE DARKNESS IS NOTHING BUT MY PAST.
GRRAGH!

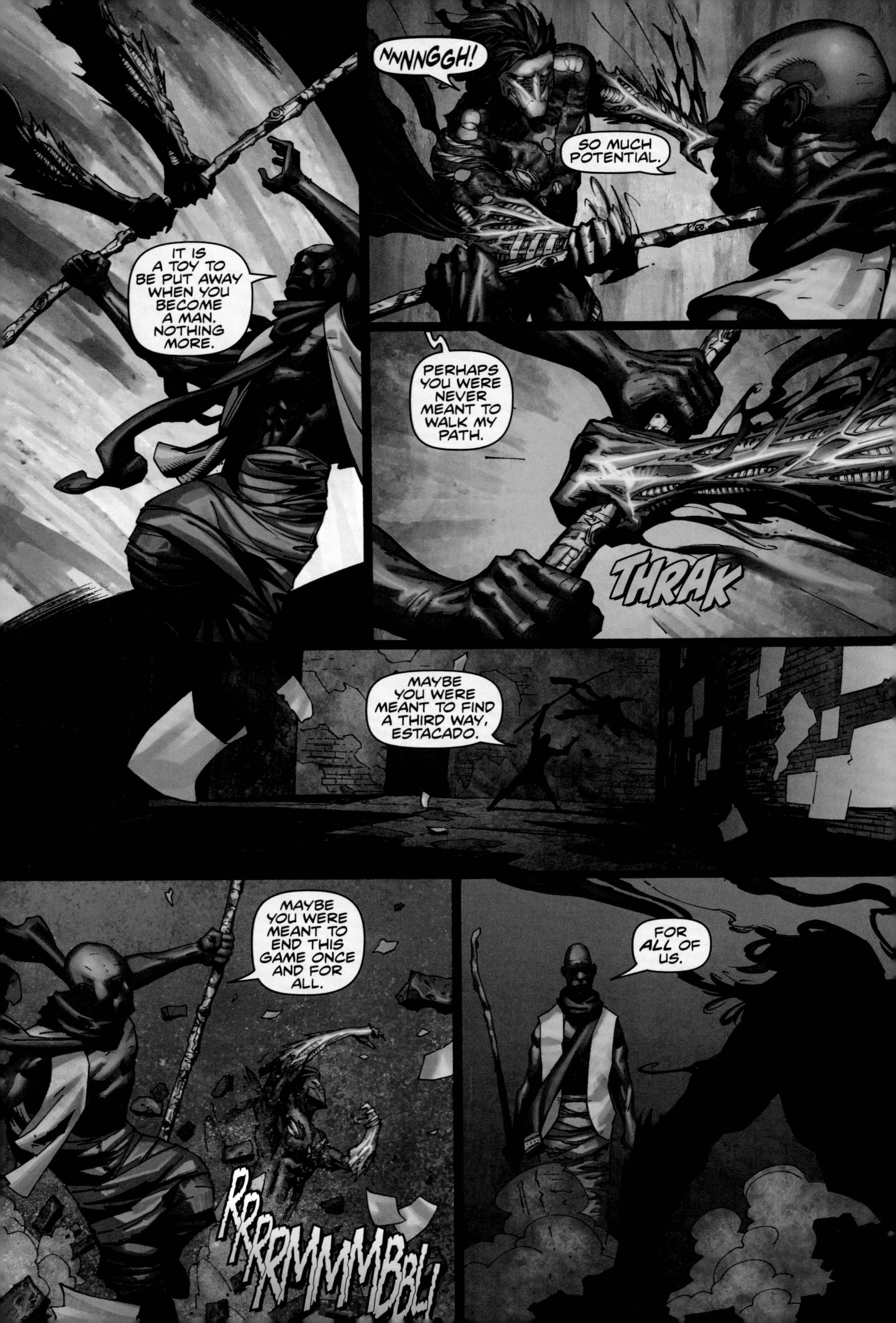
IT IS A TOY TO BE PUT AWAY WHEN YOU BECOME A MAN. NOTHING MORE.
NNNNGGH!
SO MUCH POTENTIAL.
PERHAPS YOU WERE NEVER MEANT TO WALK MY PATH.
THRAK
MAYBE YOU WERE MEANT TO FIND A THIRD WAY, ESTACADO.
MAYBE YOU WERE MEANT TO END THIS GAME ONCE AND FOR ALL.
RRRRMMMMBBLL
FOR ALL OF US.

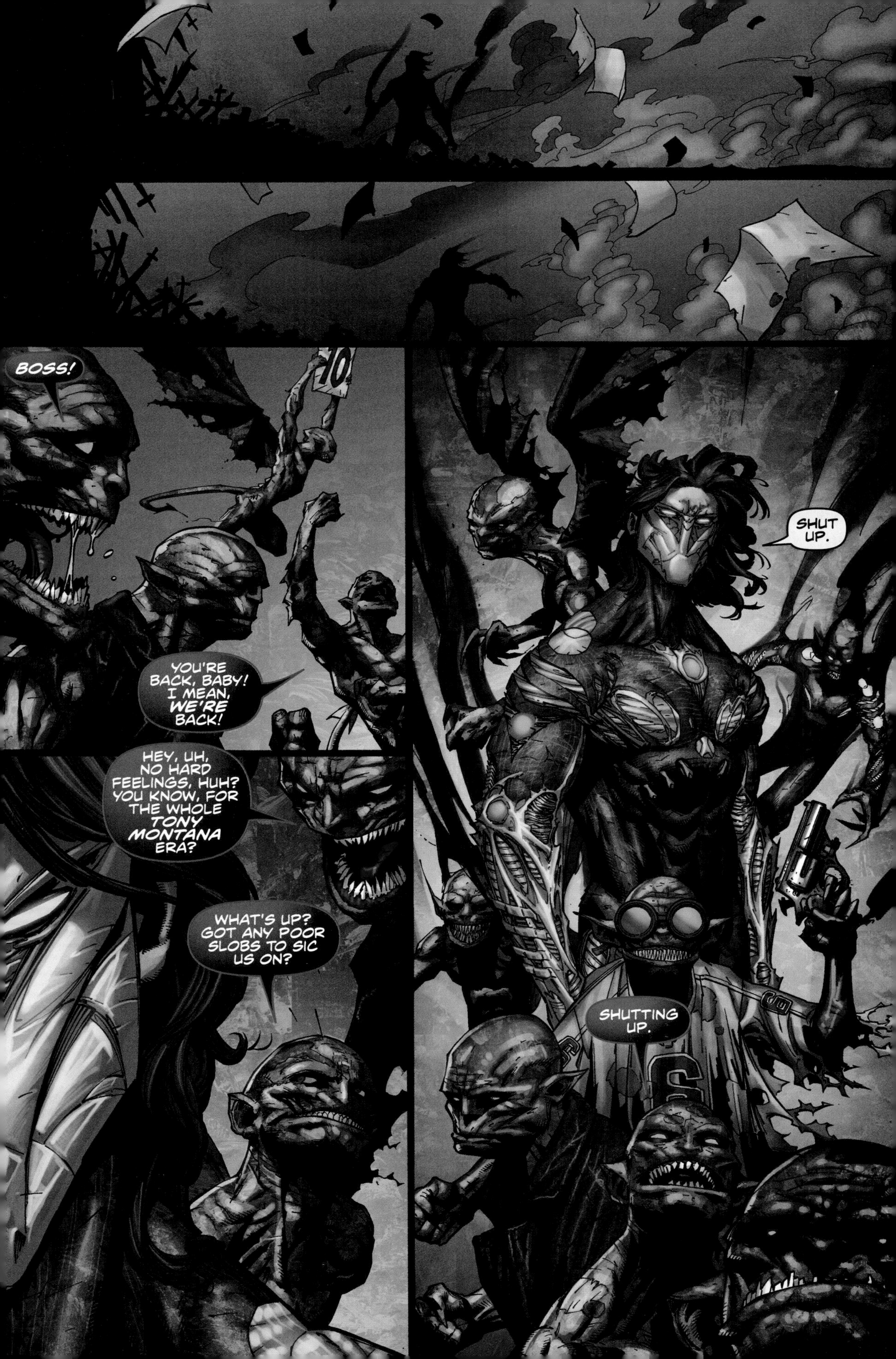
BOSS!
YOU'RE BACK, BABY! I MEAN, *WE'RE* BACK!
HEY, UH, NO HARD FEELINGS, HUH? YOU KNOW, FOR THE WHOLE *TONY MONTANA* ERA?
WHAT'S UP? GOT ANY POOR SLOBS TO SIC US ON?
SHUT UP.
SHUTTING UP.

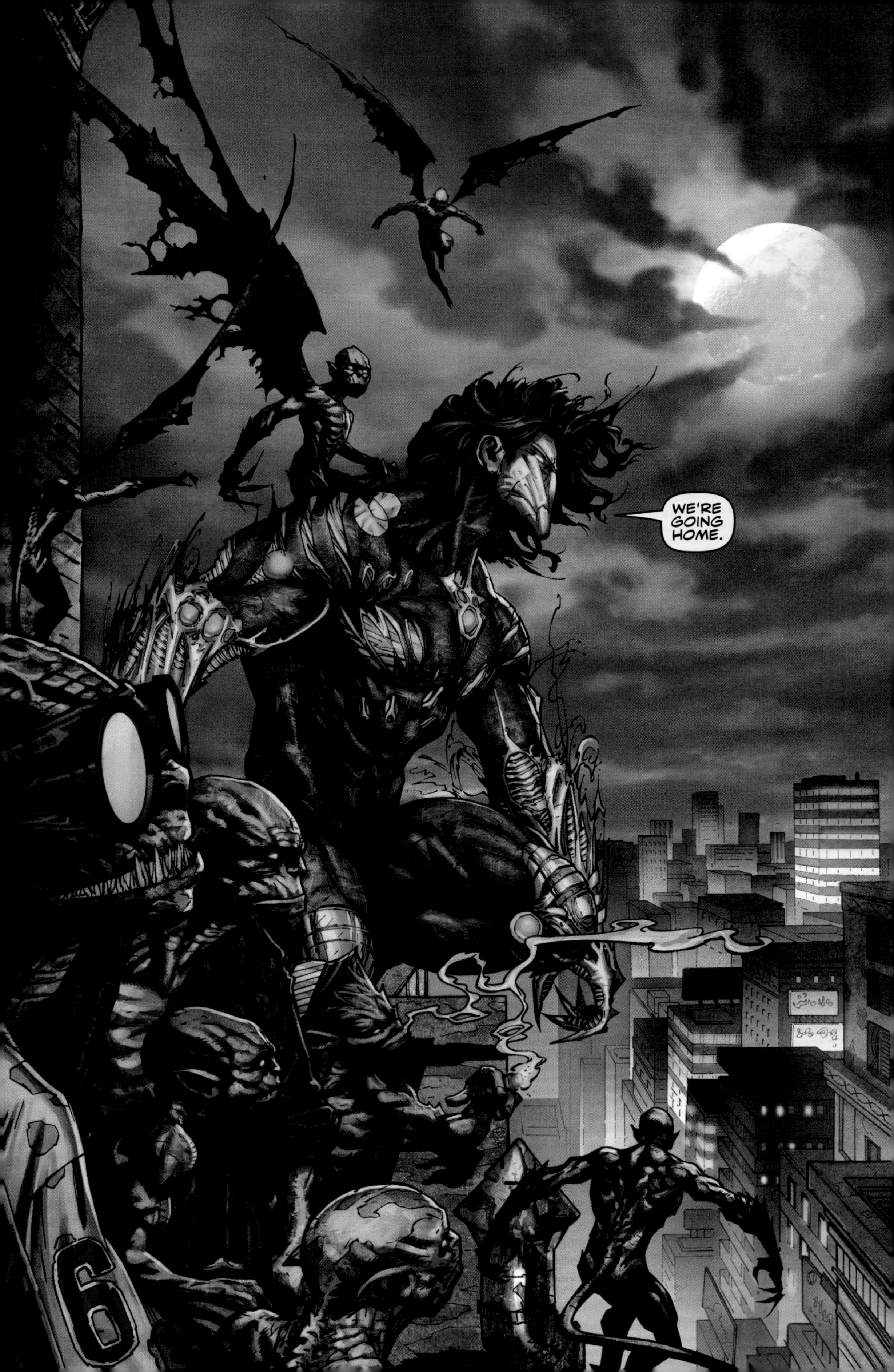
WE'RE GOING HOME.

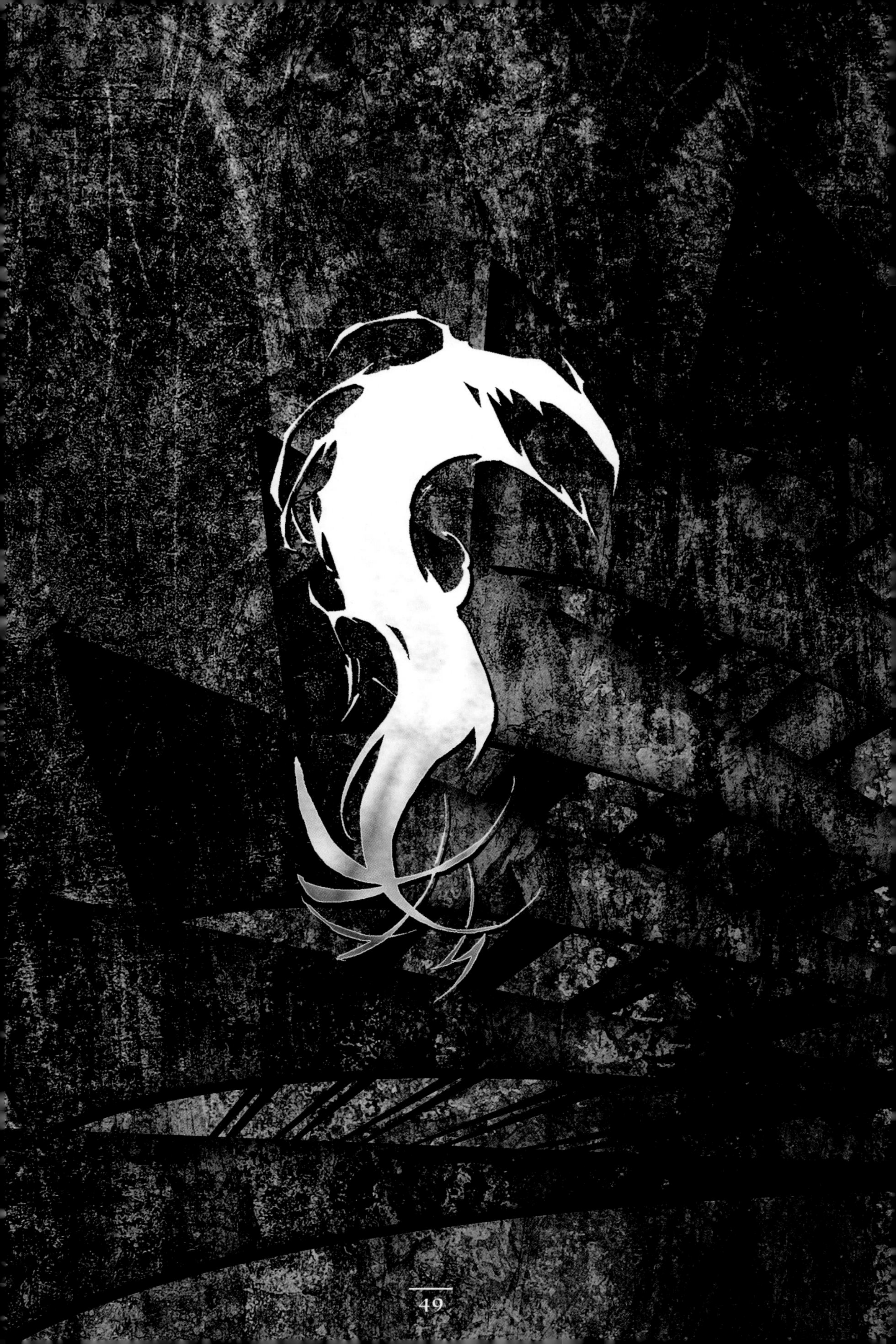

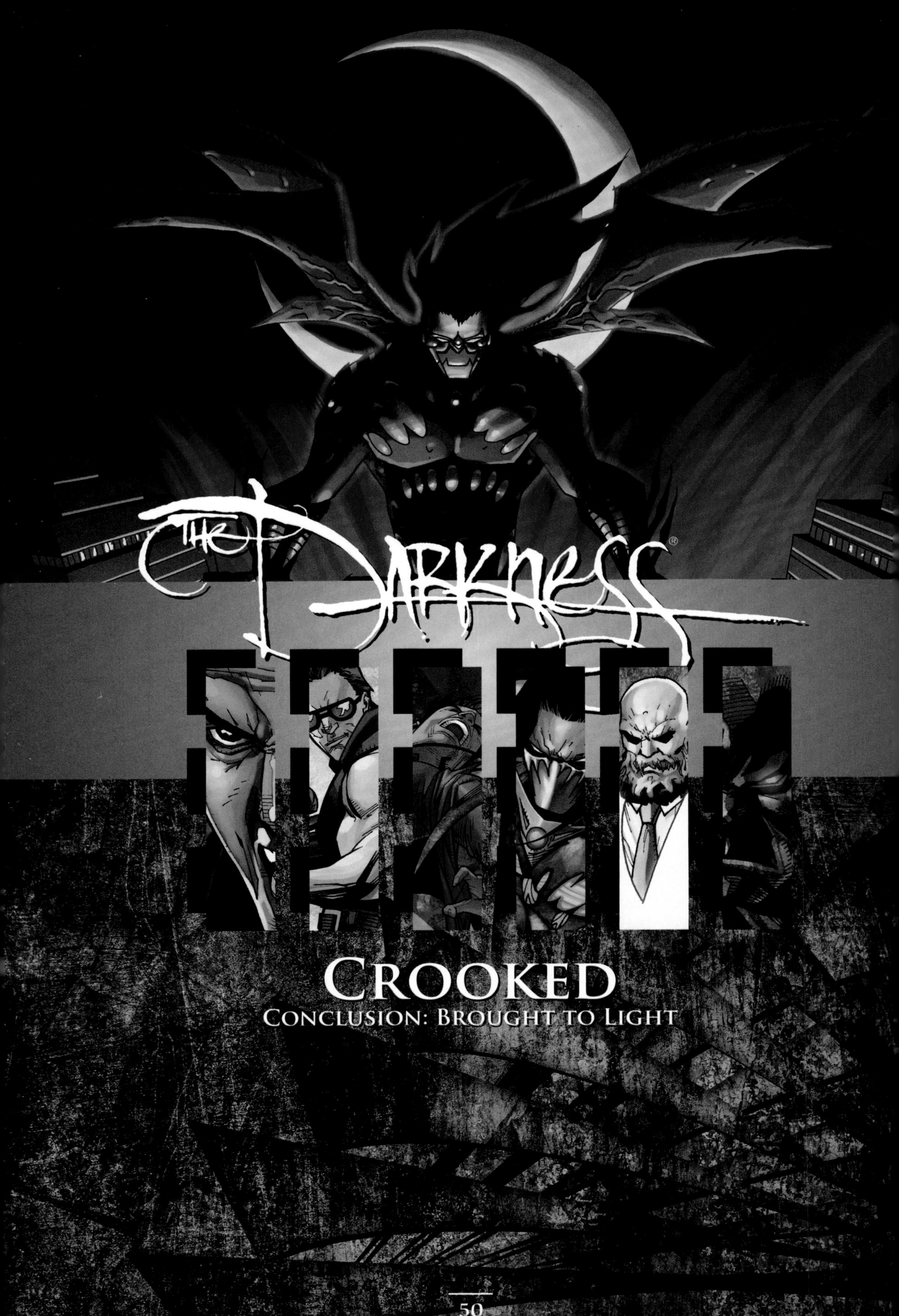
THE DARKNESS®
CROOKED
CONCLUSION: BROUGHT TO LIGHT

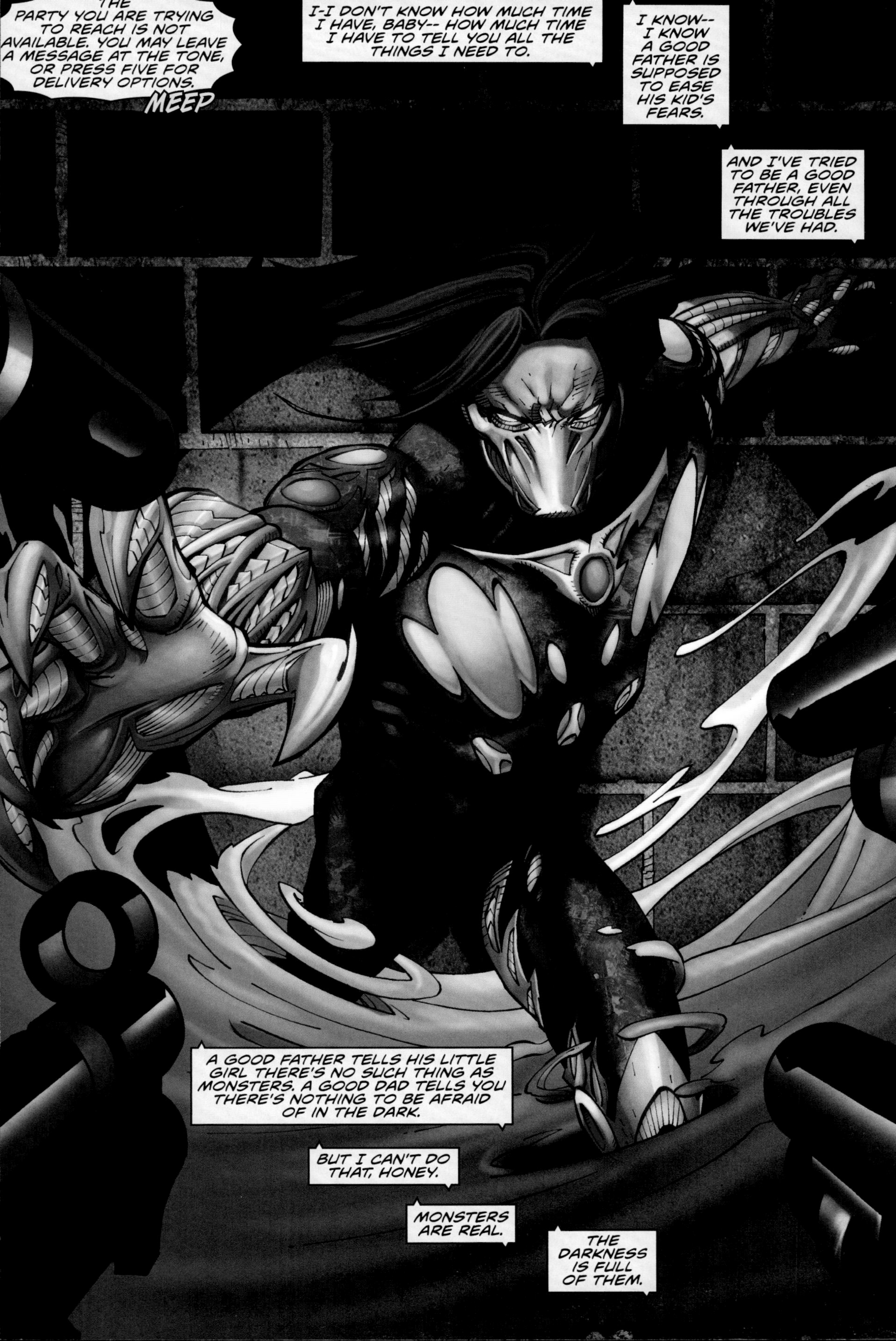

THE PARTY YOU ARE TRYING TO REACH IS NOT AVAILABLE. YOU MAY LEAVE A MESSAGE AT THE TONE, OR PRESS FIVE FOR DELIVERY OPTIONS.
MEEP
I-I DON'T KNOW HOW MUCH TIME I HAVE, BABY-- HOW MUCH TIME I HAVE TO TELL YOU ALL THE THINGS I NEED TO.
I KNOW-- I KNOW A GOOD FATHER IS SUPPOSED TO EASE HIS KID'S FEARS.
AND I'VE TRIED TO BE A GOOD FATHER, EVEN THROUGH ALL THE TROUBLES WE'VE HAD.
A GOOD FATHER TELLS HIS LITTLE GIRL THERE'S NO SUCH THING AS MONSTERS. A GOOD DAD TELLS YOU THERE'S NOTHING TO BE AFRAID OF IN THE DARK.
BUT I CAN'T DO THAT, HONEY.
MONSTERS ARE REAL.
THE DARKNESS IS FULL OF THEM.

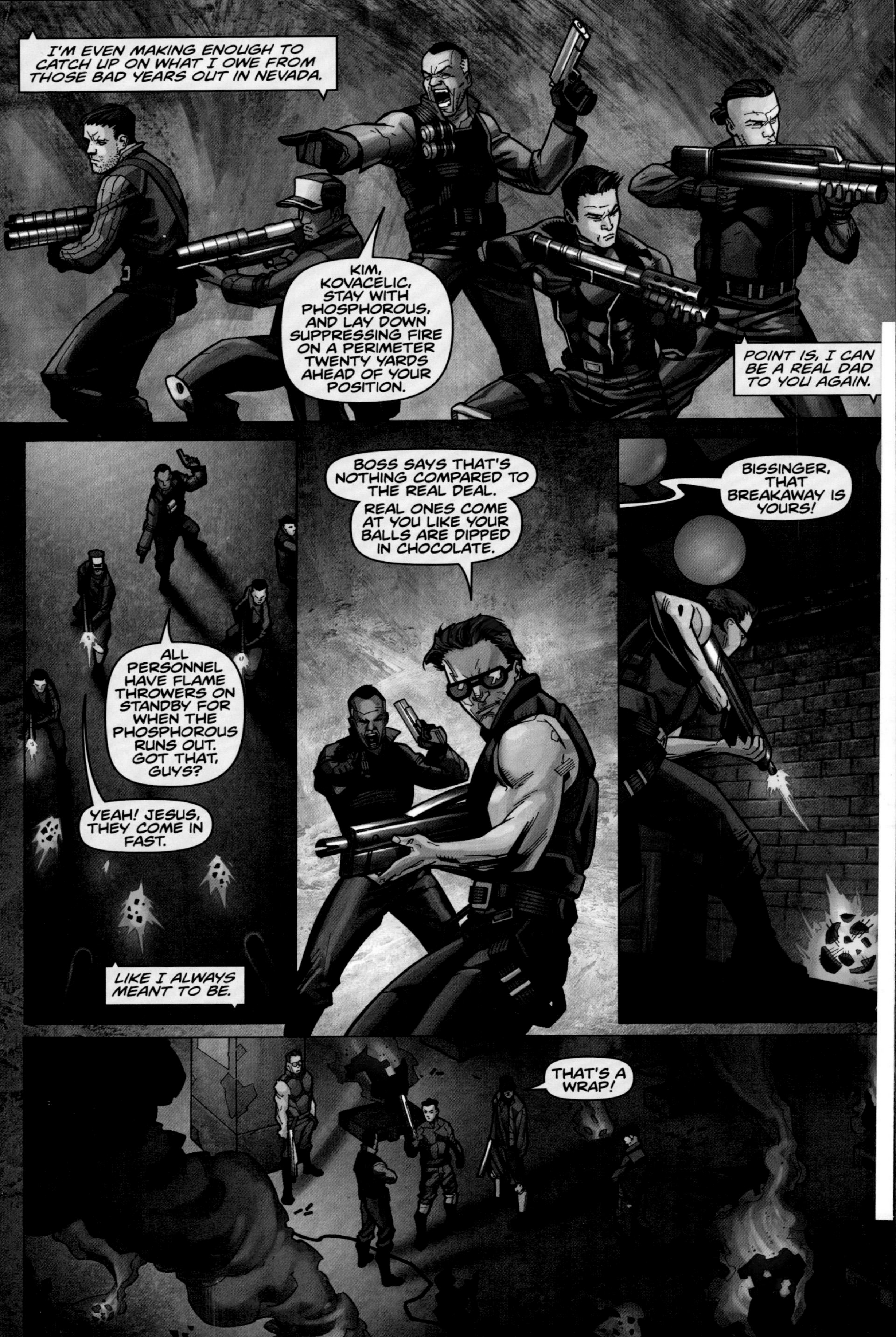

I'M EVEN MAKING ENOUGH TO CATCH UP ON WHAT I OWE FROM THOSE BAD YEARS OUT IN NEVADA.
KIM, KOVACELIC, STAY WITH PHOSPHOROUS, AND LAY DOWN SUPPRESSING FIRE ON A PERIMETER TWENTY YARDS AHEAD OF YOUR POSITION.
POINT IS, I CAN BE A REAL DAD TO YOU AGAIN.
ALL PERSONNEL HAVE FLAME THROWERS ON STANDBY FOR WHEN THE PHOSPHOROUS RUNS OUT. GOT THAT, GUYS?
YEAH! JESUS, THEY COME IN FAST.
LIKE I ALWAYS MEANT TO BE.
BOSS SAYS THAT'S NOTHING COMPARED TO THE REAL DEAL.
REAL ONES COME AT YOU LIKE YOUR BALLS ARE DIPPED IN CHOCOLATE.
BISSINGER, THAT BREAKAWAY IS YOURS!
THAT'S A WRAP!

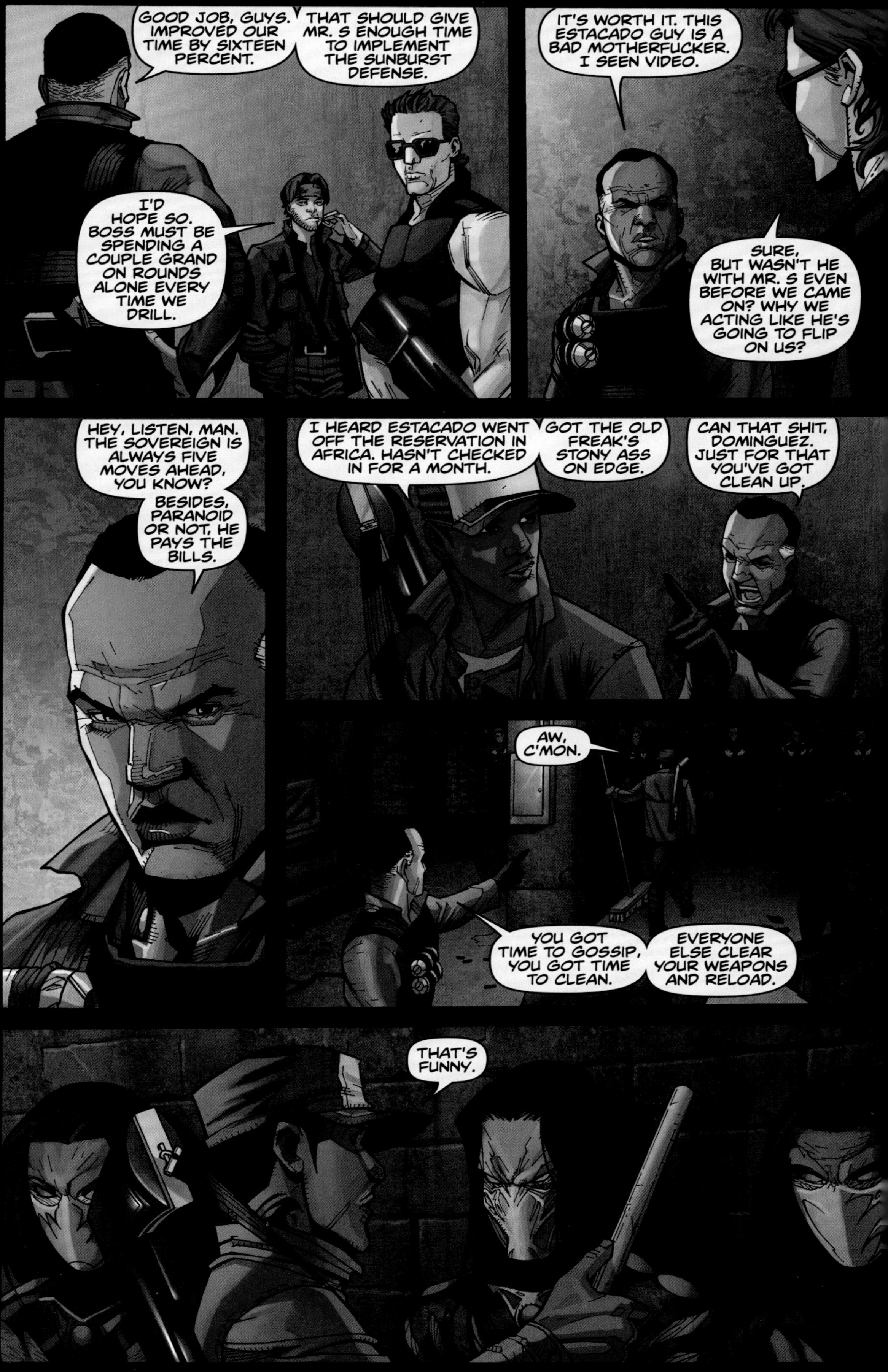
GOOD JOB, GUYS. IMPROVED OUR TIME BY SIXTEEN PERCENT.
THAT SHOULD GIVE MR. S ENOUGH TIME TO IMPLEMENT THE SUNBURST DEFENSE.
I'D HOPE SO. BOSS MUST BE SPENDING A COUPLE GRAND ON ROUNDS ALONE EVERY TIME WE DRILL.
IT'S WORTH IT. THIS ESTACADO GUY IS A BAD MOTHERFUCKER. I SEEN VIDEO.
SURE, BUT WASN'T HE WITH MR. S EVEN BEFORE WE CAME ON? WHY WE ACTING LIKE HE'S GOING TO FLIP ON US?
HEY, LISTEN, MAN. THE SOVEREIGN IS ALWAYS FIVE MOVES AHEAD, YOU KNOW?
BESIDES, PARANOID OR NOT, HE PAYS THE BILLS.
I HEARD ESTACADO WENT OFF THE RESERVATION IN AFRICA. HASN'T CHECKED IN FOR A MONTH.
GOT THE OLD FREAK'S STONY ASS ON EDGE.
CAN THAT SHIT, DOMINGUEZ. JUST FOR THAT YOU'VE GOT CLEAN UP.
AW, C'MON.
YOU GOT TIME TO GOSSIP, YOU GOT TIME TO CLEAN.
EVERYONE ELSE CLEAR YOUR WEAPONS AND RELOAD.
THAT'S FUNNY.

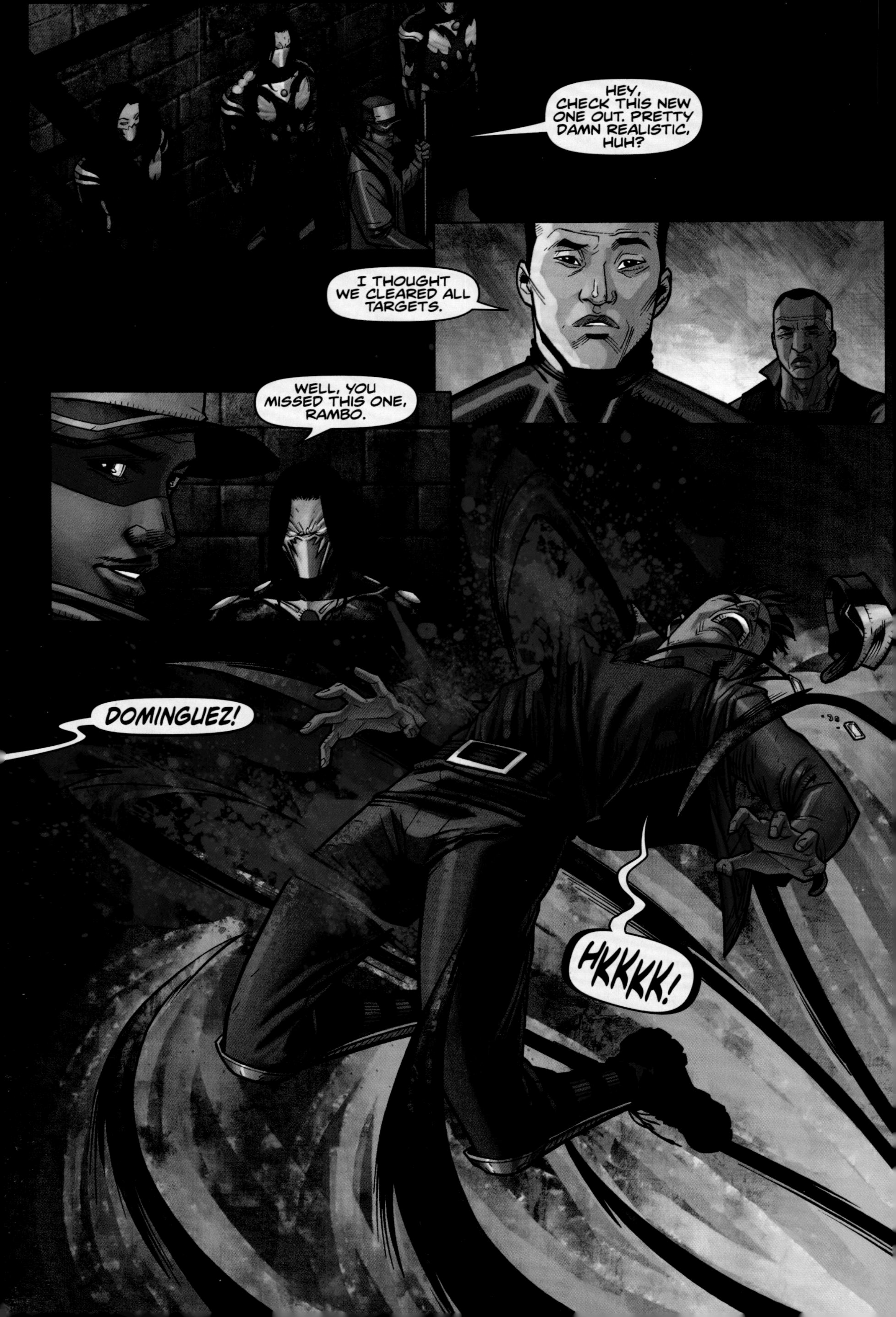
HEY, CHECK THIS NEW ONE OUT. PRETTY DAMN REALISTIC, HUH?
I THOUGHT WE CLEARED ALL TARGETS.
WELL, YOU MISSED THIS ONE, RAMBO.
DOMINGUEZ!
HKKKK!

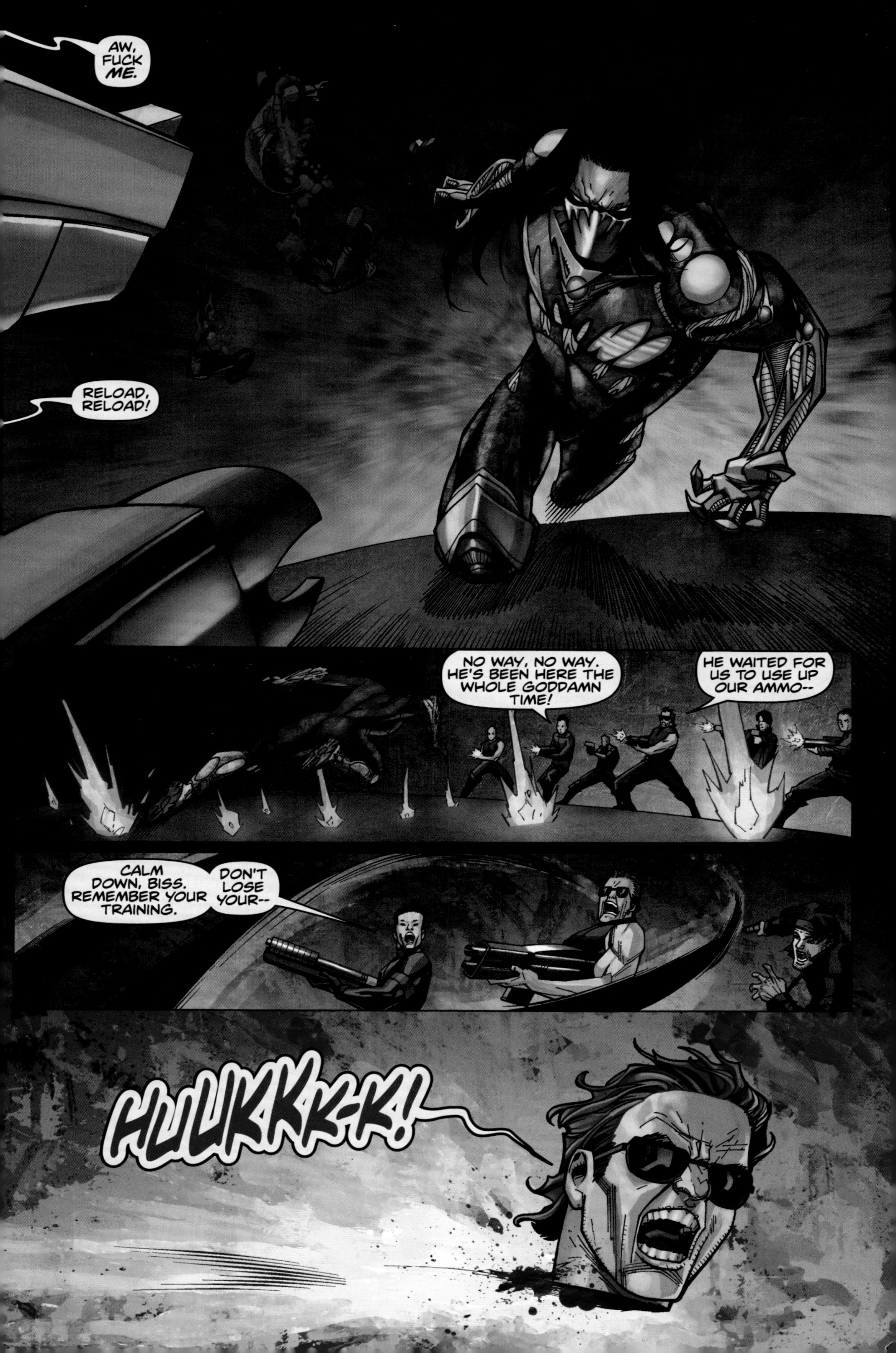
AW, FUCK ME.
RELOAD, RELOAD!
NO WAY, NO WAY. HE'S BEEN HERE THE WHOLE GODDAMN TIME!
HE WAITED FOR US TO USE UP OUR AMMO--
CALM DOWN, BISS. REMEMBER YOUR TRAINING.
DON'T LOSE YOUR--
HUUKKK-K!

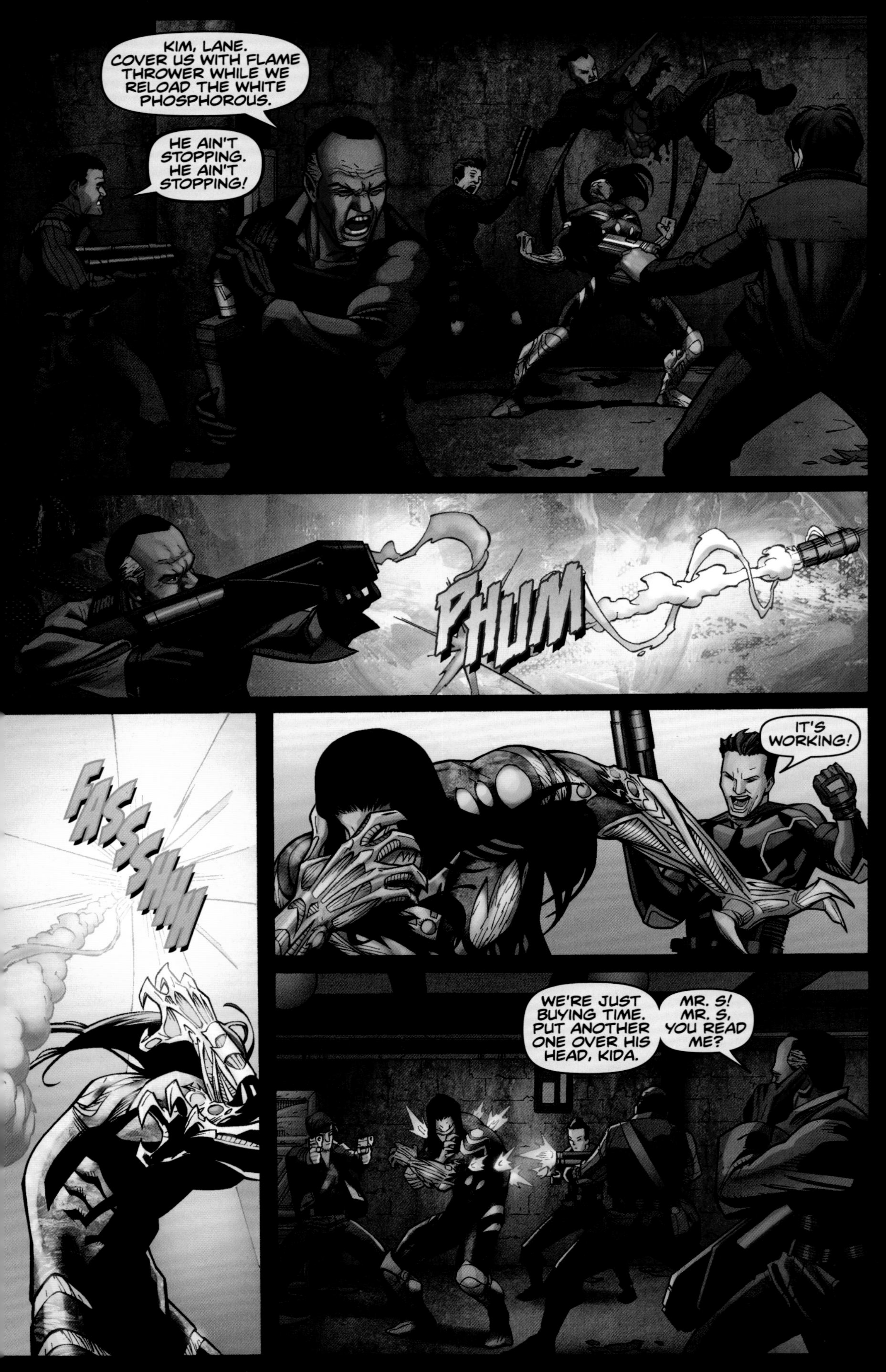
KIM, LANE. COVER US WITH FLAME THROWER WHILE WE RELOAD THE WHITE PHOSPHOROUS.
HE AIN'T STOPPING. HE AIN'T STOPPING!
PHUM
FASSSHHH
IT'S WORKING!
WE'RE JUST BUYING TIME. PUT ANOTHER ONE OVER HIS HEAD, KIDA.
MR. S! MR. S, YOU READ ME?

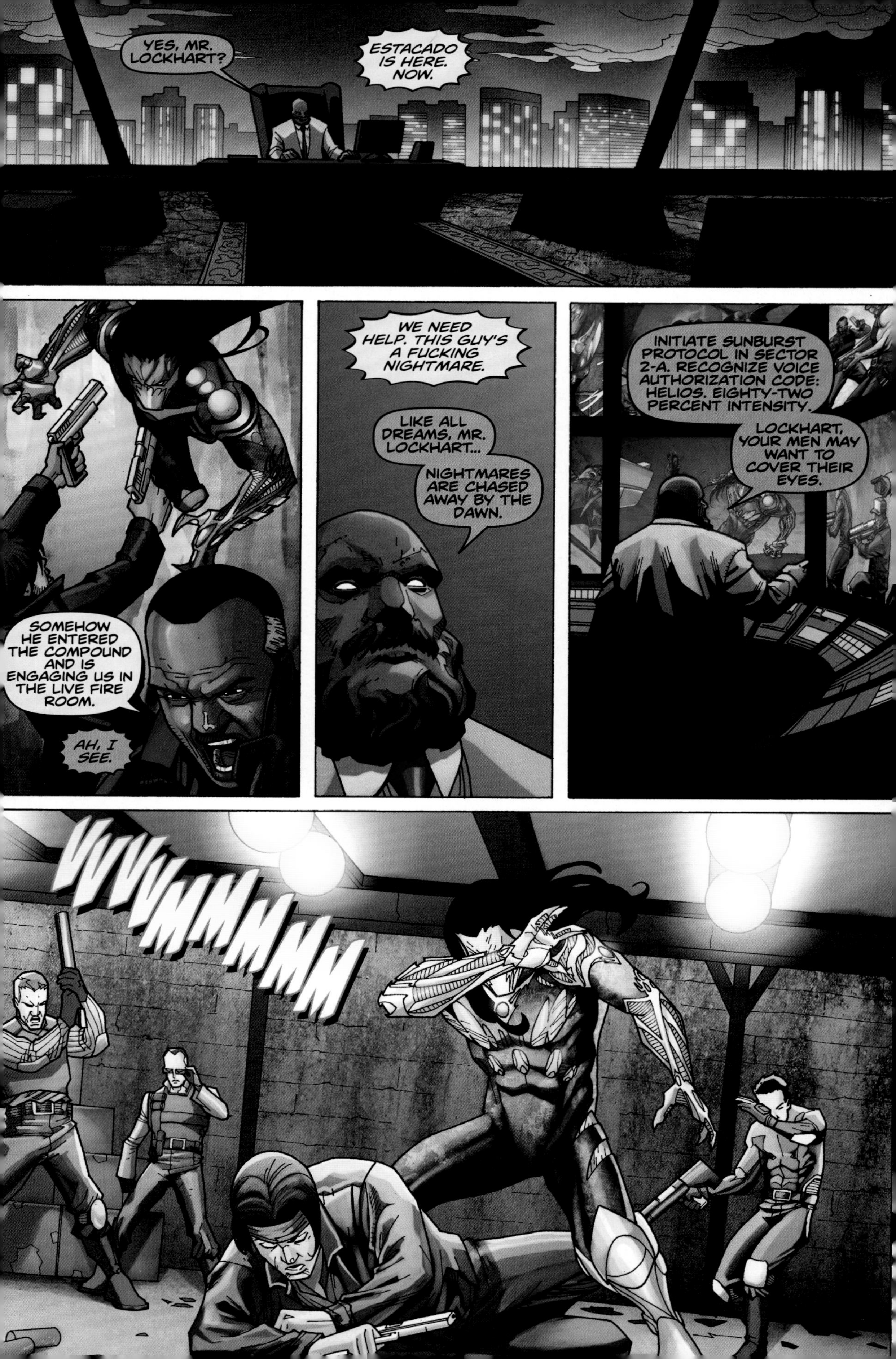
YES, MR. LOCKHART?
ESTACADO IS HERE. NOW.
SOMEHOW HE ENTERED THE COMPOUND AND IS ENGAGING US IN THE LIVE FIRE ROOM.
AH, I SEE.
WE NEED HELP. THIS GUY'S A FUCKING NIGHTMARE.
LIKE ALL DREAMS, MR. LOCKHART...
NIGHTMARES ARE CHASED AWAY BY THE DAWN.
INITIATE SUNBURST PROTOCOL IN SECTOR 2-A. RECOGNIZE VOICE AUTHORIZATION CODE: HELIOS. EIGHTY-TWO PERCENT INTENSITY.
LOCKHART, YOUR MEN MAY WANT TO COVER THEIR EYES.
VVVVMMMMMM

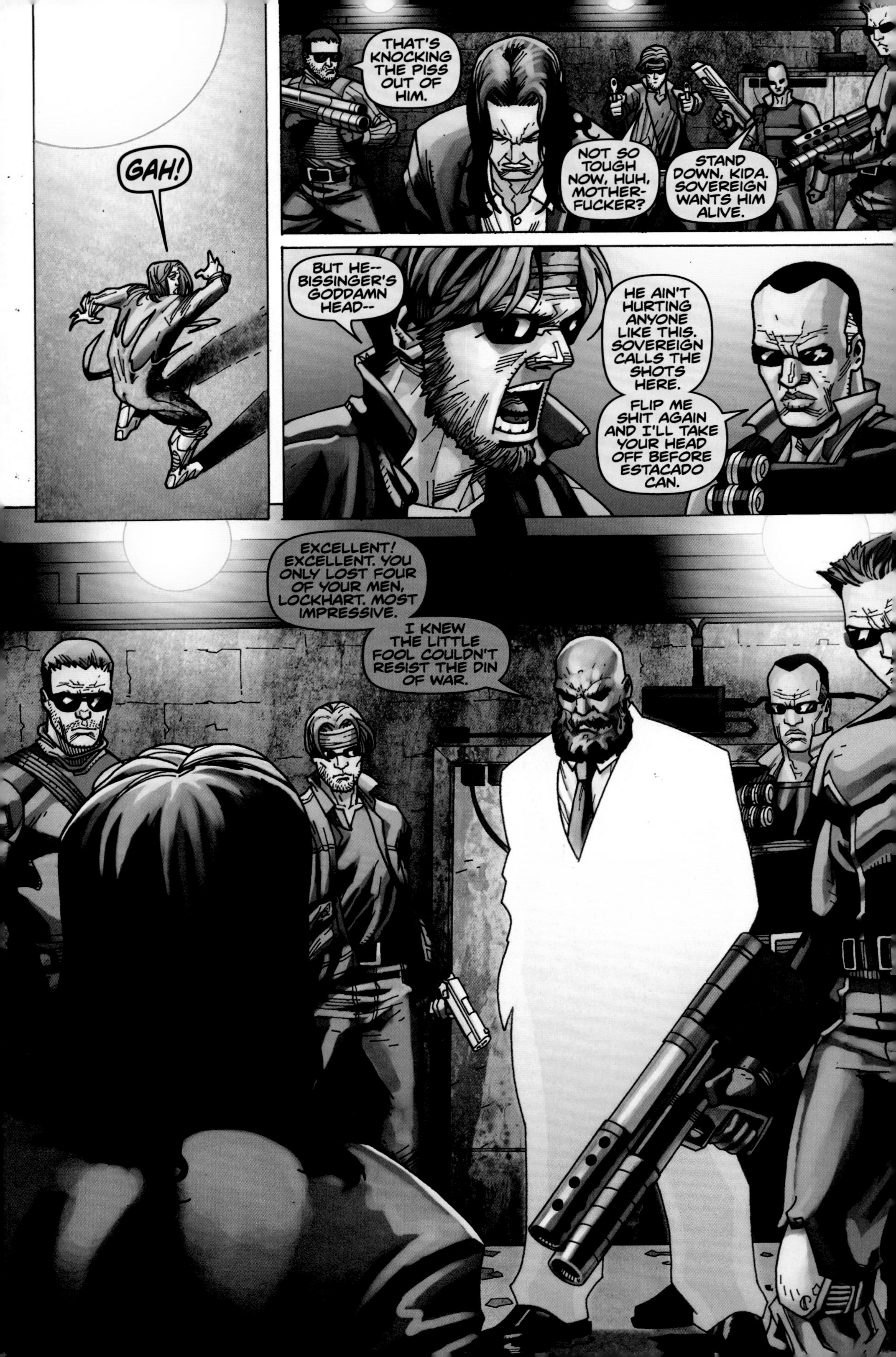
GAH!
THAT'S KNOCKING THE PISS OUT OF HIM.
NOT SO TOUGH NOW, HUH, MOTHER-FUCKER?
STAND DOWN, KIDA. SOVEREIGN WANTS HIM ALIVE.
BUT HE-- BISSINGER'S GODDAMN HEAD--
HE AIN'T HURTING ANYONE LIKE THIS. SOVEREIGN CALLS THE SHOTS HERE.
FLIP ME SHIT AGAIN AND I'LL TAKE YOUR HEAD OFF BEFORE ESTACADO CAN.
EXCELLENT! EXCELLENT. YOU ONLY LOST FOUR OF YOUR MEN, LOCKHART. MOST IMPRESSIVE.
I KNEW THE LITTLE FOOL COULDN'T RESIST THE DIN OF WAR.

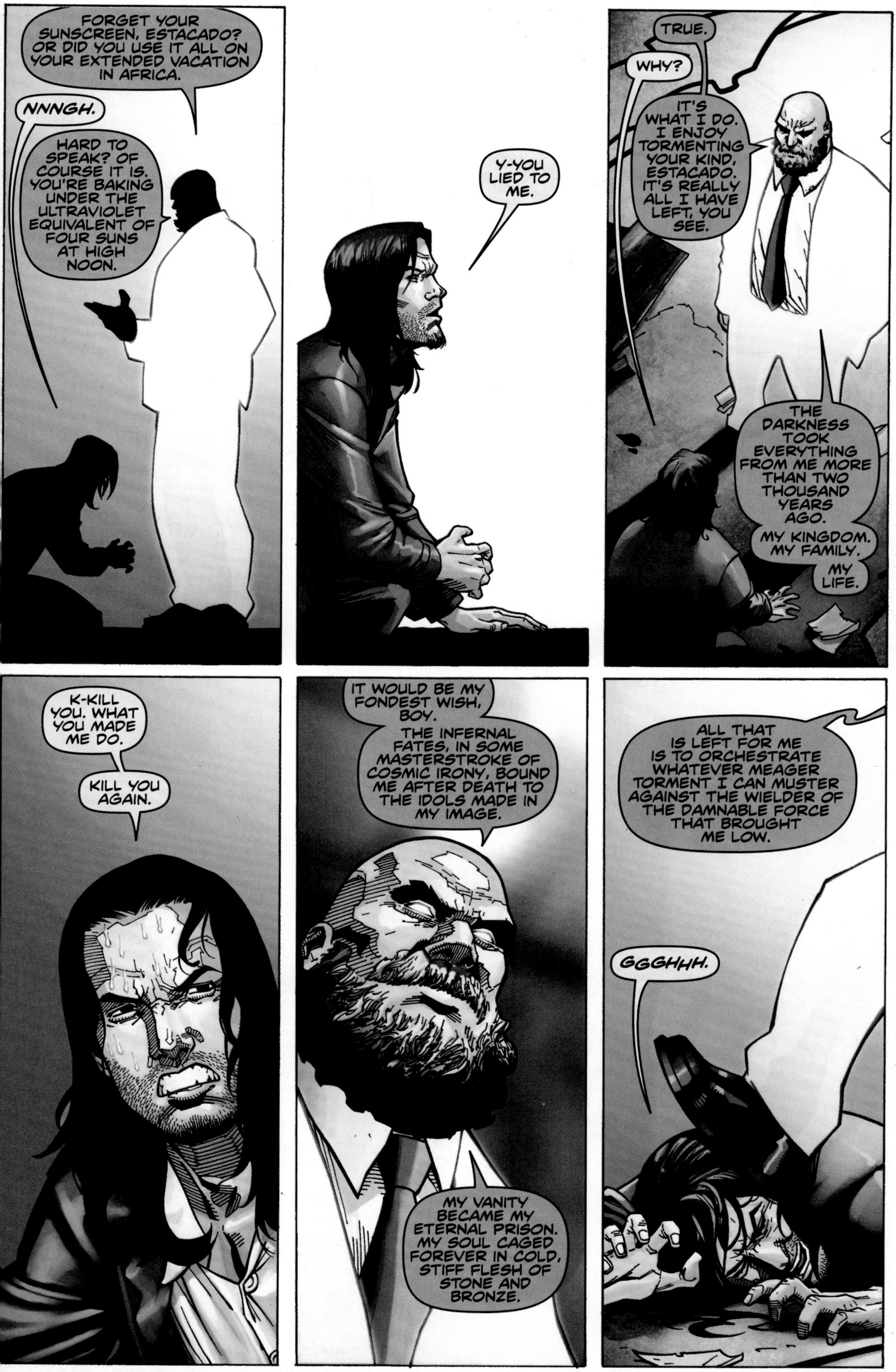
FORGET YOUR SUNSCREEN, ESTACADO? OR DID YOU USE IT ALL ON YOUR EXTENDED VACATION IN AFRICA.
NNNGH.
HARD TO SPEAK? OF COURSE IT IS. YOU'RE BAKING UNDER THE ULTRAVIOLET EQUIVALENT OF FOUR SUNS AT HIGH NOON.
Y-YOU LIED TO ME.
TRUE.
WHY?
IT'S WHAT I DO. I ENJOY TORMENTING YOUR KIND, ESTACADO. IT'S REALLY ALL I HAVE LEFT, YOU SEE.
THE DARKNESS TOOK EVERYTHING FROM ME MORE THAN TWO THOUSAND YEARS AGO.
MY KINGDOM. MY FAMILY.
MY LIFE.
K-KILL YOU. WHAT YOU MADE ME DO.
KILL YOU AGAIN.
IT WOULD BE MY FONDEST WISH, BOY.
THE INFERNAL FATES, IN SOME MASTERSTROKE OF COSMIC IRONY, BOUND ME AFTER DEATH TO THE IDOLS MADE IN MY IMAGE.
MY VANITY BECAME MY ETERNAL PRISON. MY SOUL CAGED FOREVER IN COLD, STIFF FLESH OF STONE AND BRONZE.
ALL THAT IS LEFT FOR ME IS TO ORCHESTRATE WHATEVER MEAGER TORMENT I CAN MUSTER AGAINST THE WIELDER OF THE DAMNABLE FORCE THAT BROUGHT ME LOW.
GGGHHH.

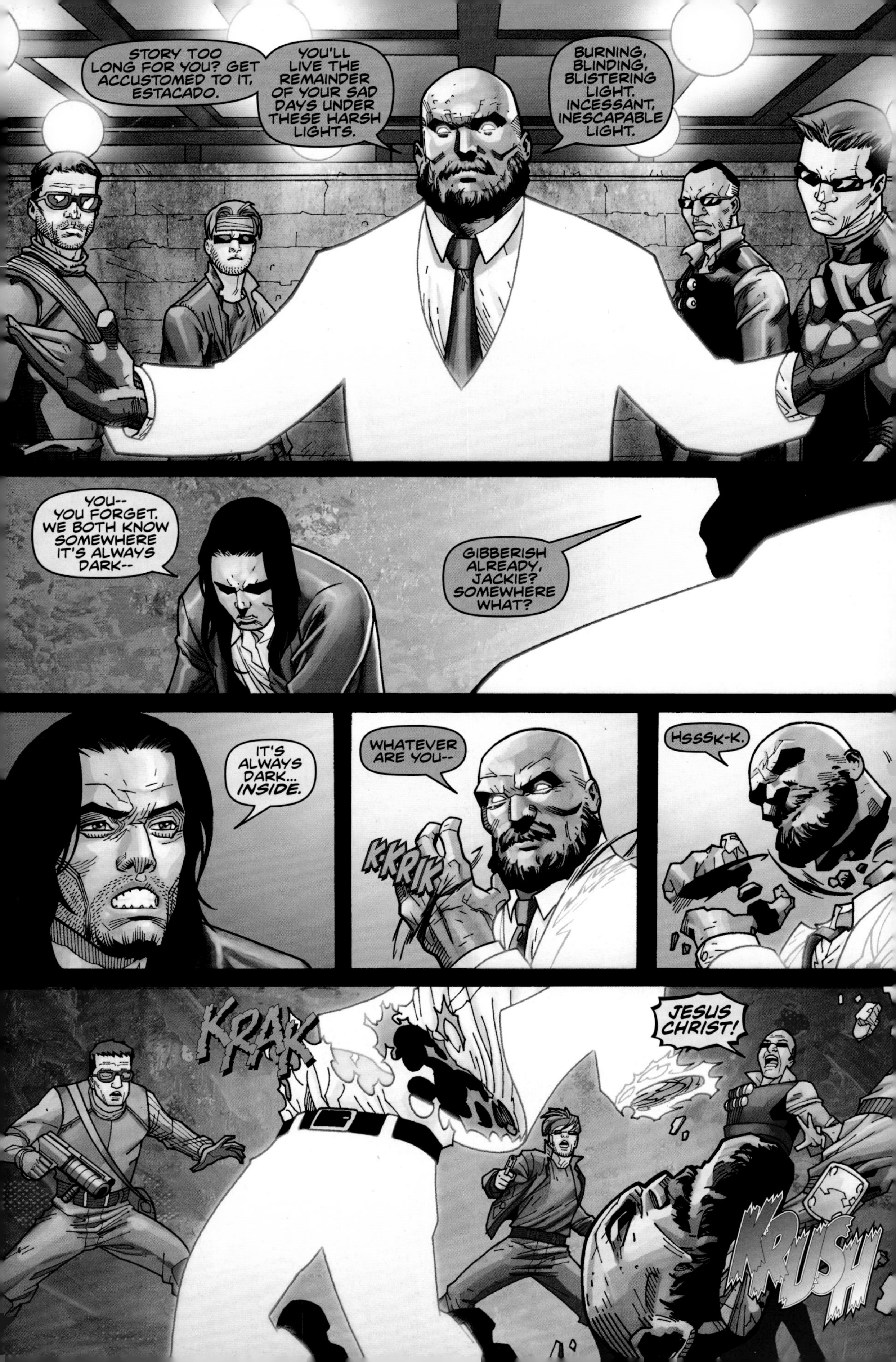
STORY TOO LONG FOR YOU? GET ACCUSTOMED TO IT, ESTACADO.
YOU'LL LIVE THE REMAINDER OF YOUR SAD DAYS UNDER THESE HARSH LIGHTS.
BURNING, BLINDING, BLISTERING LIGHT. INCESSANT, INESCAPABLE LIGHT.
YOU-- YOU FORGET. WE BOTH KNOW SOMEWHERE IT'S ALWAYS DARK--
GIBBERISH ALREADY, JACKIE? SOMEWHERE WHAT?
IT'S ALWAYS DARK... INSIDE.
WHATEVER ARE YOU--
K-KRIK
HSSSK-K.
KRAK
JESUS CHRIST!
KRUSH

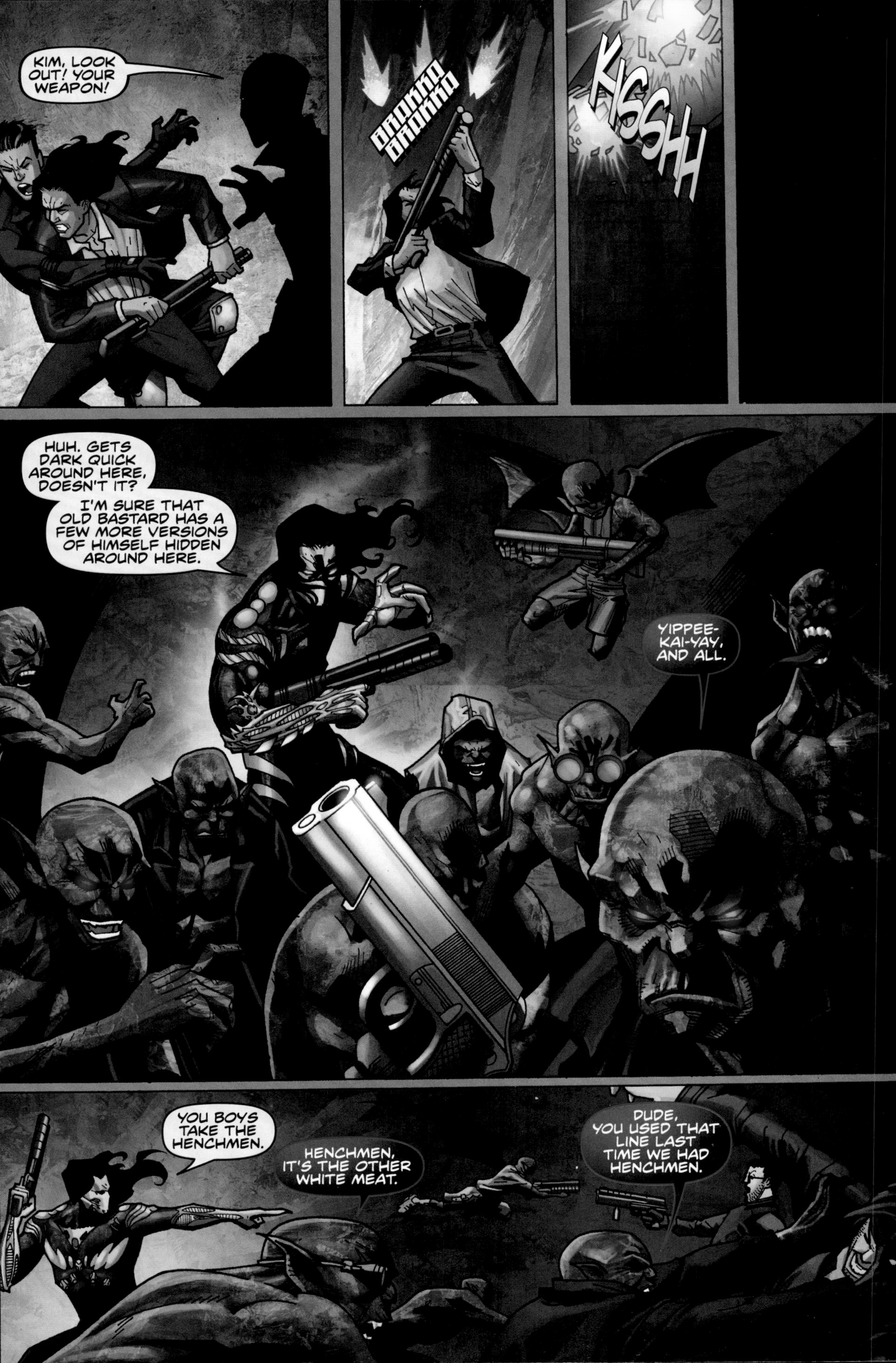
KIM, LOOK OUT! YOUR WEAPON!
BRAKKA BRAKKA
KISSHH
HUH. GETS DARK QUICK AROUND HERE, DOESN'T IT?
I'M SURE THAT OLD BASTARD HAS A FEW MORE VERSIONS OF HIMSELF HIDDEN AROUND HERE.
YIPPEE-KAI-YAY, AND ALL.
YOU BOYS TAKE THE HENCHMEN.
HENCHMEN, IT'S THE OTHER WHITE MEAT.
DUDE, YOU USED THAT LINE LAST TIME WE HAD HENCHMEN.

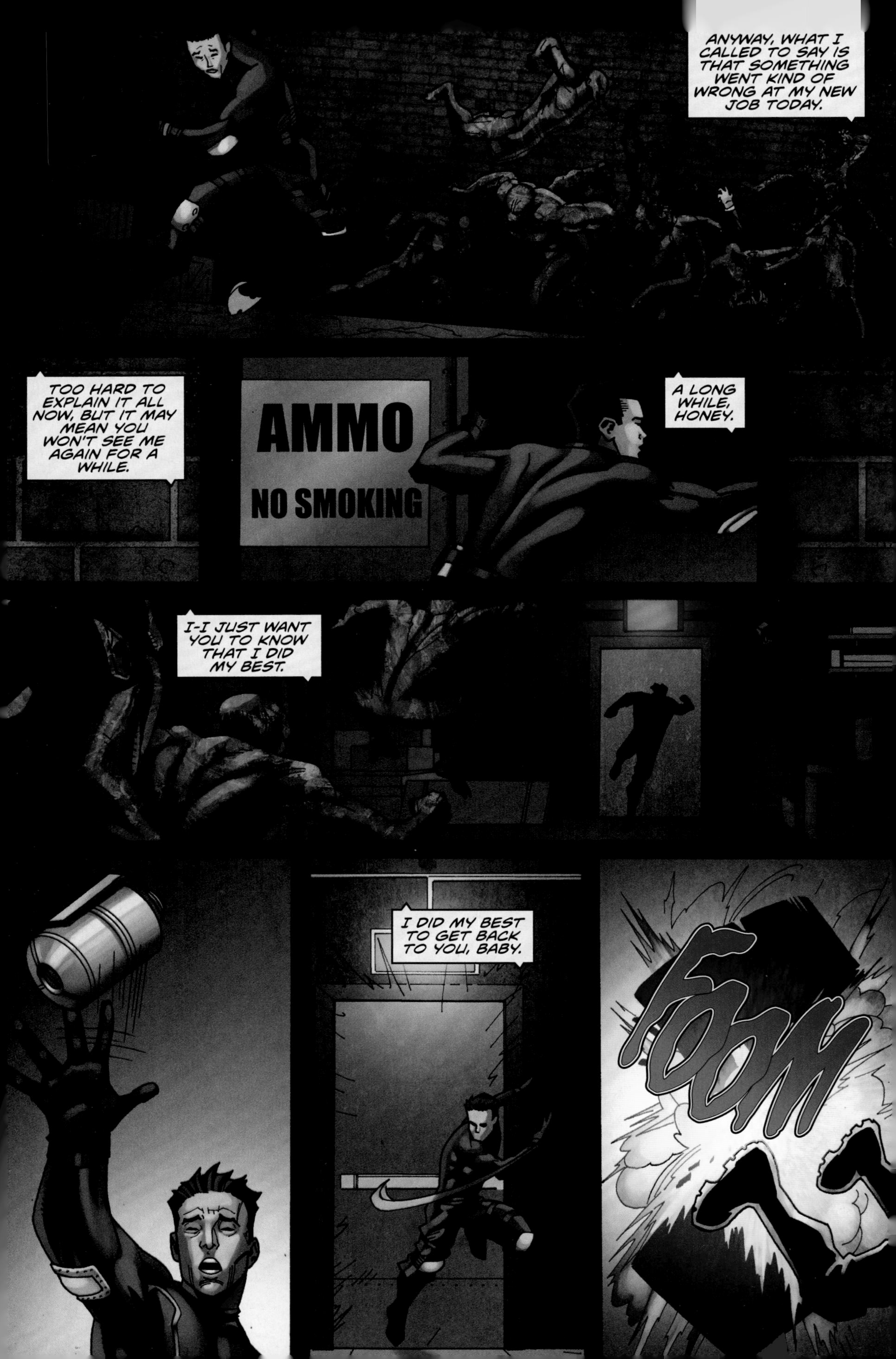

ANYWAY, WHAT I CALLED TO SAY IS THAT SOMETHING WENT KIND OF WRONG AT MY NEW JOB TODAY.
TOO HARD TO EXPLAIN IT ALL NOW, BUT IT MAY MEAN YOU WON'T SEE ME AGAIN FOR A WHILE.
AMMO
NO SMOKING
A LONG WHILE, HONEY.
I-I JUST WANT YOU TO KNOW THAT I DID MY BEST.
I DID MY BEST TO GET BACK TO YOU, BABY.
FOOM

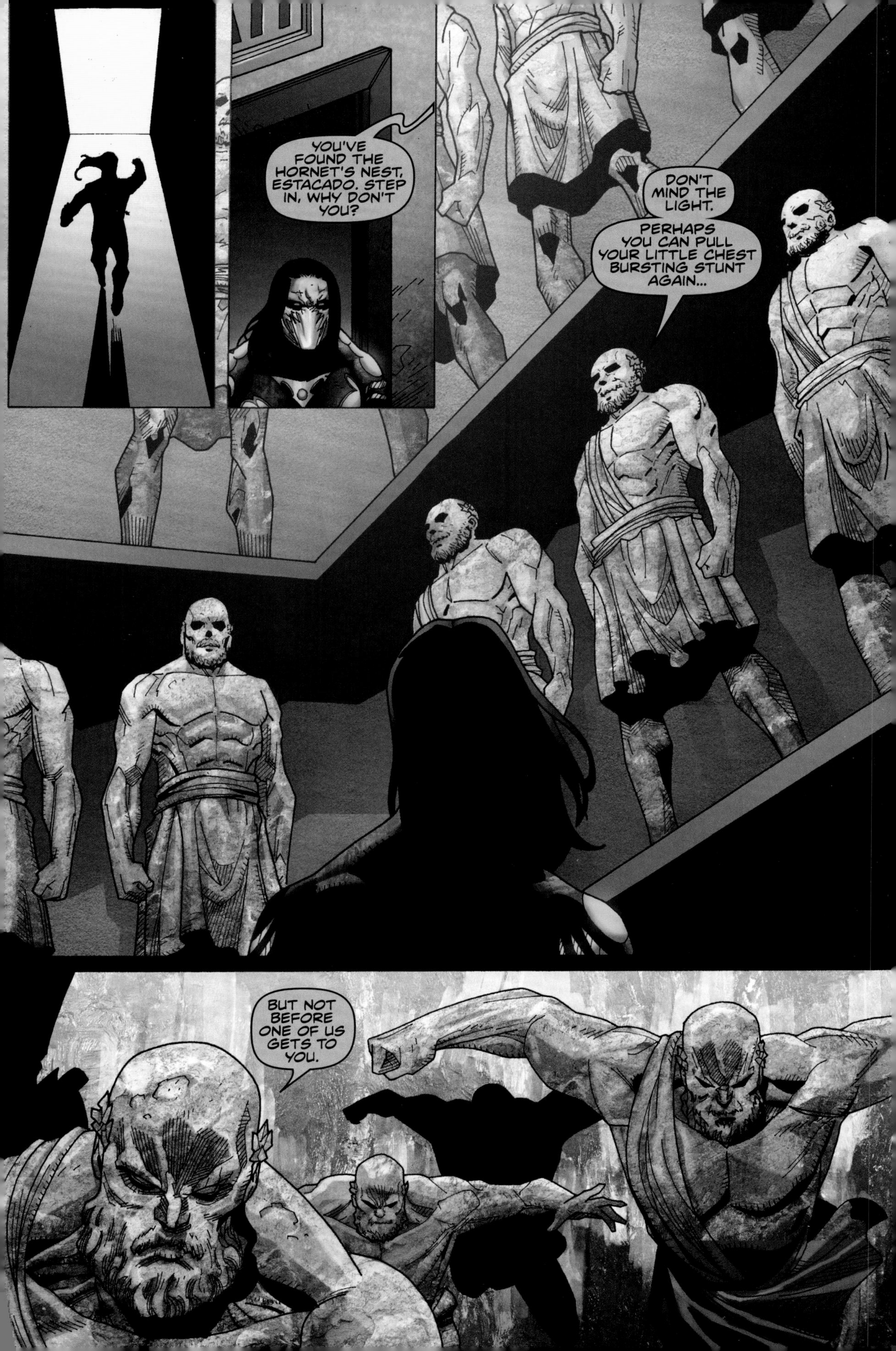
YOU'VE FOUND THE HORNET'S NEST, ESTACADO. STEP IN, WHY DON'T YOU?
DON'T MIND THE LIGHT.
PERHAPS YOU CAN PULL YOUR LITTLE CHEST BURSTING STUNT AGAIN...
BUT NOT BEFORE ONE OF US GETS TO YOU.

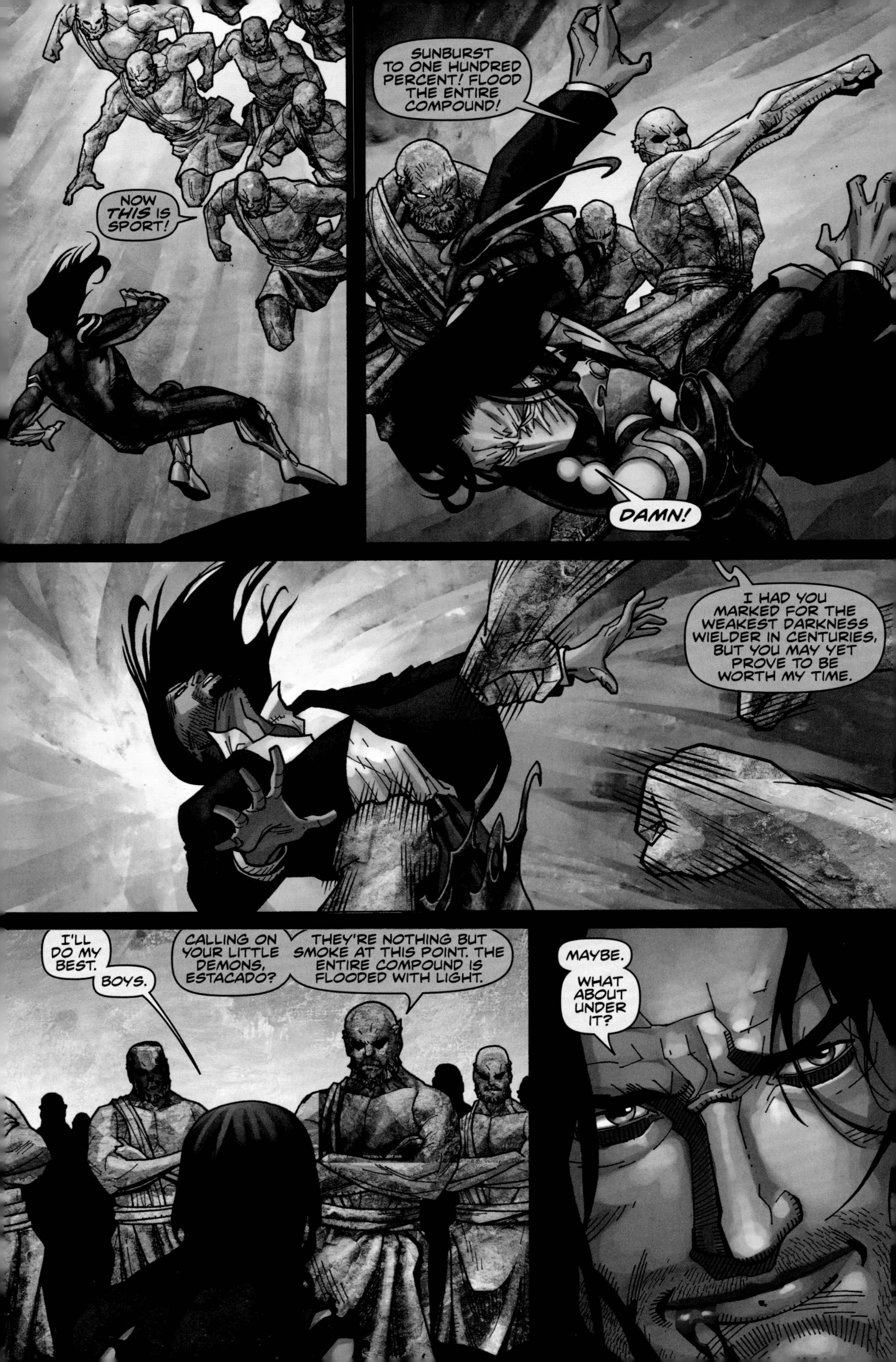

NOW *THIS* IS SPORT!
SUNBURST TO ONE HUNDRED PERCENT! FLOOD THE ENTIRE COMPOUND!
DAMN!
I HAD YOU MARKED FOR THE WEAKEST DARKNESS WIELDER IN CENTURIES, BUT YOU MAY YET PROVE TO BE WORTH MY TIME.
I'LL DO MY BEST.
BOYS.
CALLING ON YOUR LITTLE DEMONS, ESTACADO?
THEY'RE NOTHING BUT SMOKE AT THIS POINT. THE ENTIRE COMPOUND IS FLOODED WITH LIGHT.
MAYBE.
WHAT ABOUT UNDER IT?

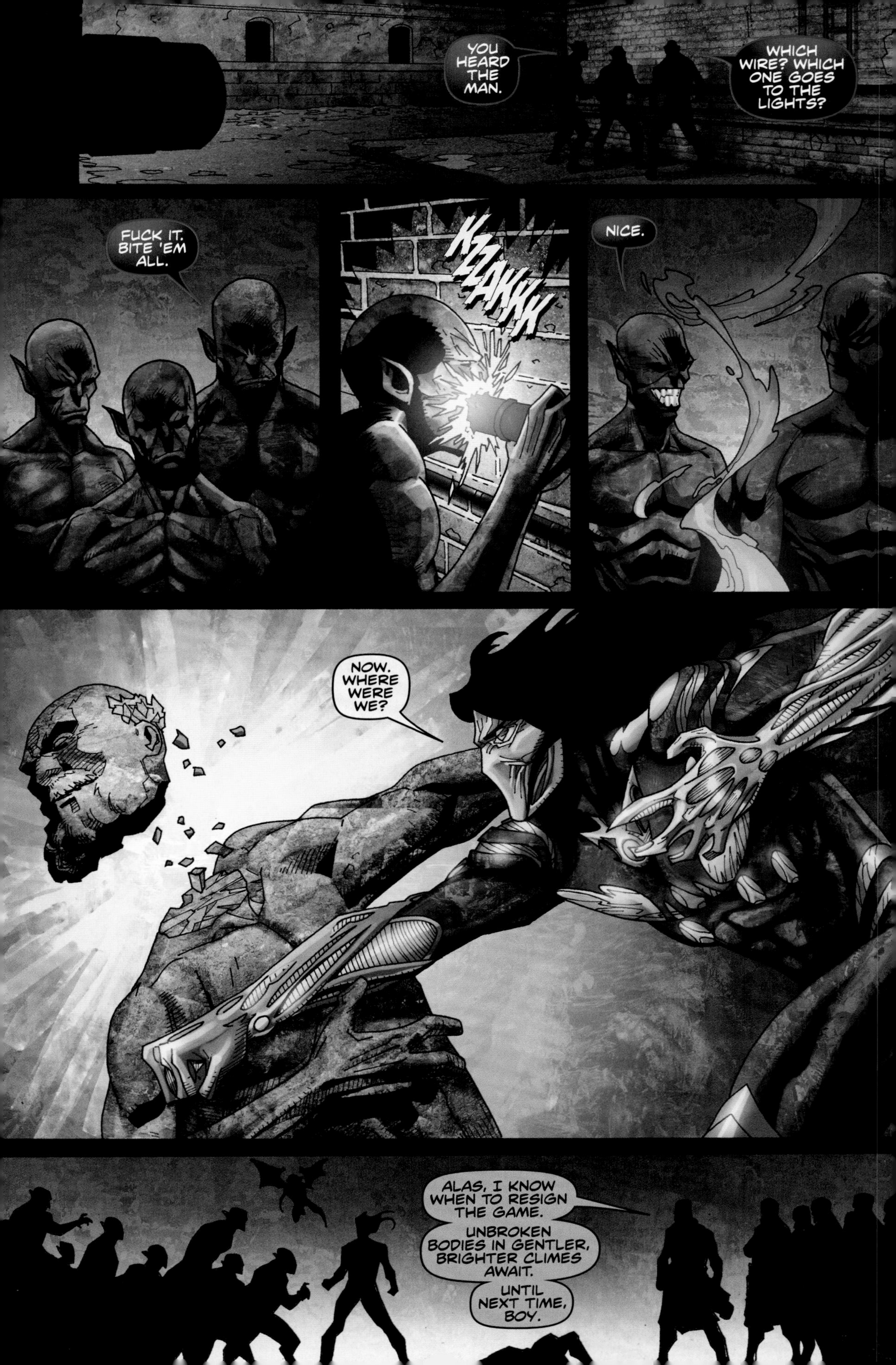
YOU HEARD THE MAN.
WHICH WIRE? WHICH ONE GOES TO THE LIGHTS?
FUCK IT. BITE 'EM ALL.
KZZAKKK
NICE.
NOW. WHERE WERE WE?
ALAS, I KNOW WHEN TO RESIGN THE GAME.
UNBROKEN BODIES IN GENTLER, BRIGHTER CLIMES AWAIT.
UNTIL NEXT TIME, BOY.

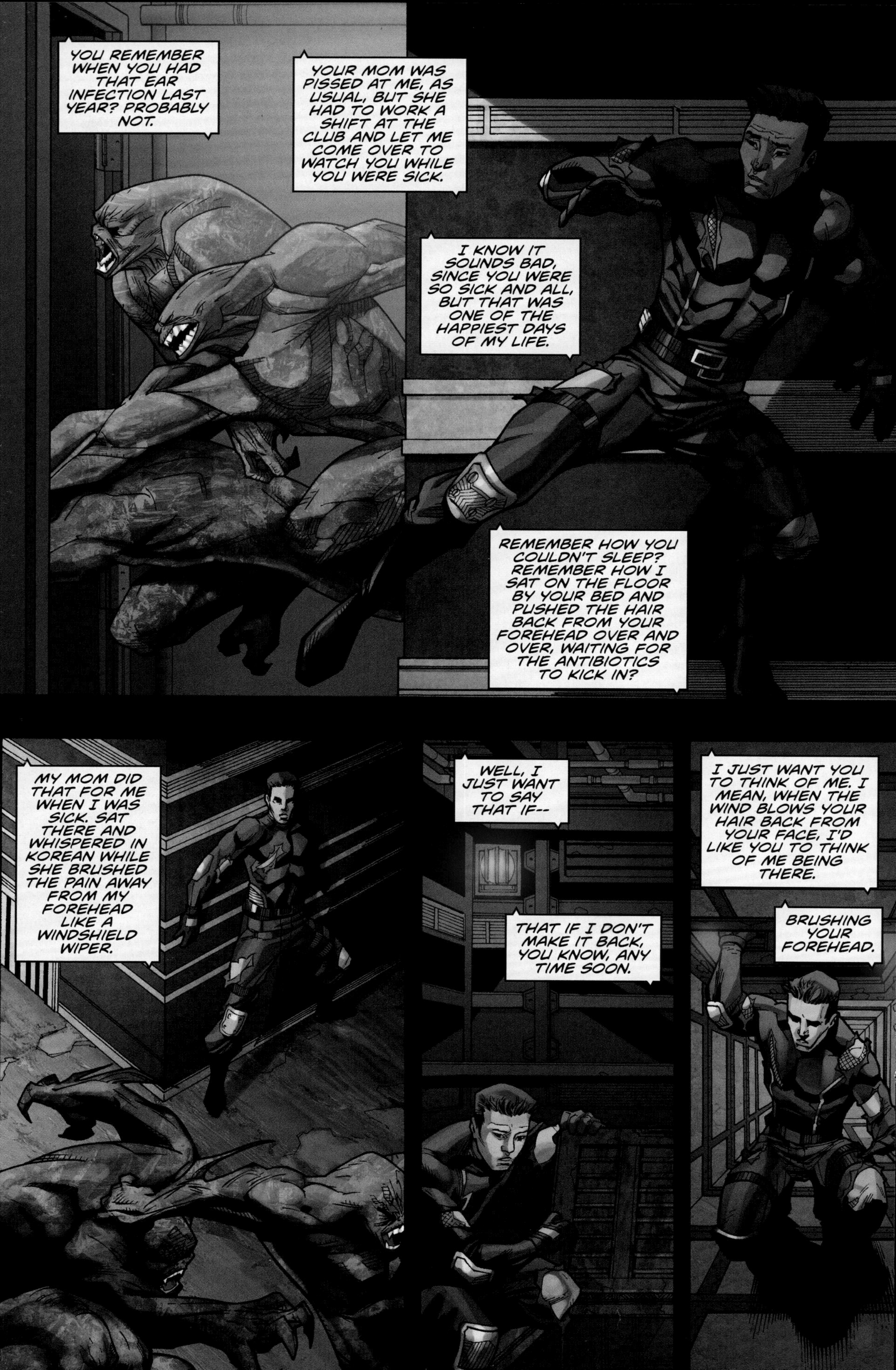
YOU REMEMBER WHEN YOU HAD THAT EAR INFECTION LAST YEAR? PROBABLY NOT.
YOUR MOM WAS PISSED AT ME, AS USUAL, BUT SHE HAD TO WORK A SHIFT AT THE CLUB AND LET ME COME OVER TO WATCH YOU WHILE YOU WERE SICK.
I KNOW IT SOUNDS BAD, SINCE YOU WERE SO SICK AND ALL, BUT THAT WAS ONE OF THE HAPPIEST DAYS OF MY LIFE.
REMEMBER HOW YOU COULDN'T SLEEP? REMEMBER HOW I SAT ON THE FLOOR BY YOUR BED AND PUSHED THE HAIR BACK FROM YOUR FOREHEAD OVER AND OVER, WAITING FOR THE ANTIBIOTICS TO KICK IN?
MY MOM DID THAT FOR ME WHEN I WAS SICK. SAT THERE AND WHISPERED IN KOREAN WHILE SHE BRUSHED THE PAIN AWAY FROM MY FOREHEAD LIKE A WINDSHIELD WIPER.
WELL, I JUST WANT TO SAY THAT IF--
THAT IF I DON'T MAKE IT BACK, YOU KNOW, ANY TIME SOON.
I JUST WANT YOU TO THINK OF ME. I MEAN, WHEN THE WIND BLOWS YOUR HAIR BACK FROM YOUR FACE, I'D LIKE YOU TO THINK OF ME BEING THERE.
BRUSHING YOUR FOREHEAD.

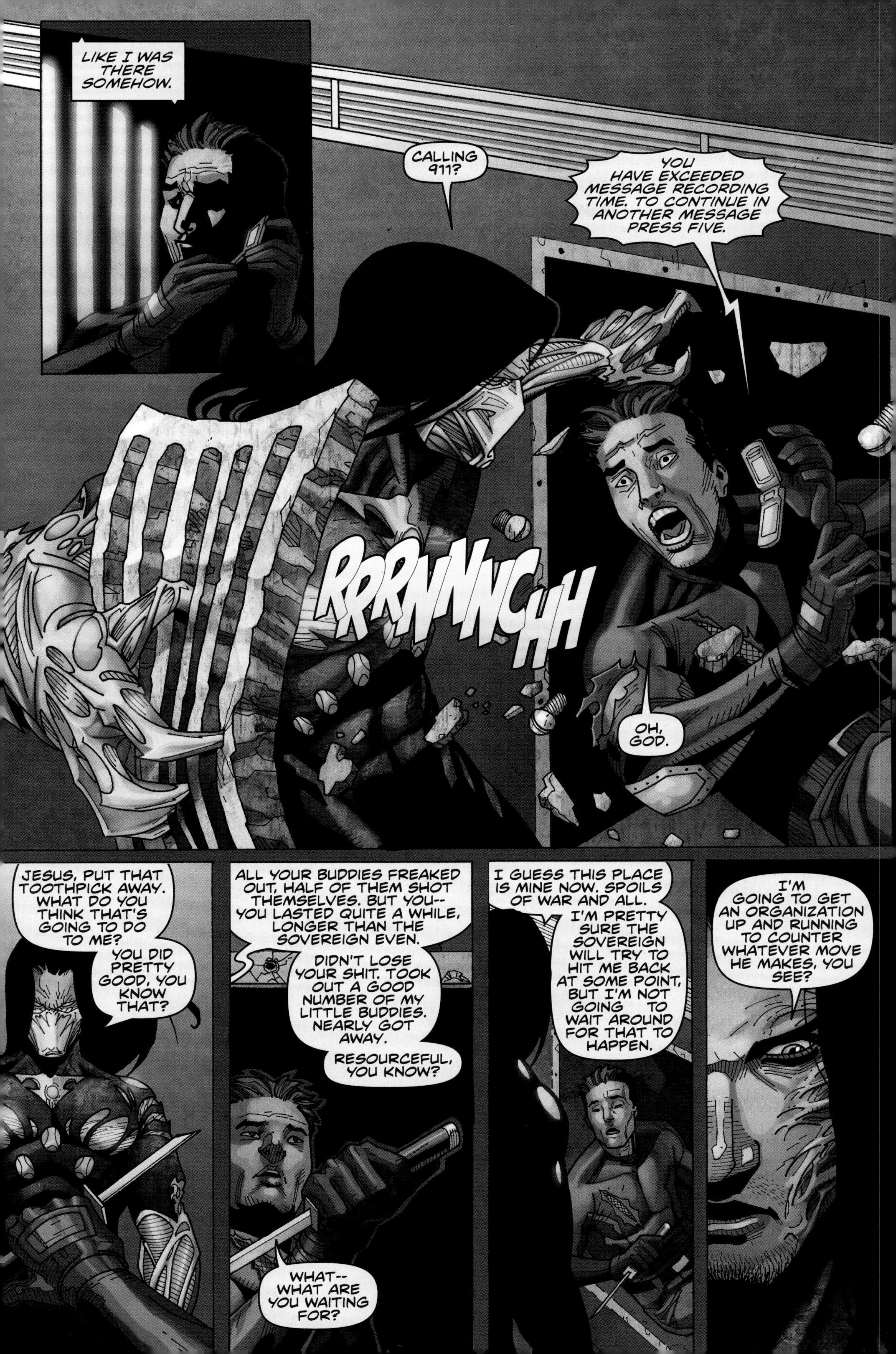
LIKE I WAS THERE SOMEHOW.
CALLING 911?
YOU HAVE EXCEEDED MESSAGE RECORDING TIME. TO CONTINUE IN ANOTHER MESSAGE PRESS FIVE.
RRRNNNNCHH
OH, GOD.
JESUS, PUT THAT TOOTHPICK AWAY. WHAT DO YOU THINK THAT'S GOING TO DO TO ME?
YOU DID PRETTY GOOD, YOU KNOW THAT?
ALL YOUR BUDDIES FREAKED OUT, HALF OF THEM SHOT THEMSELVES. BUT YOU-- YOU LASTED QUITE A WHILE, LONGER THAN THE SOVEREIGN EVEN.
DIDN'T LOSE YOUR SHIT. TOOK OUT A GOOD NUMBER OF MY LITTLE BUDDIES. NEARLY GOT AWAY.
RESOURCEFUL, YOU KNOW?
WHAT-- WHAT ARE YOU WAITING FOR?
I GUESS THIS PLACE IS MINE NOW. SPOILS OF WAR AND ALL.
I'M PRETTY SURE THE SOVEREIGN WILL TRY TO HIT ME BACK AT SOME POINT, BUT I'M NOT GOING TO WAIT AROUND FOR THAT TO HAPPEN.
I'M GOING TO GET AN ORGANIZATION UP AND RUNNING TO COUNTER WHATEVER MOVE HE MAKES, YOU SEE?

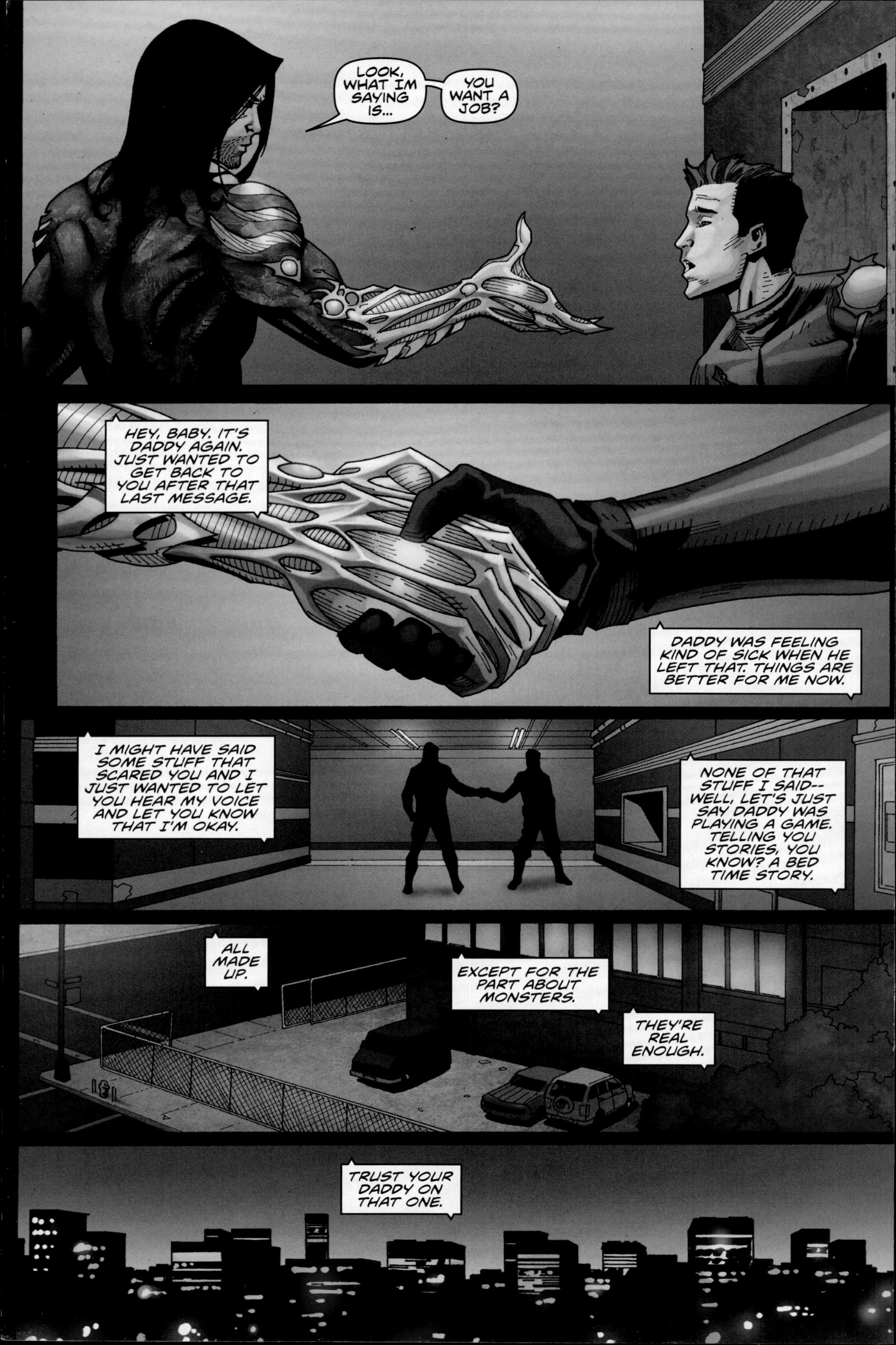

LOOK, WHAT I'M SAYING IS...
YOU WANT A JOB?
HEY, BABY. IT'S DADDY AGAIN. JUST WANTED TO GET BACK TO YOU AFTER THAT LAST MESSAGE.
DADDY WAS FEELING KIND OF SICK WHEN HE LEFT THAT. THINGS ARE BETTER FOR ME NOW.
I MIGHT HAVE SAID SOME STUFF THAT SCARED YOU AND I JUST WANTED TO LET YOU HEAR MY VOICE AND LET YOU KNOW THAT I'M OKAY.
NONE OF THAT STUFF I SAID-- WELL, LET'S JUST SAY DADDY WAS PLAYING A GAME. TELLING YOU STORIES, YOU KNOW? A BED TIME STORY.
ALL MADE UP.
EXCEPT FOR THE PART ABOUT MONSTERS.
THEY'RE REAL ENOUGH.
TRUST YOUR DADDY ON THAT ONE.

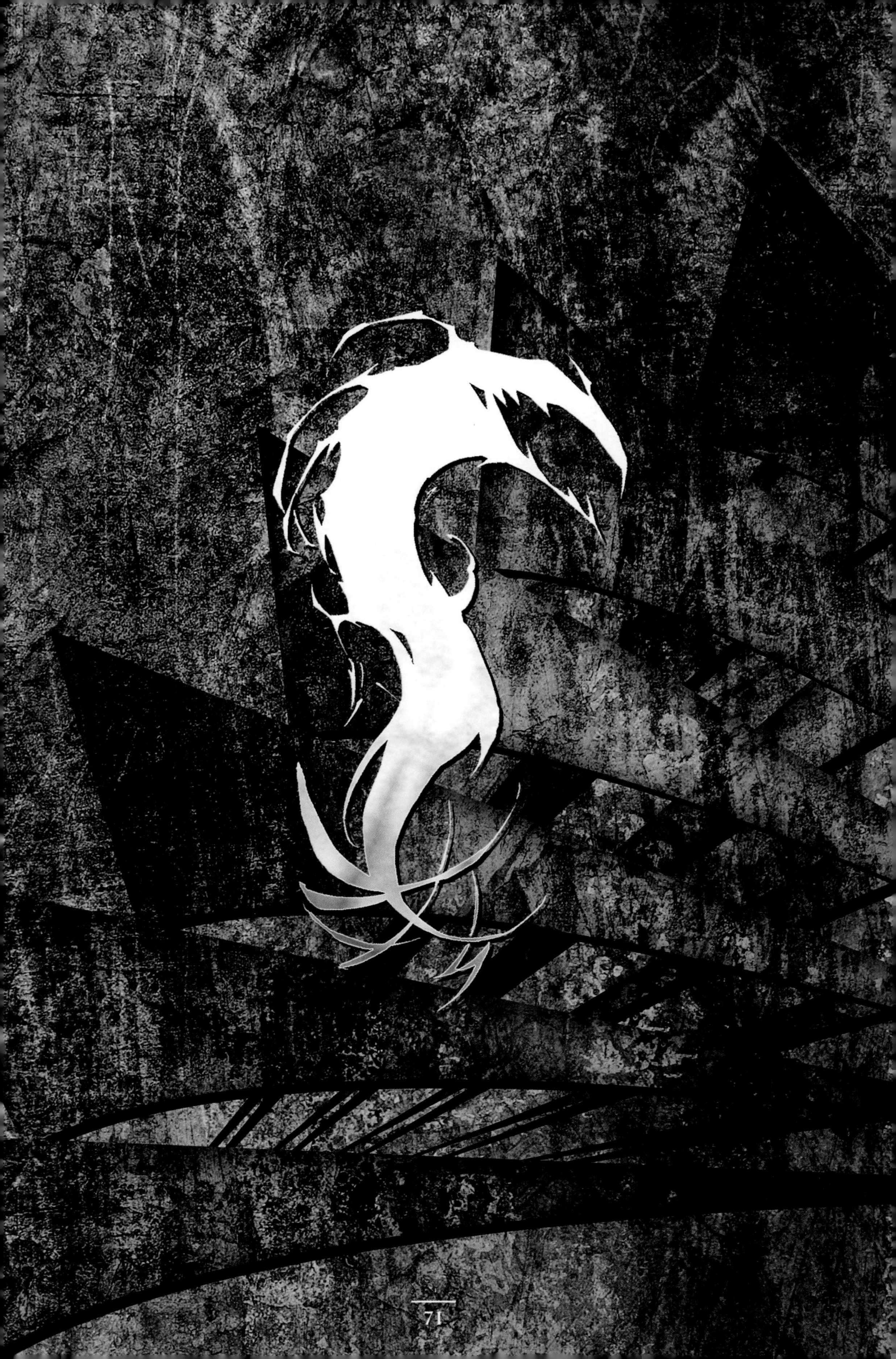

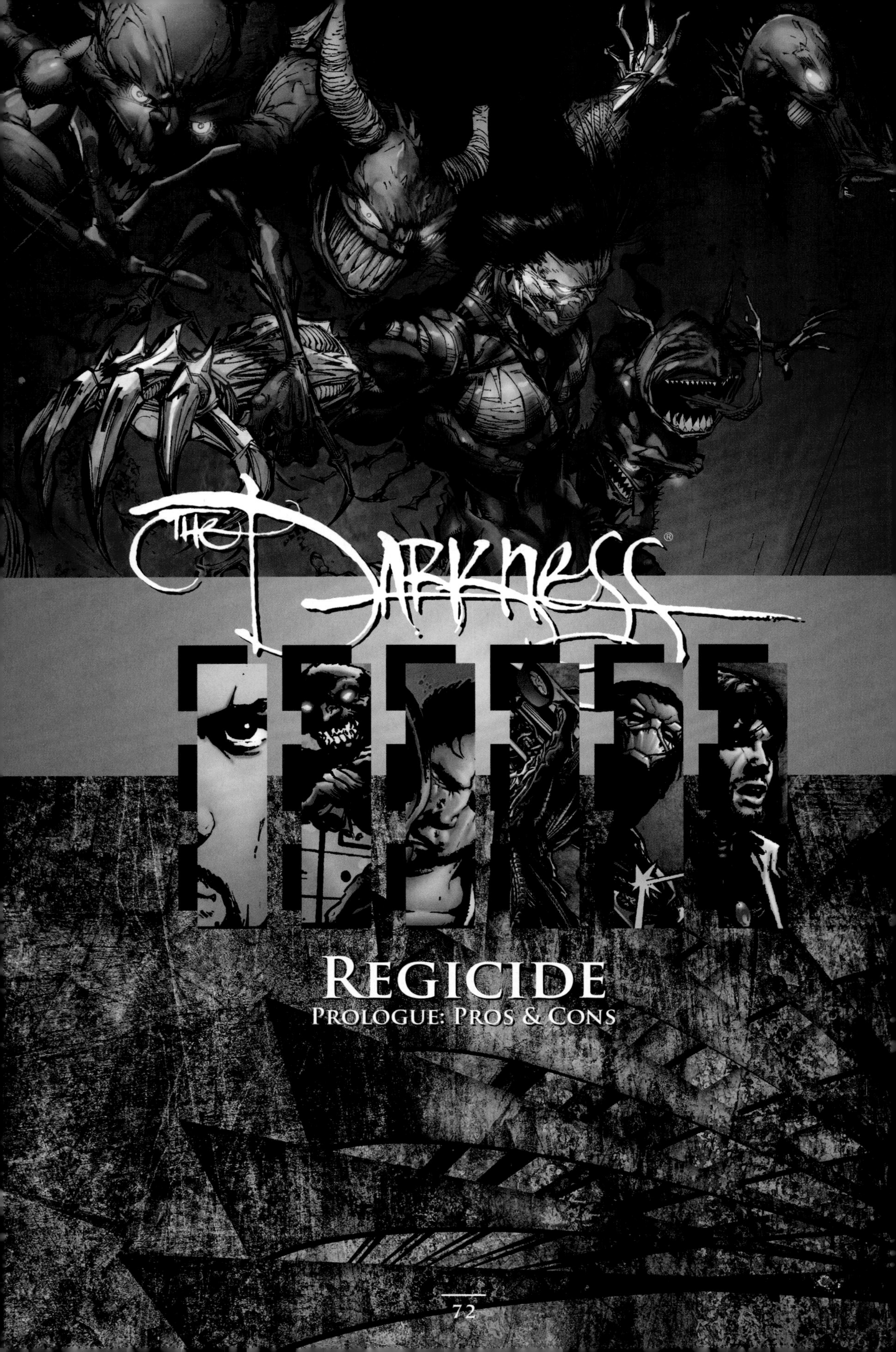
The Darkness®
REGICIDE
PROLOGUE: PROS & CONS

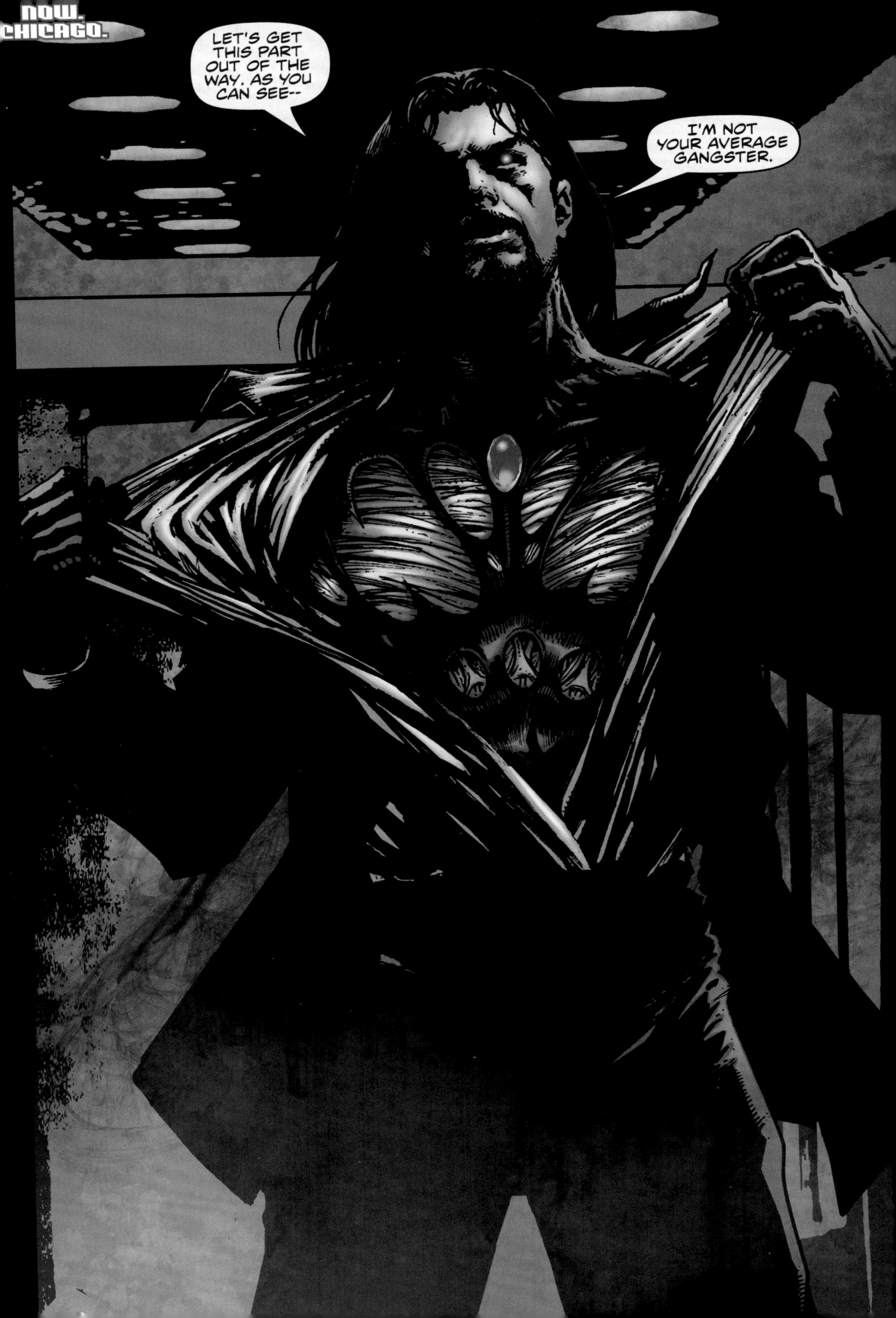
NOW. CHICAGO.
LET'S GET THIS PART OUT OF THE WAY. AS YOU CAN SEE--
I'M NOT YOUR AVERAGE GANGSTER.

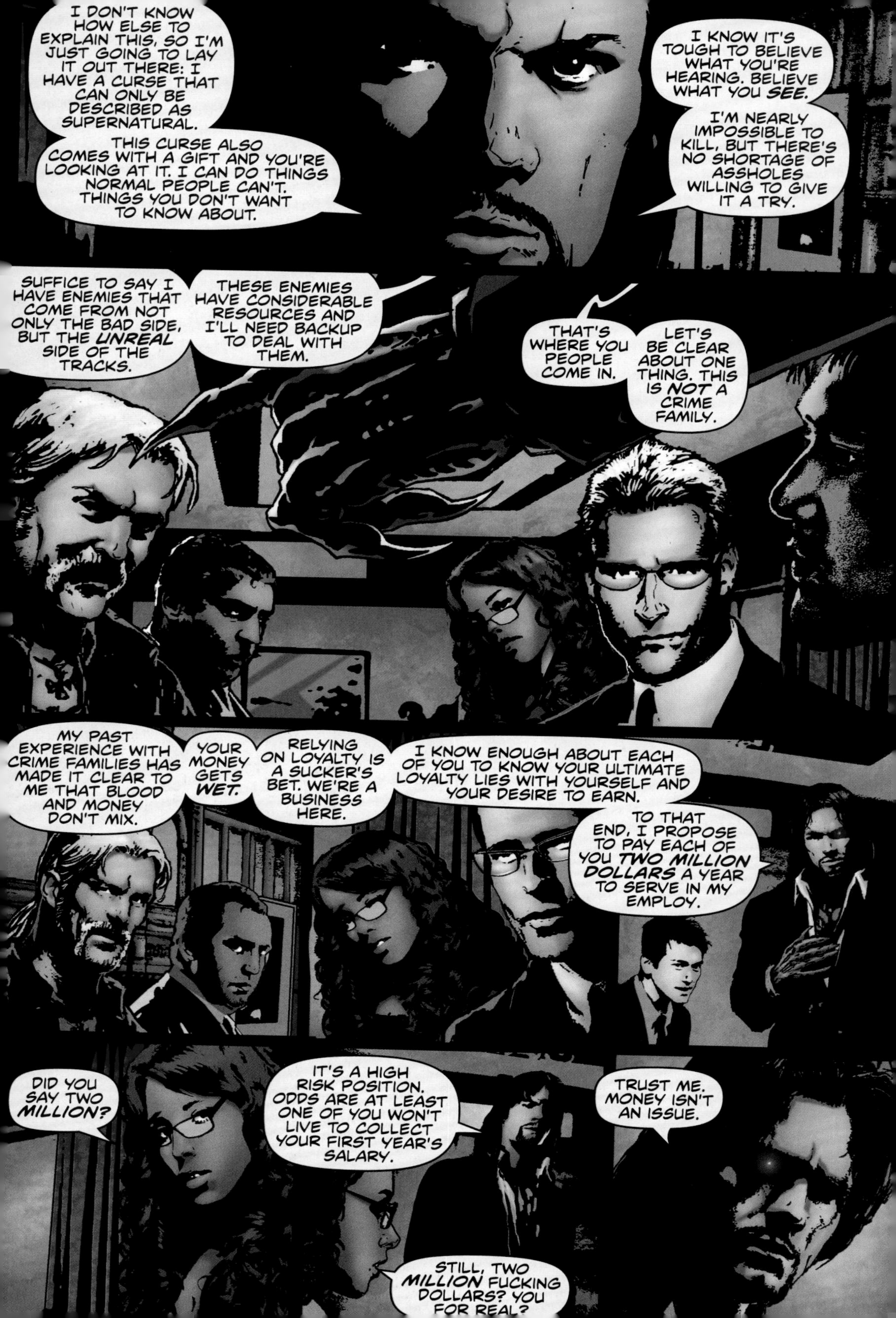
I DON'T KNOW HOW ELSE TO EXPLAIN THIS, SO I'M JUST GOING TO LAY IT OUT THERE: I HAVE A CURSE THAT CAN ONLY BE DESCRIBED AS SUPERNATURAL.
THIS CURSE ALSO COMES WITH A GIFT AND YOU'RE LOOKING AT IT. I CAN DO THINGS NORMAL PEOPLE CAN'T. THINGS YOU DON'T WANT TO KNOW ABOUT.
I KNOW IT'S TOUGH TO BELIEVE WHAT YOU'RE HEARING. BELIEVE WHAT YOU *SEE*.
I'M NEARLY IMPOSSIBLE TO KILL, BUT THERE'S NO SHORTAGE OF ASSHOLES WILLING TO GIVE IT A TRY.
SUFFICE TO SAY I HAVE ENEMIES THAT COME FROM NOT ONLY THE BAD SIDE, BUT THE *UNREAL* SIDE OF THE TRACKS.
THESE ENEMIES HAVE CONSIDERABLE RESOURCES AND I'LL NEED BACKUP TO DEAL WITH THEM.
THAT'S WHERE YOU PEOPLE COME IN.
LET'S BE CLEAR ABOUT ONE THING. THIS IS *NOT* A CRIME FAMILY.
MY PAST EXPERIENCE WITH CRIME FAMILIES HAS MADE IT CLEAR TO ME THAT BLOOD AND MONEY DON'T MIX.
YOUR MONEY GETS *WET.*
RELYING ON LOYALTY IS A SUCKER'S BET. WE'RE A BUSINESS HERE.
I KNOW ENOUGH ABOUT EACH OF YOU TO KNOW YOUR ULTIMATE LOYALTY LIES WITH YOURSELF AND YOUR DESIRE TO EARN.
TO THAT END, I PROPOSE TO PAY EACH OF YOU *TWO MILLION DOLLARS* A YEAR TO SERVE IN MY EMPLOY.
DID YOU SAY TWO *MILLION?*
IT'S A HIGH RISK POSITION. ODDS ARE AT LEAST ONE OF YOU WON'T LIVE TO COLLECT YOUR FIRST YEAR'S SALARY.
TRUST ME. MONEY ISN'T AN ISSUE.
STILL, TWO *MILLION* FUCKING DOLLARS? YOU FOR REAL?

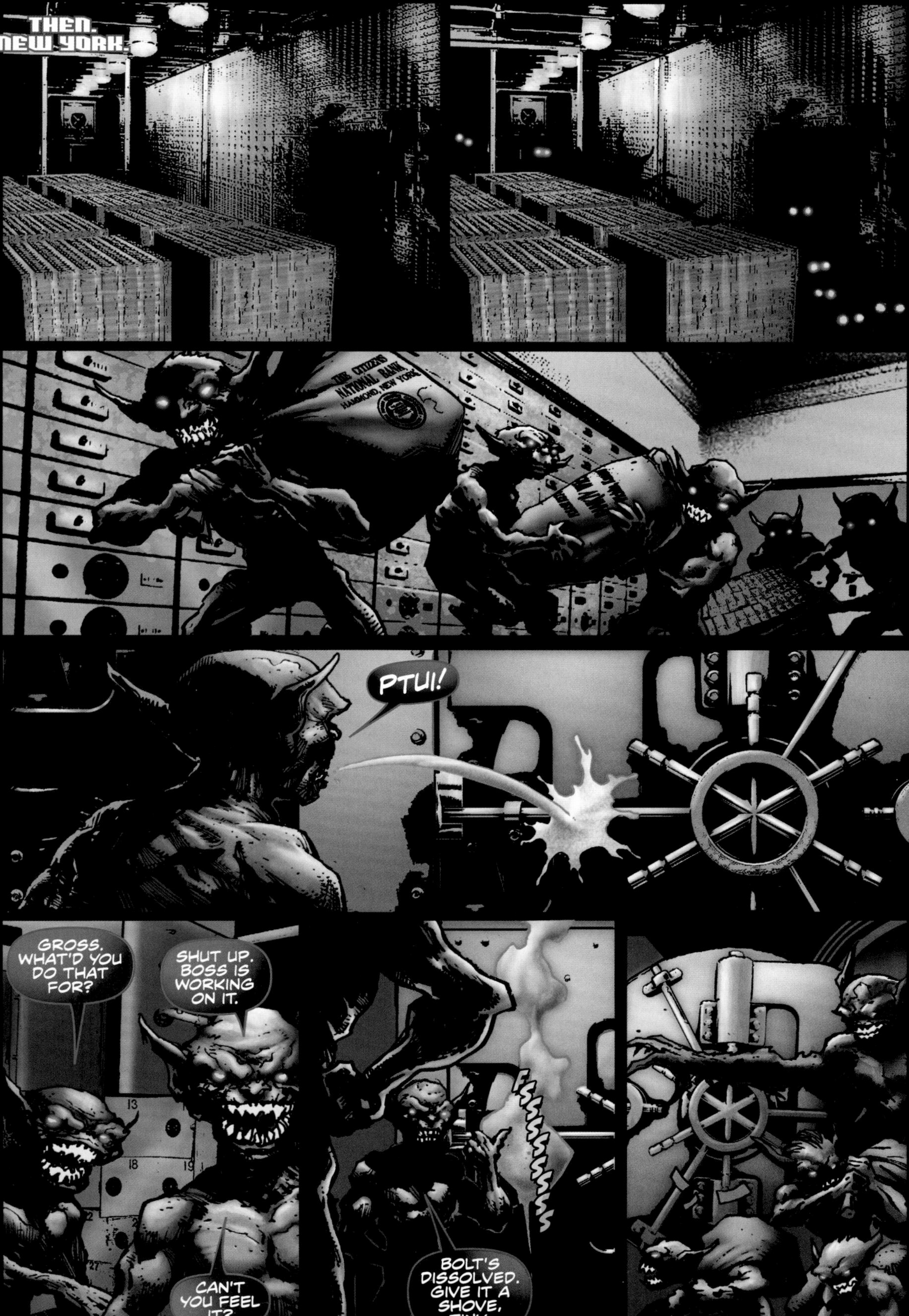
THEN.
NEW YORK.
THE CITIZENS NATIONAL BANK HAMMOND, NEW YORK
PTUI!
GROSS. WHAT'D YOU DO THAT FOR?
SHUT UP. BOSS IS WORKING ON IT.
CAN'T YOU FEEL IT?
FSSSSSSSSS
BOLT'S DISSOLVED. GIVE IT A SHOVE, TINY.

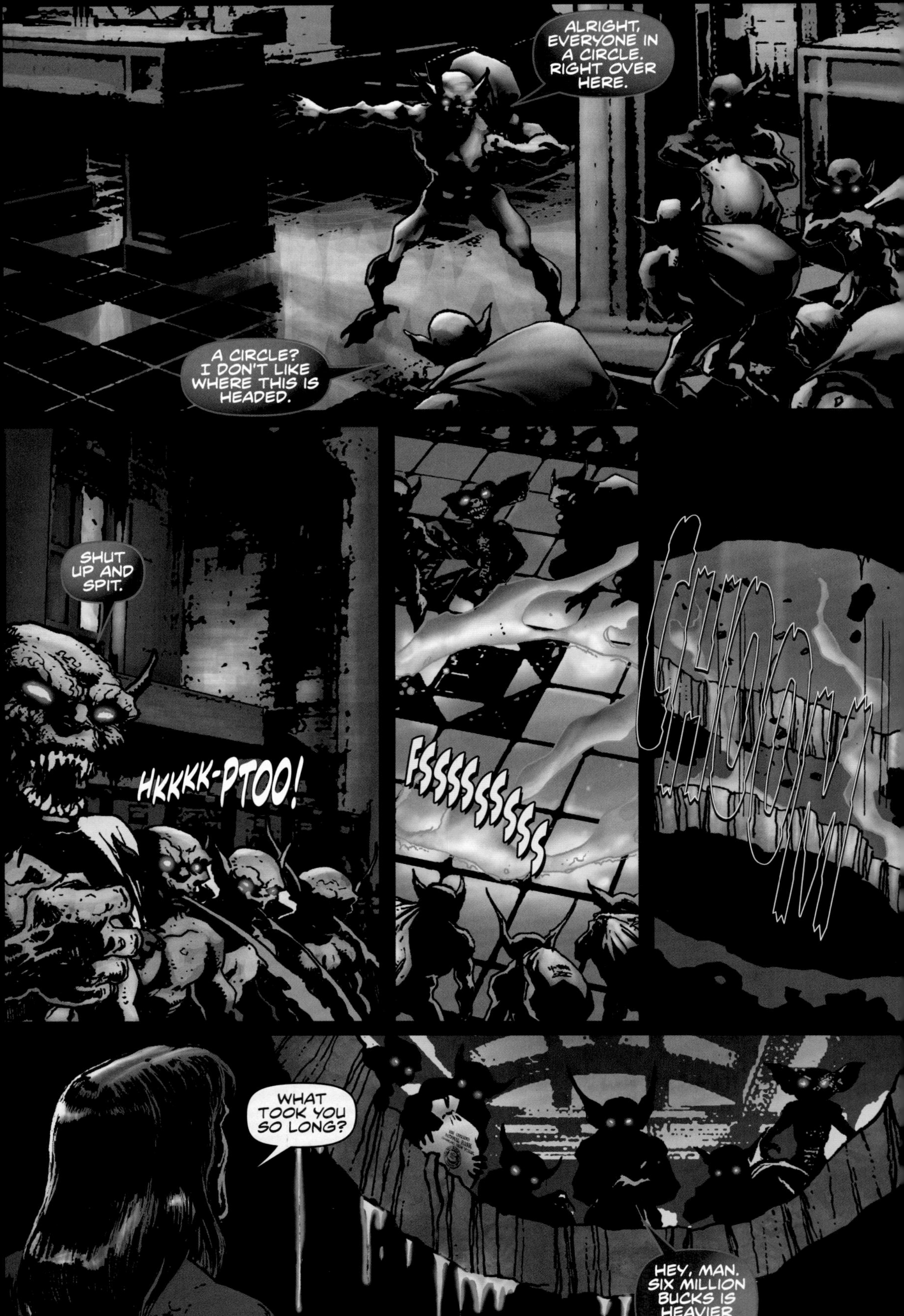
ALRIGHT, EVERYONE IN A CIRCLE. RIGHT OVER HERE.
A CIRCLE? I DON'T LIKE WHERE THIS IS HEADED.
SHUT UP AND SPIT.
HKKKK-PTOO!
FSSSSSSSSSS
WHAT TOOK YOU SO LONG?
HEY, MAN. SIX MILLION BUCKS IS HEAVIER THAN IT LOOKS.

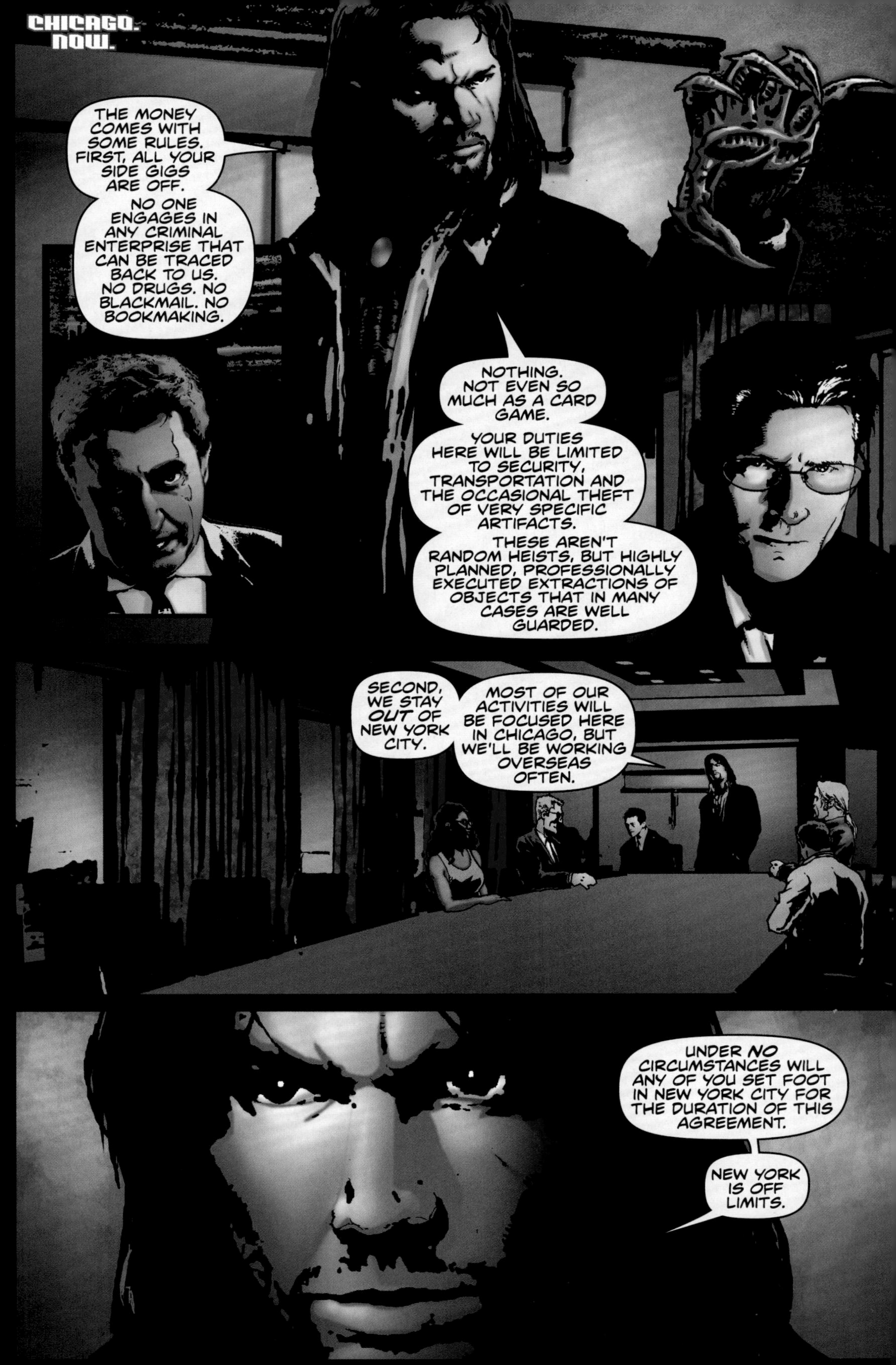
CHICAGO. NOW.
THE MONEY COMES WITH SOME RULES. FIRST, ALL YOUR SIDE GIGS ARE OFF.
NO ONE ENGAGES IN ANY CRIMINAL ENTERPRISE THAT CAN BE TRACED BACK TO US. NO DRUGS. NO BLACKMAIL. NO BOOKMAKING.
NOTHING. NOT EVEN SO MUCH AS A CARD GAME.
YOUR DUTIES HERE WILL BE LIMITED TO SECURITY, TRANSPORTATION AND THE OCCASIONAL THEFT OF VERY SPECIFIC ARTIFACTS.
THESE AREN'T RANDOM HEISTS, BUT HIGHLY PLANNED, PROFESSIONALLY EXECUTED EXTRACTIONS OF OBJECTS THAT IN MANY CASES ARE WELL GUARDED.
SECOND, WE STAY *OUT* OF NEW YORK CITY.
MOST OF OUR ACTIVITIES WILL BE FOCUSED HERE IN CHICAGO, BUT WE'LL BE WORKING OVERSEAS OFTEN.
UNDER *NO* CIRCUMSTANCES WILL ANY OF YOU SET FOOT IN NEW YORK CITY FOR THE DURATION OF THIS AGREEMENT.
NEW YORK IS OFF LIMITS.

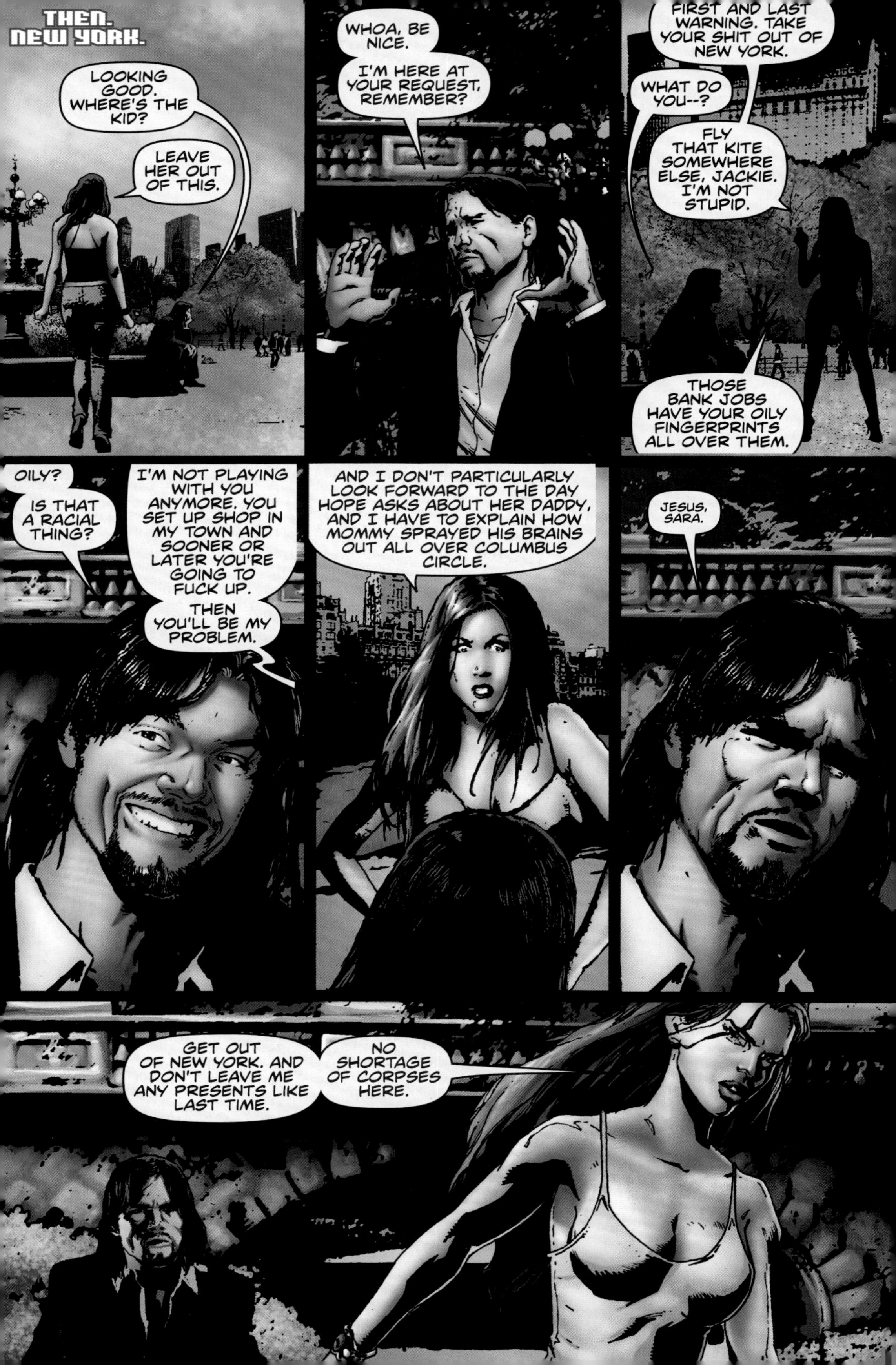
THEN. NEW YORK.
LOOKING GOOD. WHERE'S THE KID?
LEAVE HER OUT OF THIS.
WHOA, BE NICE.
I'M HERE AT YOUR REQUEST, REMEMBER?
FIRST AND LAST WARNING. TAKE YOUR SHIT OUT OF NEW YORK.
WHAT DO YOU--?
FLY THAT KITE SOMEWHERE ELSE, JACKIE. I'M NOT STUPID.
THOSE BANK JOBS HAVE YOUR OILY FINGERPRINTS ALL OVER THEM.
OILY?
IS THAT A RACIAL THING?
I'M NOT PLAYING WITH YOU ANYMORE. YOU SET UP SHOP IN MY TOWN AND SOONER OR LATER YOU'RE GOING TO FUCK UP.
THEN YOU'LL BE MY PROBLEM.
AND I DON'T PARTICULARLY LOOK FORWARD TO THE DAY HOPE ASKS ABOUT HER DADDY, AND I HAVE TO EXPLAIN HOW MOMMY SPRAYED HIS BRAINS OUT ALL OVER COLUMBUS CIRCLE.
JESUS, SARA.
GET OUT OF NEW YORK. AND DON'T LEAVE ME ANY PRESENTS LIKE LAST TIME.
NO SHORTAGE OF CORPSES HERE.

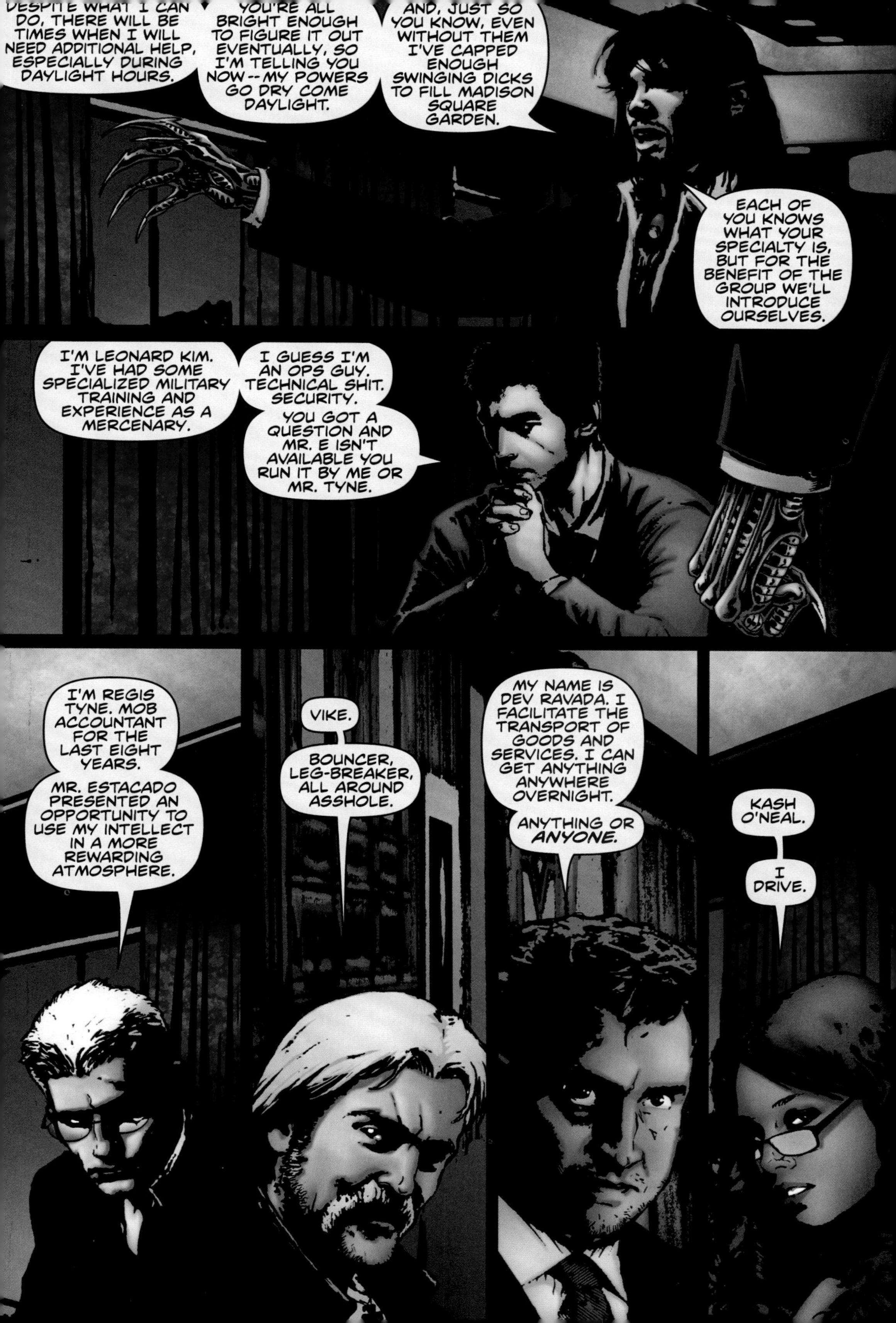
DESPITE WHAT I CAN DO, THERE WILL BE TIMES WHEN I WILL NEED ADDITIONAL HELP, ESPECIALLY DURING DAYLIGHT HOURS.
YOU'RE ALL BRIGHT ENOUGH TO FIGURE IT OUT EVENTUALLY, SO I'M TELLING YOU NOW--MY POWERS GO DRY COME DAYLIGHT.
AND, JUST SO YOU KNOW, EVEN WITHOUT THEM I'VE CAPPED ENOUGH SWINGING DICKS TO FILL MADISON SQUARE GARDEN.
EACH OF YOU KNOWS WHAT YOUR SPECIALTY IS, BUT FOR THE BENEFIT OF THE GROUP WE'LL INTRODUCE OURSELVES.
I'M LEONARD KIM. I'VE HAD SOME SPECIALIZED MILITARY TRAINING AND EXPERIENCE AS A MERCENARY.
I GUESS I'M AN OPS GUY. TECHNICAL SHIT. SECURITY.
YOU GOT A QUESTION AND MR. E ISN'T AVAILABLE YOU RUN IT BY ME OR MR. TYNE.
I'M REGIS TYNE. MOB ACCOUNTANT FOR THE LAST EIGHT YEARS.
MR. ESTACADO PRESENTED AN OPPORTUNITY TO USE MY INTELLECT IN A MORE REWARDING ATMOSPHERE.
VIKE.
BOUNCER, LEG-BREAKER, ALL AROUND ASSHOLE.
MY NAME IS DEV RAVADA. I FACILITATE THE TRANSPORT OF GOODS AND SERVICES. I CAN GET ANYTHING ANYWHERE OVERNIGHT.
ANYTHING OR *ANYONE*.
KASH O'NEAL.
I DRIVE.

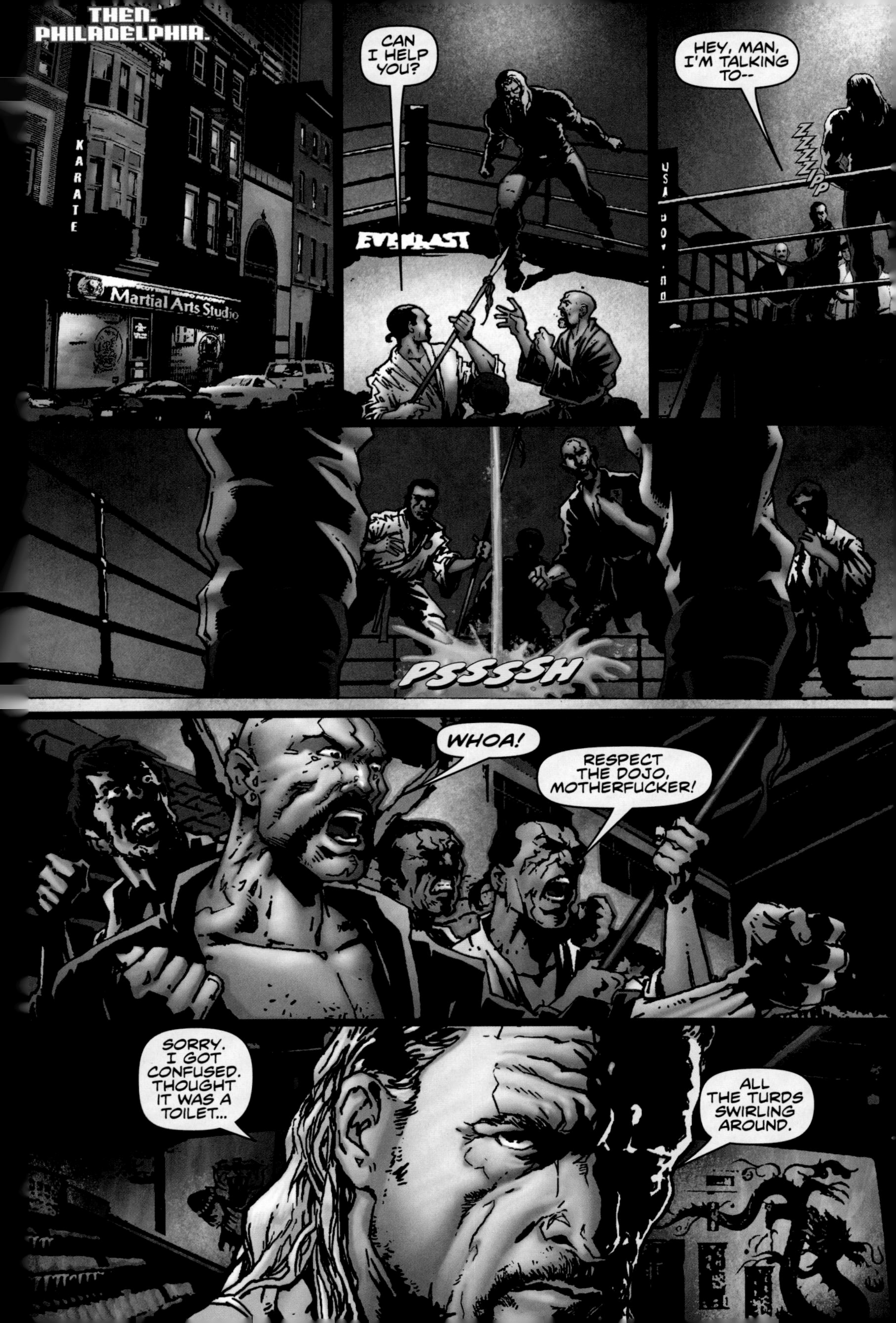
THEN.
PHILADELPHIA.
KARATE
Martial Arts Studio
CAN I HELP YOU?
EVERLAST
HEY, MAN, I'M TALKING TO--
ZZZZIPP
PSSSSH
WHOA!
RESPECT THE DOJO, MOTHERFUCKER!
SORRY. I GOT CONFUSED. THOUGHT IT WAS A TOILET...
ALL THE TURDS SWIRLING AROUND.

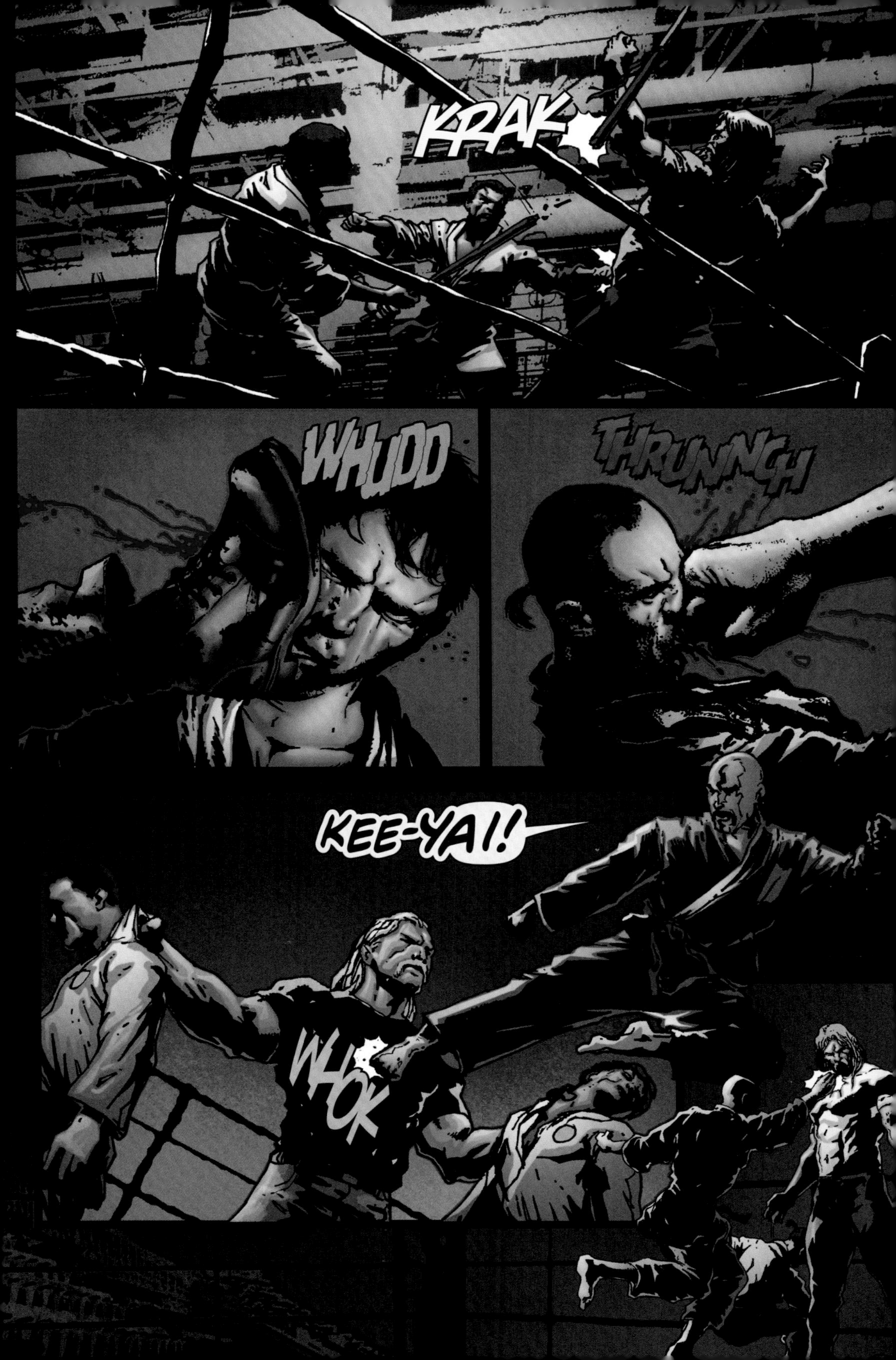
KRAK
WHUDD
THRUNNCH
KEE-YAI!
WHOK

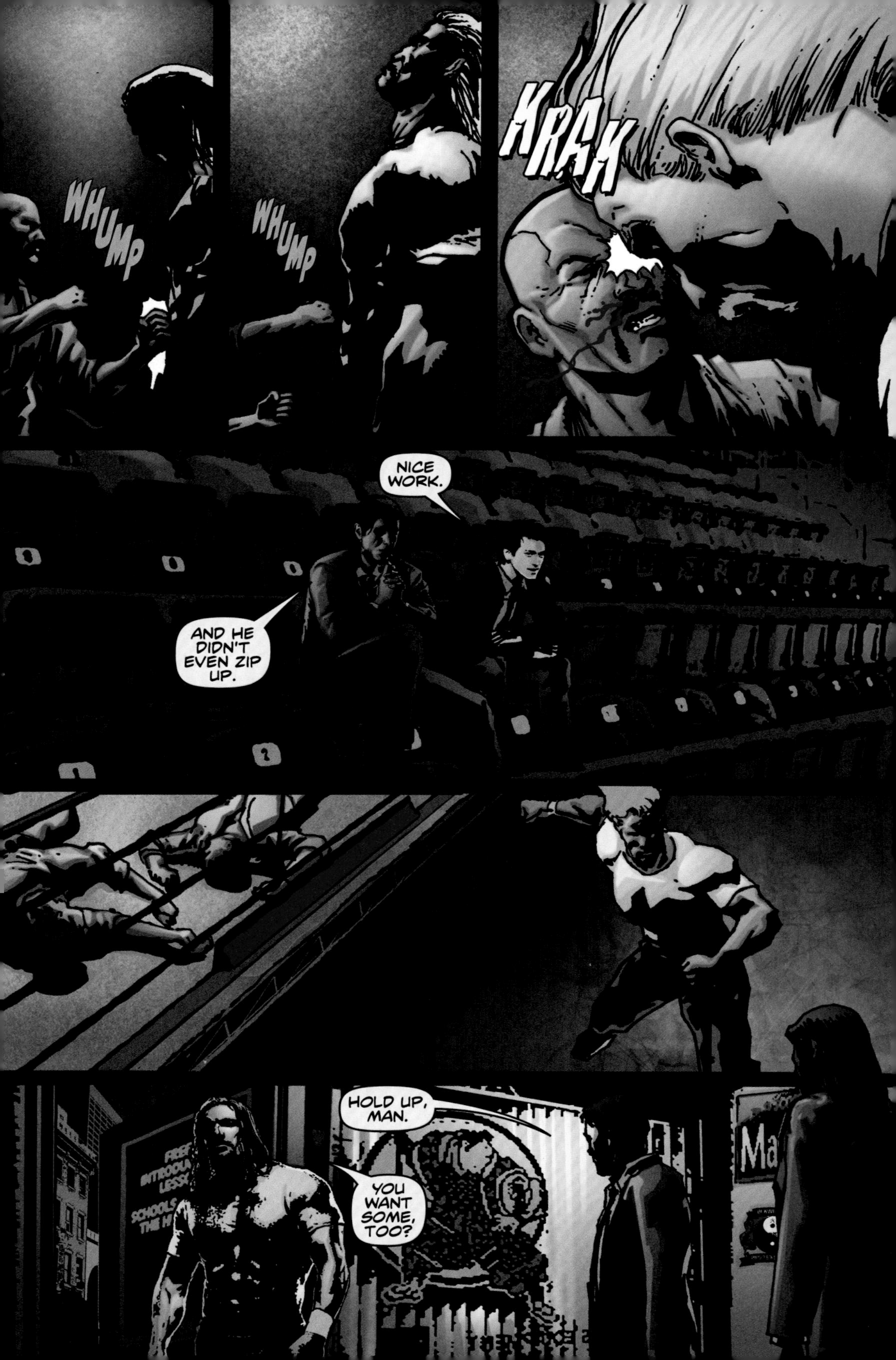
WHUMP
WHUMP
KRAK
NICE WORK.
AND HE DIDN'T EVEN ZIP UP.
HOLD UP, MAN.
YOU WANT SOME, TOO?

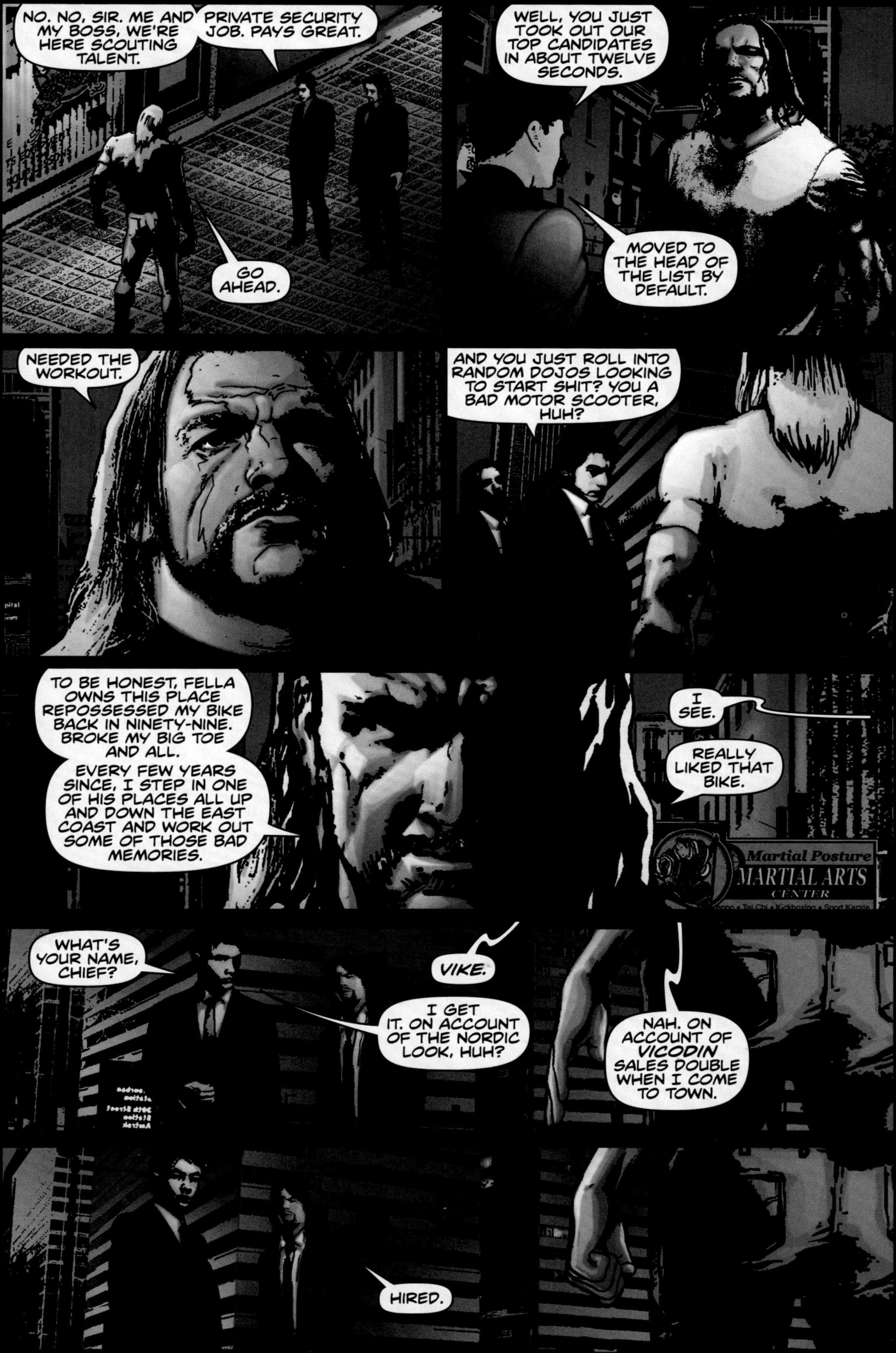
NO. NO, SIR. ME AND MY BOSS, WE'RE HERE SCOUTING TALENT.
PRIVATE SECURITY JOB. PAYS GREAT.
GO AHEAD.
WELL, YOU JUST TOOK OUT OUR TOP CANDIDATES IN ABOUT TWELVE SECONDS.
MOVED TO THE HEAD OF THE LIST BY DEFAULT.
NEEDED THE WORKOUT.
AND YOU JUST ROLL INTO RANDOM DOJOS LOOKING TO START SHIT? YOU A BAD MOTOR SCOOTER, HUH?
TO BE HONEST, FELLA OWNS THIS PLACE REPOSSESSED MY BIKE BACK IN NINETY-NINE. BROKE MY BIG TOE AND ALL.
EVERY FEW YEARS SINCE, I STEP IN ONE OF HIS PLACES ALL UP AND DOWN THE EAST COAST AND WORK OUT SOME OF THOSE BAD MEMORIES.
I SEE.
REALLY LIKED THAT BIKE.
Martial Posture
MARTIAL ARTS
CENTER
WHAT'S YOUR NAME, CHIEF?
VIKE.
I GET IT. ON ACCOUNT OF THE NORDIC LOOK, HUH?
NAH. ON ACCOUNT OF VICODIN SALES DOUBLE WHEN I COME TO TOWN.
HIRED.

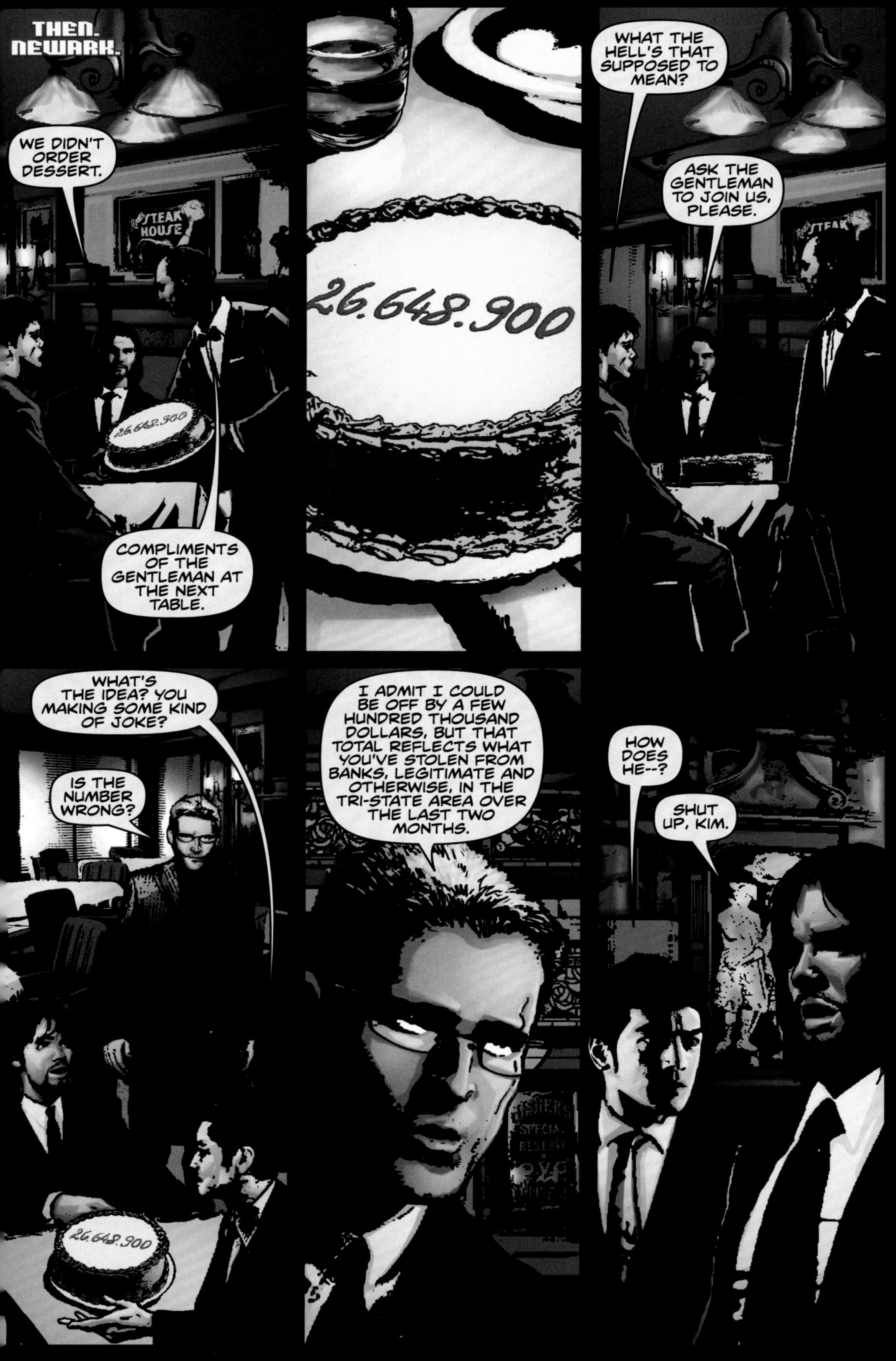
THEN. NEWARK.
WE DIDN'T ORDER DESSERT.
26.648.900
COMPLIMENTS OF THE GENTLEMAN AT THE NEXT TABLE.
26.648.900
WHAT THE HELL'S THAT SUPPOSED TO MEAN?
ASK THE GENTLEMAN TO JOIN US, PLEASE.
WHAT'S THE IDEA? YOU MAKING SOME KIND OF JOKE?
IS THE NUMBER WRONG?
26.648.900
I ADMIT I COULD BE OFF BY A FEW HUNDRED THOUSAND DOLLARS, BUT THAT TOTAL REFLECTS WHAT YOU'VE STOLEN FROM BANKS, LEGITIMATE AND OTHERWISE, IN THE TRI-STATE AREA OVER THE LAST TWO MONTHS.
HOW DOES HE--?
SHUT UP, KIM.

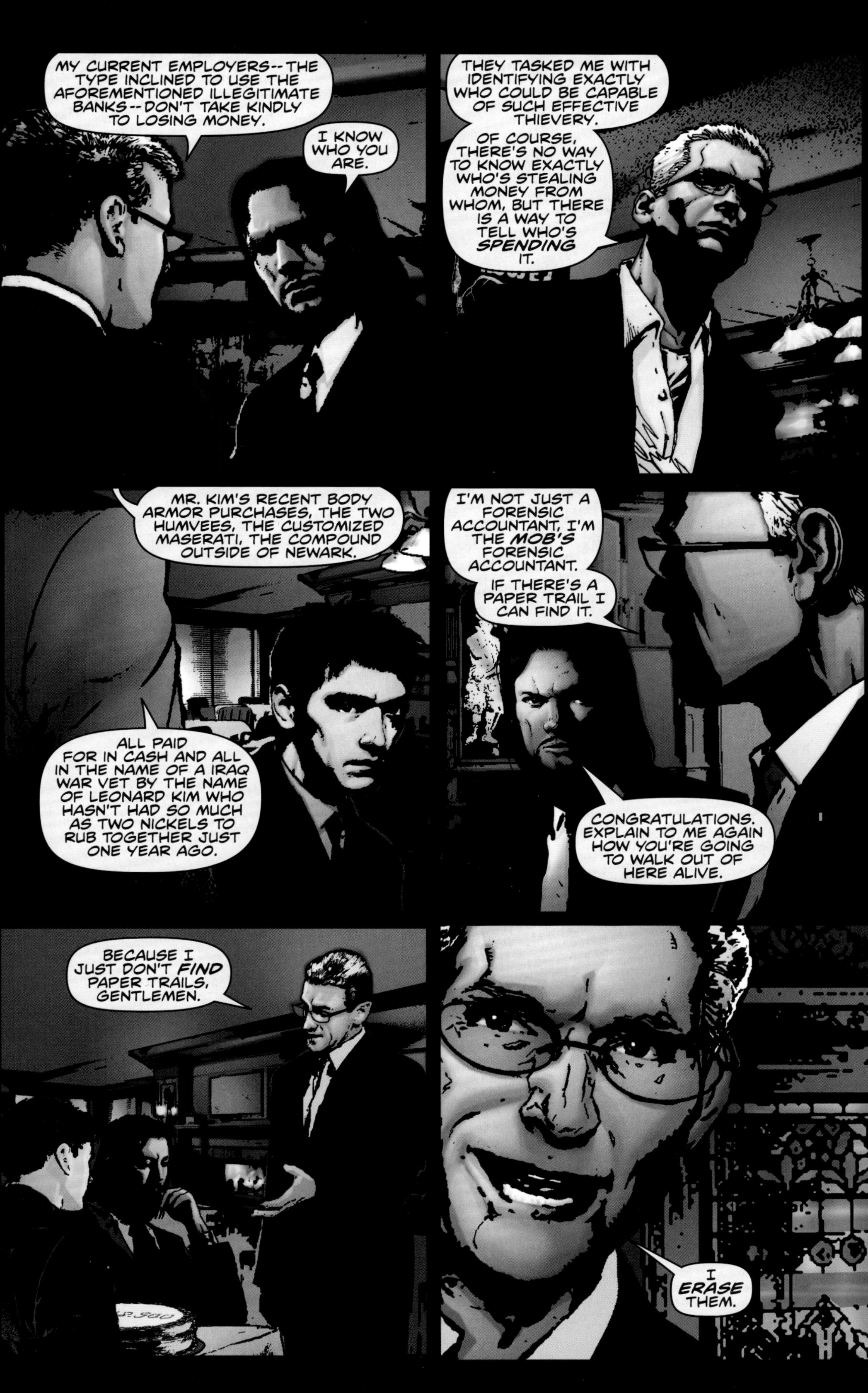
MY CURRENT EMPLOYERS--THE TYPE INCLINED TO USE THE AFOREMENTIONED ILLEGITIMATE BANKS--DON'T TAKE KINDLY TO LOSING MONEY.
I KNOW WHO YOU ARE.
THEY TASKED ME WITH IDENTIFYING EXACTLY WHO COULD BE CAPABLE OF SUCH EFFECTIVE THIEVERY.
OF COURSE, THERE'S NO WAY TO KNOW EXACTLY WHO'S STEALING MONEY FROM WHOM, BUT THERE IS A WAY TO TELL WHO'S *SPENDING* IT.
MR. KIM'S RECENT BODY ARMOR PURCHASES, THE TWO HUMVEES, THE CUSTOMIZED MASERATI, THE COMPOUND OUTSIDE OF NEWARK.
ALL PAID FOR IN CASH AND ALL IN THE NAME OF A IRAQ WAR VET BY THE NAME OF LEONARD KIM WHO HASN'T HAD SO MUCH AS TWO NICKELS TO RUB TOGETHER JUST ONE YEAR AGO.
I'M NOT JUST A FORENSIC ACCOUNTANT, I'M THE *MOB'S* FORENSIC ACCOUNTANT.
IF THERE'S A PAPER TRAIL I CAN FIND IT.
CONGRATULATIONS. EXPLAIN TO ME AGAIN HOW YOU'RE GOING TO WALK OUT OF HERE ALIVE.
BECAUSE I JUST DON'T *FIND* PAPER TRAILS, GENTLEMEN.
I *ERASE* THEM.

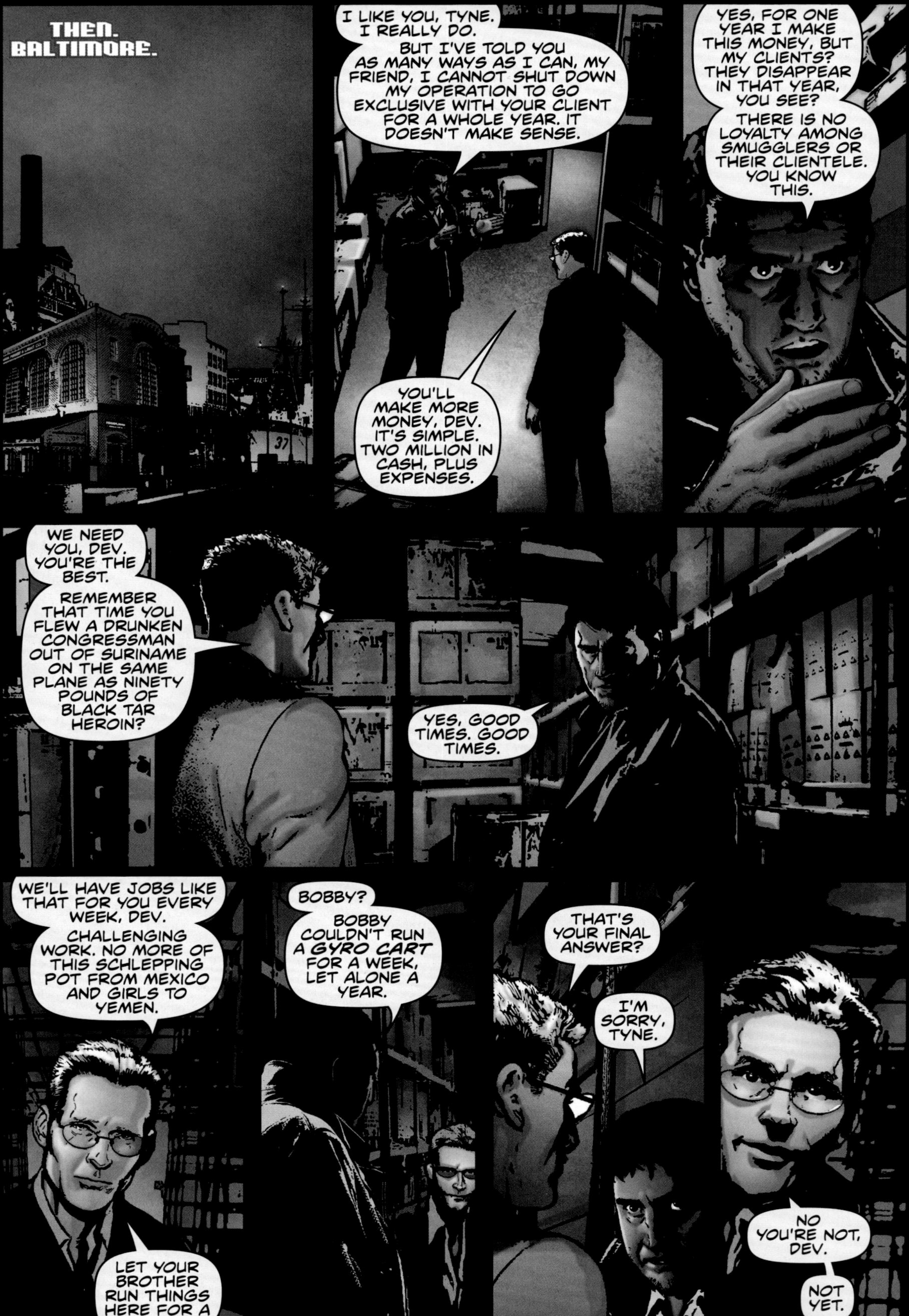
THEN.
BALTIMORE.
I LIKE YOU, TYNE. I REALLY DO.
BUT I'VE TOLD YOU AS MANY WAYS AS I CAN, MY FRIEND, I CANNOT SHUT DOWN MY OPERATION TO GO EXCLUSIVE WITH YOUR CLIENT FOR A WHOLE YEAR. IT DOESN'T MAKE SENSE.
YOU'LL MAKE MORE MONEY, DEV. IT'S SIMPLE. TWO MILLION IN CASH, PLUS EXPENSES.
YES, FOR ONE YEAR I MAKE THIS MONEY, BUT MY CLIENTS? THEY DISAPPEAR IN THAT YEAR, YOU SEE?
THERE IS NO LOYALTY AMONG SMUGGLERS OR THEIR CLIENTELE. YOU KNOW THIS.
WE NEED YOU, DEV. YOU'RE THE BEST.
REMEMBER THAT TIME YOU FLEW A DRUNKEN CONGRESSMAN OUT OF SURINAME ON THE SAME PLANE AS NINETY POUNDS OF BLACK TAR HEROIN?
YES, GOOD TIMES. GOOD TIMES.
WE'LL HAVE JOBS LIKE THAT FOR YOU EVERY WEEK, DEV.
CHALLENGING WORK. NO MORE OF THIS SCHLEPPING POT FROM MEXICO AND GIRLS TO YEMEN.
LET YOUR BROTHER RUN THINGS HERE FOR A YEAR.
BOBBY?
BOBBY COULDN'T RUN A *GYRO CART* FOR A WEEK, LET ALONE A YEAR.
THAT'S YOUR FINAL ANSWER?
I'M SORRY, TYNE.
NO YOU'RE NOT, DEV.
NOT YET.

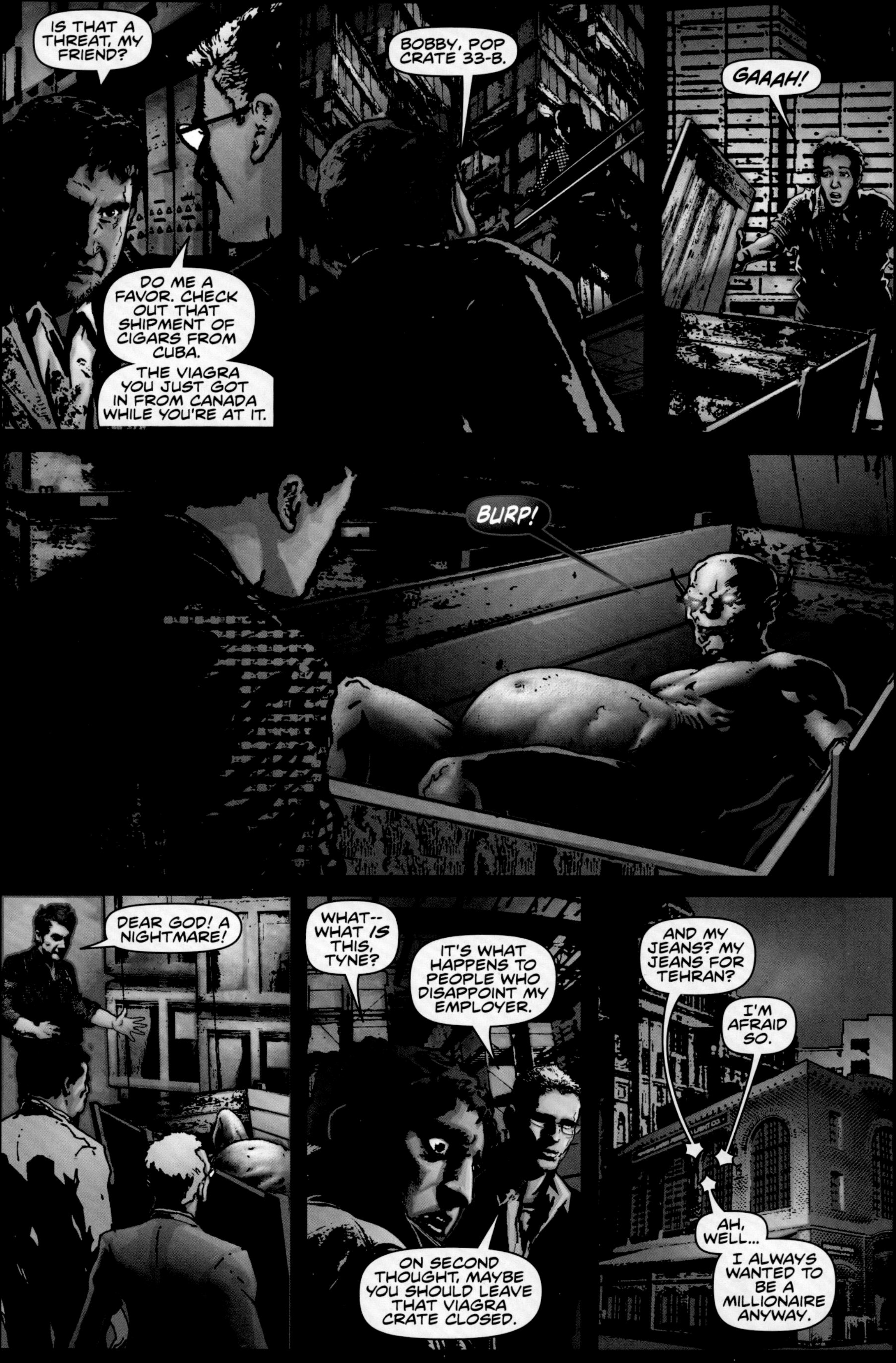
IS THAT A THREAT, MY FRIEND?
DO ME A FAVOR. CHECK OUT THAT SHIPMENT OF CIGARS FROM CUBA.
THE VIAGRA YOU JUST GOT IN FROM CANADA WHILE YOU'RE AT IT.
BOBBY, POP CRATE 33-B.
GAAAH!
BURP!
DEAR GOD! A NIGHTMARE!
WHAT-- WHAT *IS* THIS, TYNE?
IT'S WHAT HAPPENS TO PEOPLE WHO DISAPPOINT MY EMPLOYER.
ON SECOND THOUGHT, MAYBE YOU SHOULD LEAVE THAT VIAGRA CRATE CLOSED.
AND MY JEANS? MY JEANS FOR TEHRAN?
I'M AFRAID SO.
AH, WELL...
I ALWAYS WANTED TO BE A MILLIONAIRE ANYWAY.

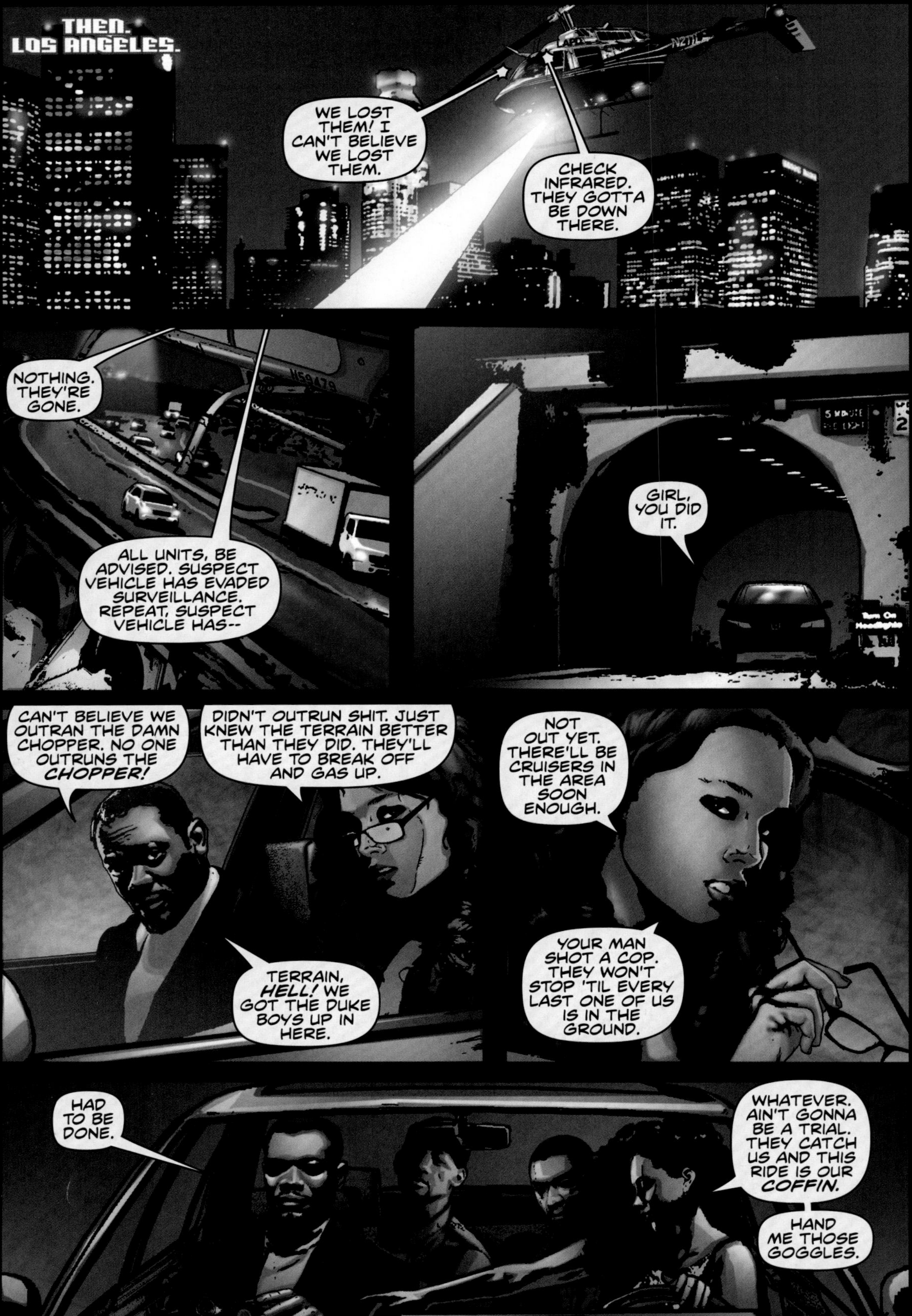
THEN. LOS ANGELES.
WE LOST THEM! I CAN'T BELIEVE WE LOST THEM.
CHECK INFRARED. THEY GOTTA BE DOWN THERE.
NOTHING. THEY'RE GONE.
ALL UNITS, BE ADVISED. SUSPECT VEHICLE HAS EVADED SURVEILLANCE. REPEAT, SUSPECT VEHICLE HAS--
GIRL, YOU DID IT.
Turn On Headlights
CAN'T BELIEVE WE OUTRAN THE DAMN CHOPPER. NO ONE OUTRUNS THE *CHOPPER!*
DIDN'T OUTRUN SHIT. JUST KNEW THE TERRAIN BETTER THAN THEY DID. THEY'LL HAVE TO BREAK OFF AND GAS UP.
TERRAIN, *HELL!* WE GOT THE DUKE BOYS UP IN HERE.
NOT OUT YET. THERE'LL BE CRUISERS IN THE AREA SOON ENOUGH.
YOUR MAN SHOT A COP. THEY WON'T STOP 'TIL EVERY LAST ONE OF US IS IN THE GROUND.
HAD TO BE DONE.
WHATEVER. AIN'T GONNA BE A TRIAL. THEY CATCH US AND THIS RIDE IS OUR *COFFIN.*
HAND ME THOSE GOGGLES.

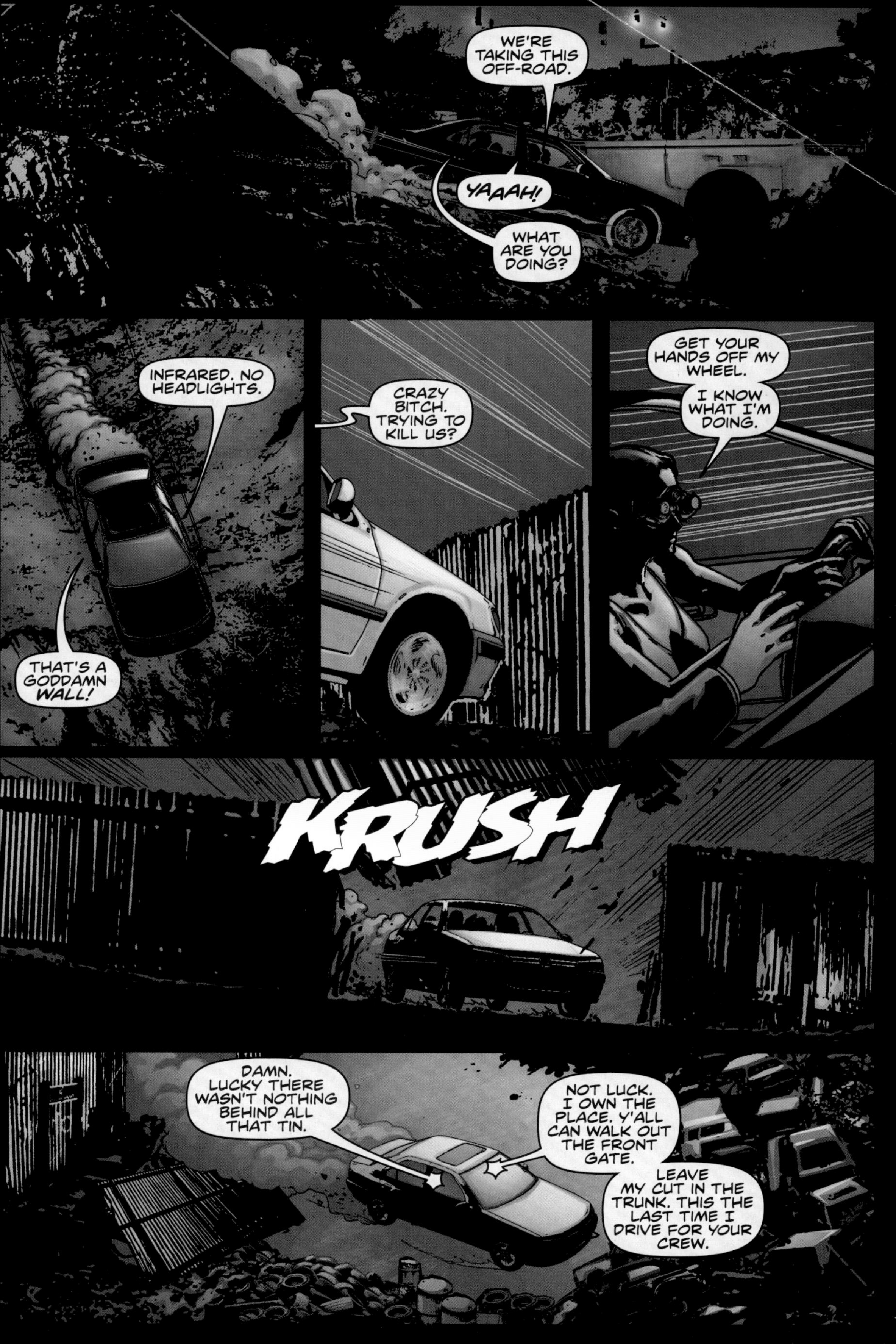
WE'RE TAKING THIS OFF-ROAD.
YAAAH!
WHAT ARE YOU DOING?
INFRARED. NO HEADLIGHTS.
THAT'S A GODDAMN WALL!
CRAZY BITCH. TRYING TO KILL US?
GET YOUR HANDS OFF MY WHEEL.
I KNOW WHAT I'M DOING.
KRUSH
DAMN. LUCKY THERE WASN'T NOTHING BEHIND ALL THAT TIN.
NOT LUCK. I OWN THE PLACE. Y'ALL CAN WALK OUT THE FRONT GATE.
LEAVE MY CUT IN THE TRUNK. THIS THE LAST TIME I DRIVE FOR YOUR CREW.

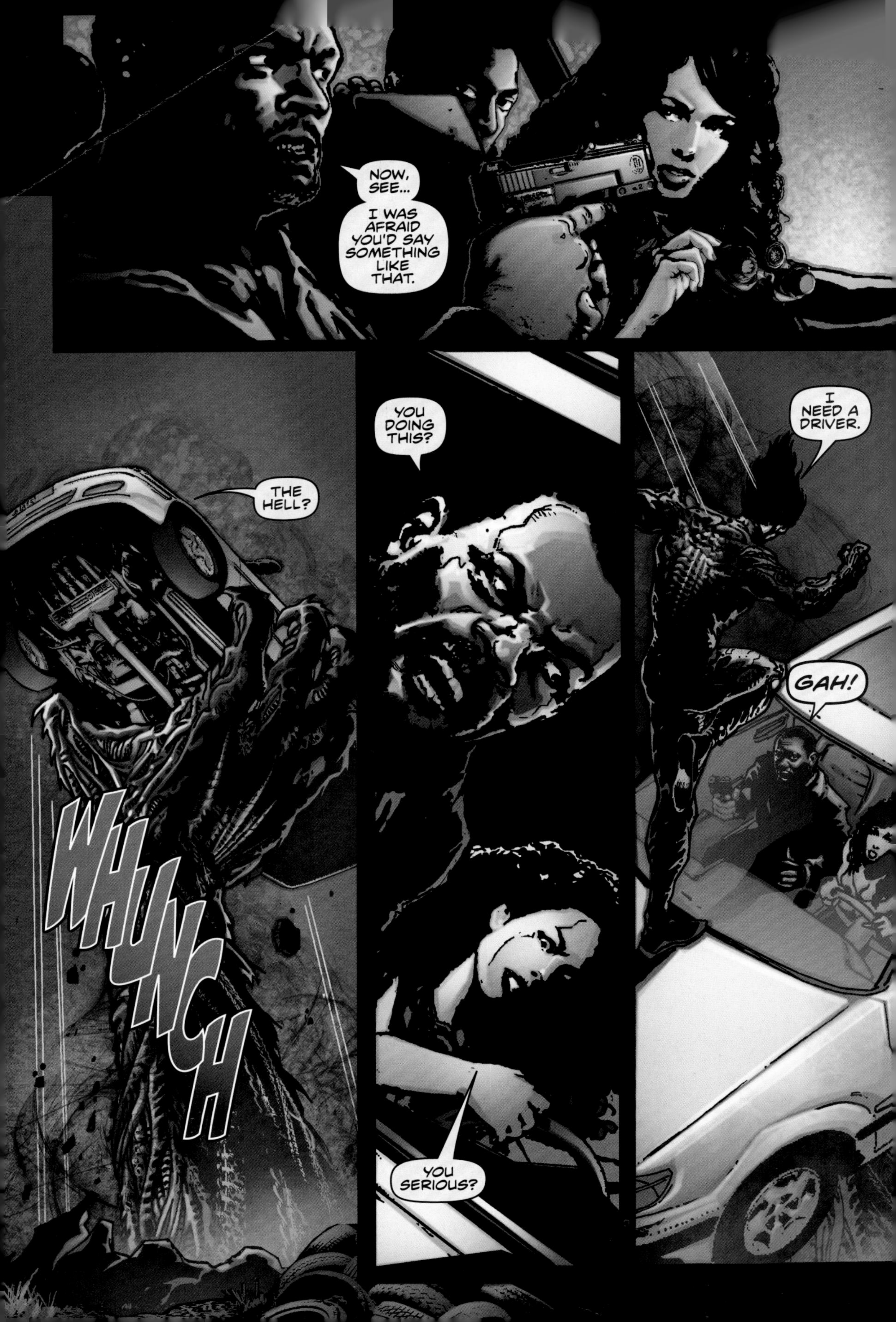
NOW, SEE...
I WAS AFRAID YOU'D SAY SOMETHING LIKE THAT.
THE HELL?
WHUNCH
YOU DOING THIS?
YOU SERIOUS?
I NEED A DRIVER.
GAH!

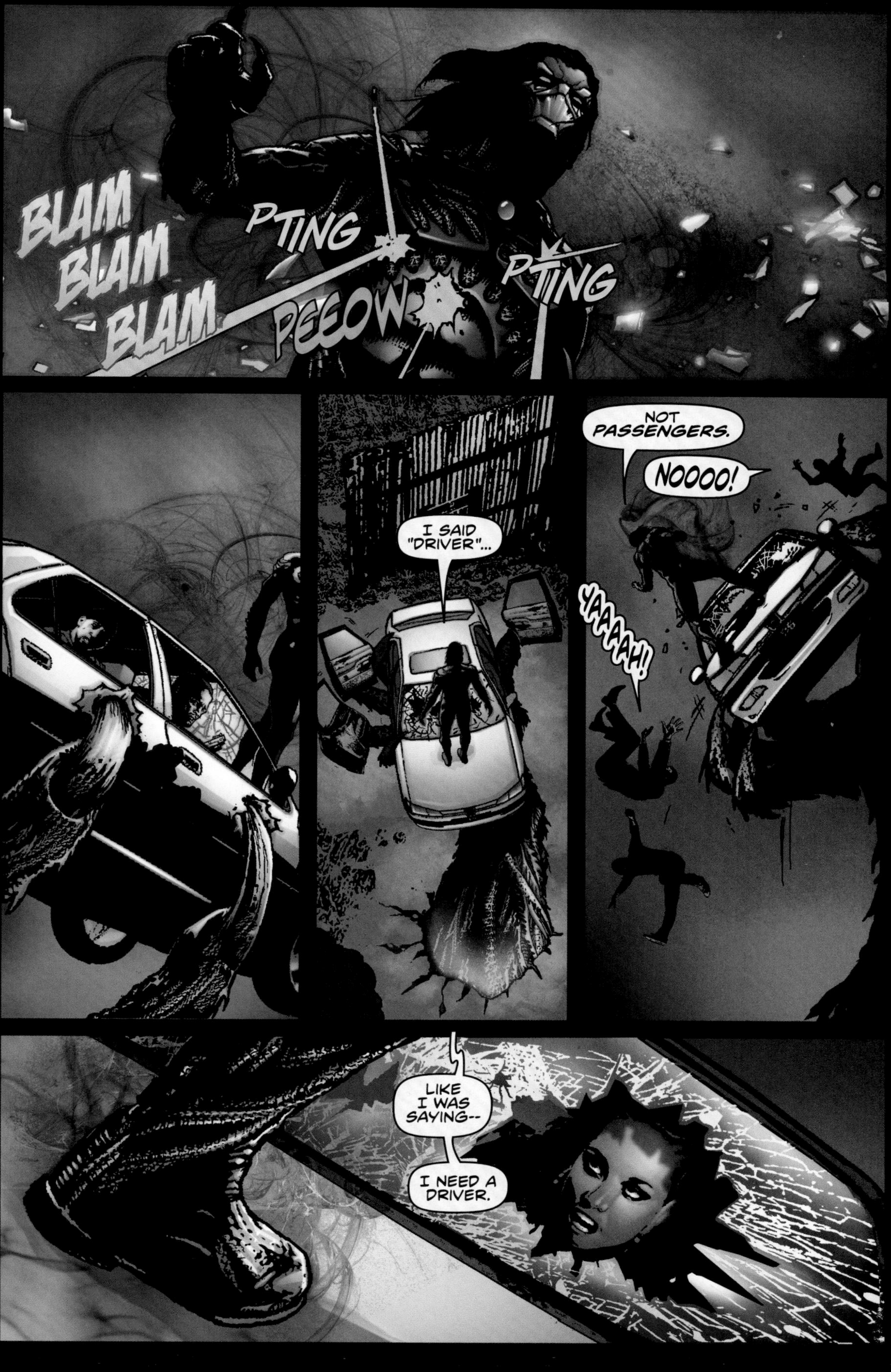
BLAM
BLAM
BLAM
PTING
PEEOW
PTING
I SAID "DRIVER"...
NOT PASSENGERS.
NOOOO!
YAAAAAH!
LIKE I WAS SAYING--
I NEED A DRIVER.

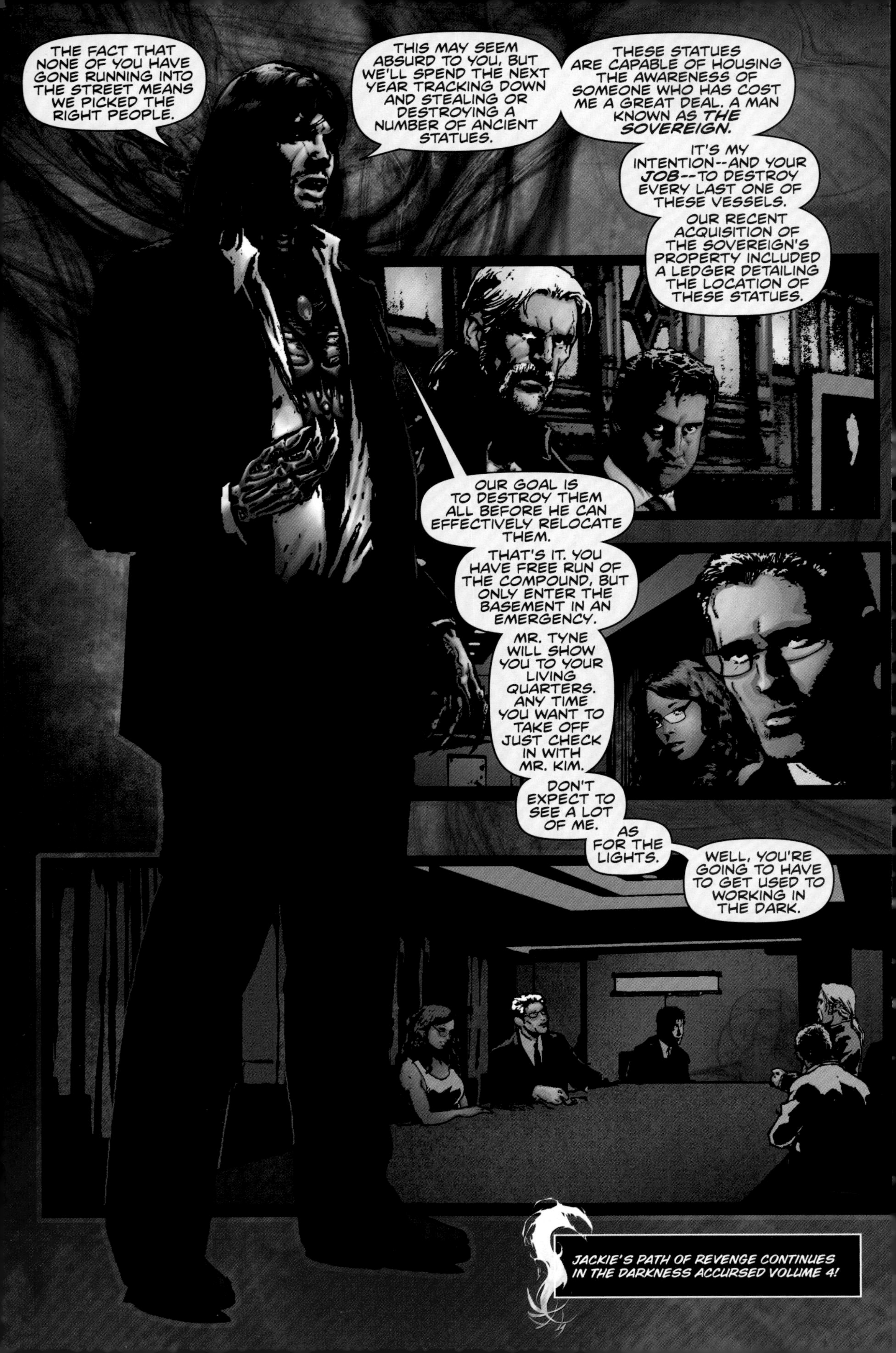
THE FACT THAT NONE OF YOU HAVE GONE RUNNING INTO THE STREET MEANS WE PICKED THE RIGHT PEOPLE.
THIS MAY SEEM ABSURD TO YOU, BUT WE'LL SPEND THE NEXT YEAR TRACKING DOWN AND STEALING OR DESTROYING A NUMBER OF ANCIENT STATUES.
THESE STATUES ARE CAPABLE OF HOUSING THE AWARENESS OF SOMEONE WHO HAS COST ME A GREAT DEAL. A MAN KNOWN AS THE SOVEREIGN.
IT'S MY INTENTION--AND YOUR JOB--TO DESTROY EVERY LAST ONE OF THESE VESSELS.
OUR RECENT ACQUISITION OF THE SOVEREIGN'S PROPERTY INCLUDED A LEDGER DETAILING THE LOCATION OF THESE STATUES.
OUR GOAL IS TO DESTROY THEM ALL BEFORE HE CAN EFFECTIVELY RELOCATE THEM.
THAT'S IT. YOU HAVE FREE RUN OF THE COMPOUND, BUT ONLY ENTER THE BASEMENT IN AN EMERGENCY.
MR. TYNE WILL SHOW YOU TO YOUR LIVING QUARTERS. ANY TIME YOU WANT TO TAKE OFF JUST CHECK IN WITH MR. KIM.
DON'T EXPECT TO SEE A LOT OF ME.
AS FOR THE LIGHTS.
WELL, YOU'RE GOING TO HAVE TO GET USED TO WORKING IN THE DARK.
JACKIE'S PATH OF REVENGE CONTINUES IN THE DARKNESS ACCURSED VOLUME 4!

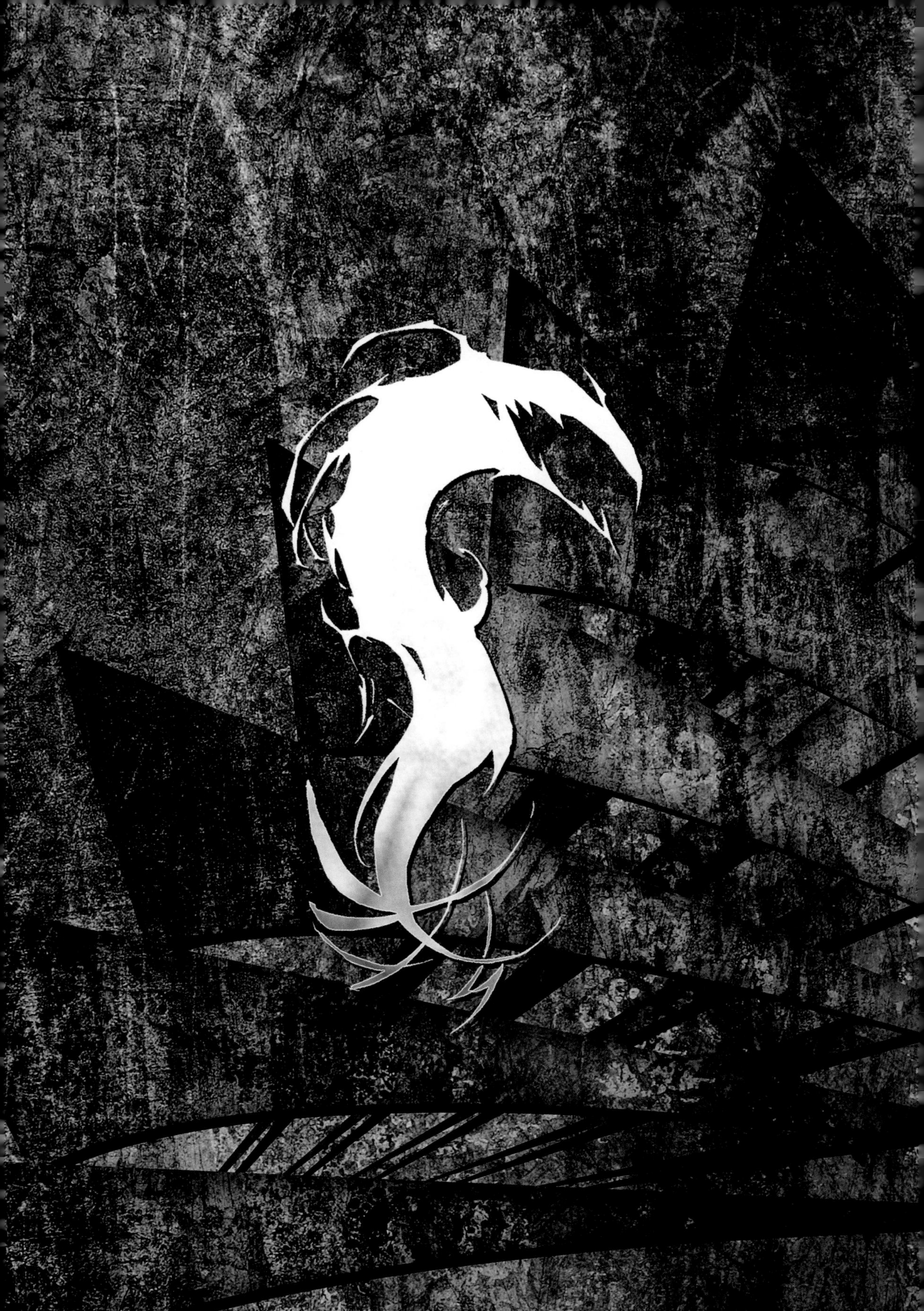

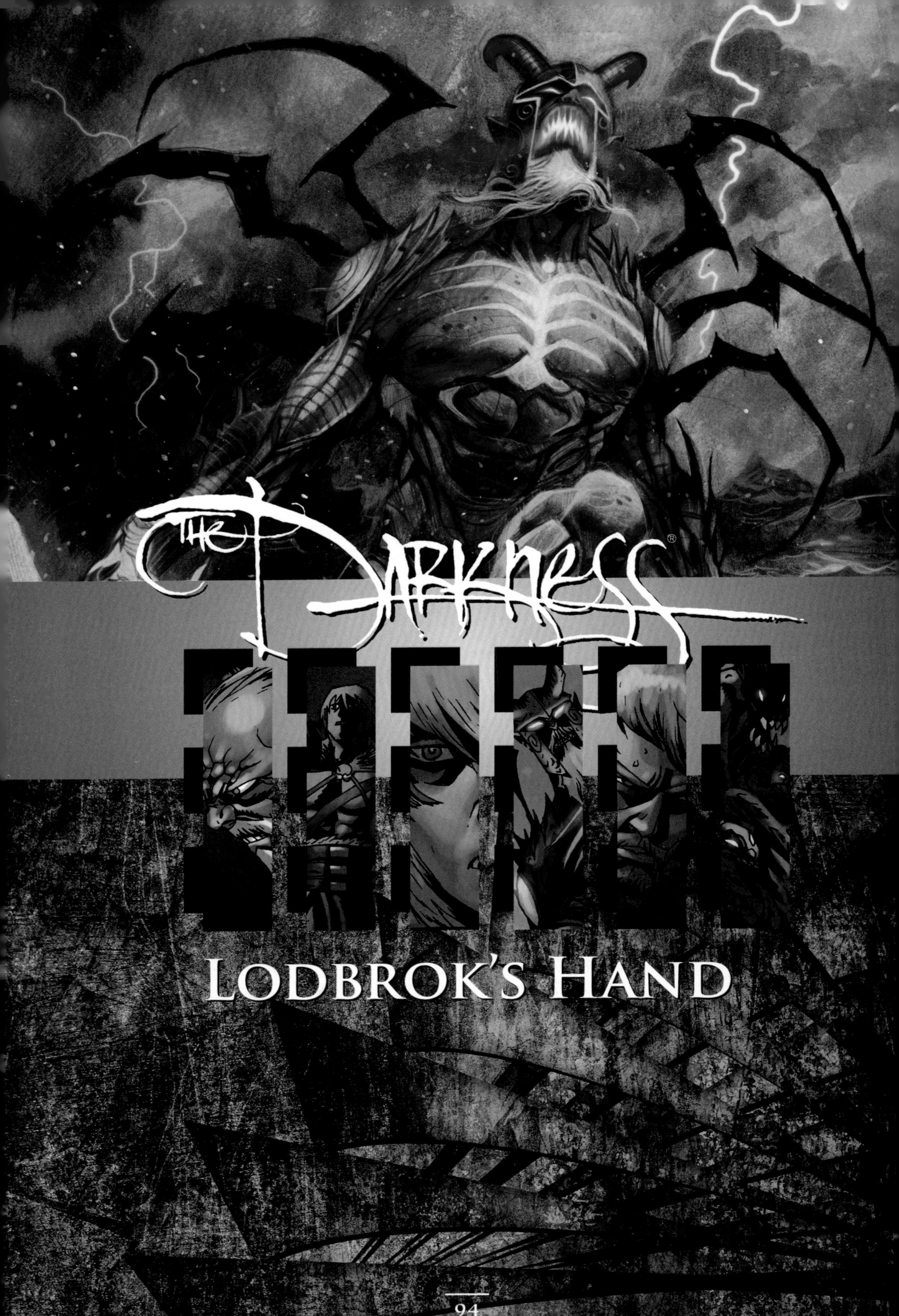
THE DARKNESS®
LODBROK'S HAND

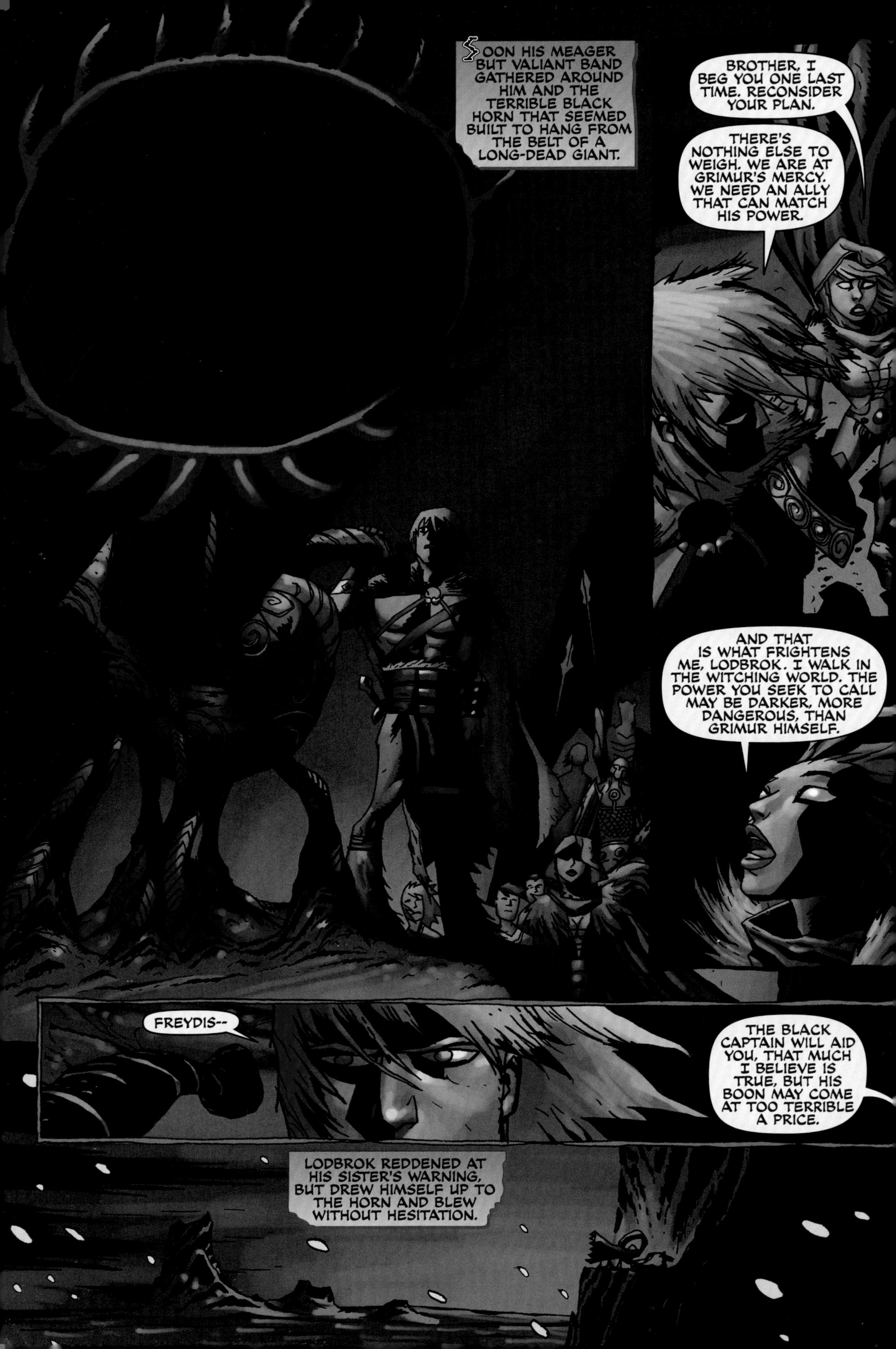
SOON HIS MEAGER BUT VALIANT BAND GATHERED AROUND HIM AND THE TERRIBLE BLACK HORN THAT SEEMED BUILT TO HANG FROM THE BELT OF A LONG-DEAD GIANT.
BROTHER, I BEG YOU ONE LAST TIME. RECONSIDER YOUR PLAN.
THERE'S NOTHING ELSE TO WEIGH. WE ARE AT GRIMUR'S MERCY. WE NEED AN ALLY THAT CAN MATCH HIS POWER.
AND THAT IS WHAT FRIGHTENS ME, LODBROK. I WALK IN THE WITCHING WORLD. THE POWER YOU SEEK TO CALL MAY BE DARKER, MORE DANGEROUS, THAN GRIMUR HIMSELF.
FREYDIS--
THE BLACK CAPTAIN WILL AID YOU, THAT MUCH I BELIEVE IS TRUE, BUT HIS BOON MAY COME AT TOO TERRIBLE A PRICE.
LODBROK REDDENED AT HIS SISTER'S WARNING, BUT DREW HIMSELF UP TO THE HORN AND BLEW WITHOUT HESITATION.

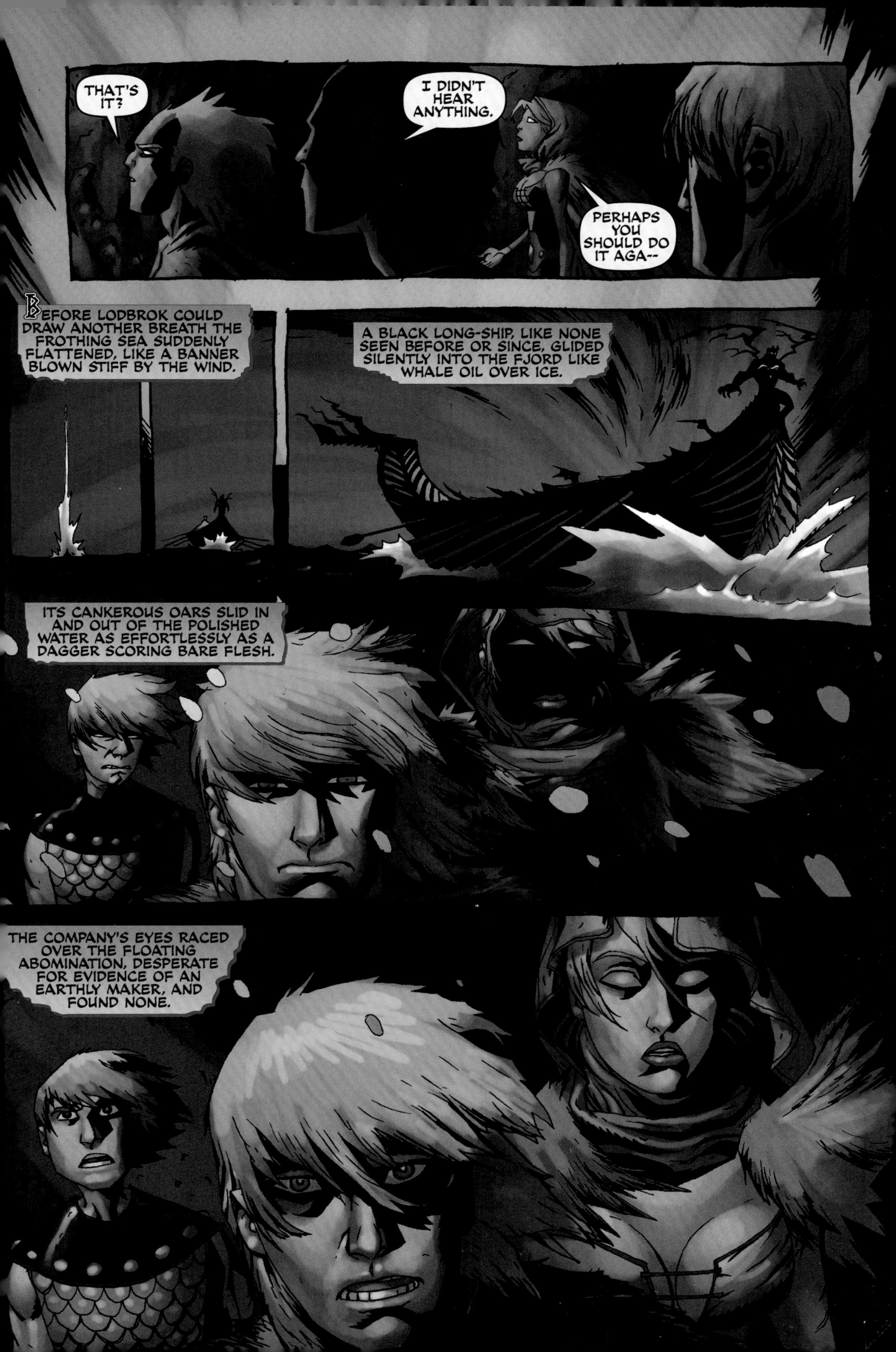
THAT'S IT?
I DIDN'T HEAR ANYTHING.
PERHAPS YOU SHOULD DO IT AGA--
BEFORE LODBROK COULD DRAW ANOTHER BREATH THE FROTHING SEA SUDDENLY FLATTENED, LIKE A BANNER BLOWN STIFF BY THE WIND.
A BLACK LONG-SHIP, LIKE NONE SEEN BEFORE OR SINCE, GLIDED SILENTLY INTO THE FJORD LIKE WHALE OIL OVER ICE.
ITS CANKEROUS OARS SLID IN AND OUT OF THE POLISHED WATER AS EFFORTLESSLY AS A DAGGER SCORING BARE FLESH.
THE COMPANY'S EYES RACED OVER THE FLOATING ABOMINATION, DESPERATE FOR EVIDENCE OF AN EARTHLY MAKER, AND FOUND NONE.

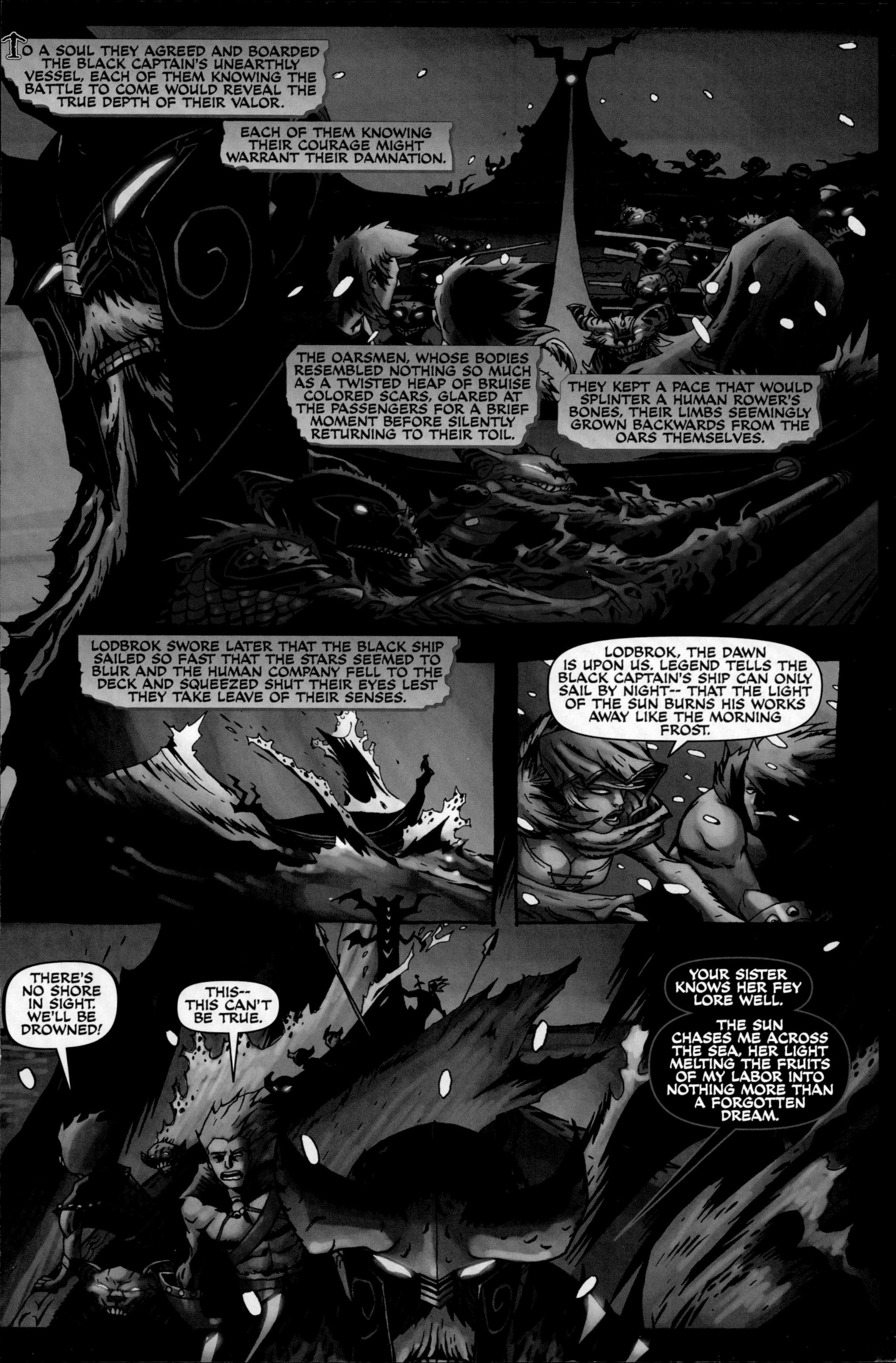
TO A SOUL THEY AGREED AND BOARDED THE BLACK CAPTAIN'S UNEARTHLY VESSEL, EACH OF THEM KNOWING THE BATTLE TO COME WOULD REVEAL THE TRUE DEPTH OF THEIR VALOR.
EACH OF THEM KNOWING THEIR COURAGE MIGHT WARRANT THEIR DAMNATION.
THE OARSMEN, WHOSE BODIES RESEMBLED NOTHING SO MUCH AS A TWISTED HEAP OF BRUISE COLORED SCARS, GLARED AT THE PASSENGERS FOR A BRIEF MOMENT BEFORE SILENTLY RETURNING TO THEIR TOIL.
THEY KEPT A PACE THAT WOULD SPLINTER A HUMAN ROWER'S BONES, THEIR LIMBS SEEMINGLY GROWN BACKWARDS FROM THE OARS THEMSELVES.
LODBROK SWORE LATER THAT THE BLACK SHIP SAILED SO FAST THAT THE STARS SEEMED TO BLUR AND THE HUMAN COMPANY FELL TO THE DECK AND SQUEEZED SHUT THEIR EYES LEST THEY TAKE LEAVE OF THEIR SENSES.
LODBROK, THE DAWN IS UPON US. LEGEND TELLS THE BLACK CAPTAIN'S SHIP CAN ONLY SAIL BY NIGHT-- THAT THE LIGHT OF THE SUN BURNS HIS WORKS AWAY LIKE THE MORNING FROST.
THERE'S NO SHORE IN SIGHT. WE'LL BE DROWNED!
THIS-- THIS CAN'T BE TRUE.
YOUR SISTER KNOWS HER FEY LORE WELL.
THE SUN CHASES ME ACROSS THE SEA, HER LIGHT MELTING THE FRUITS OF MY LABOR INTO NOTHING MORE THAN A FORGOTTEN DREAM.

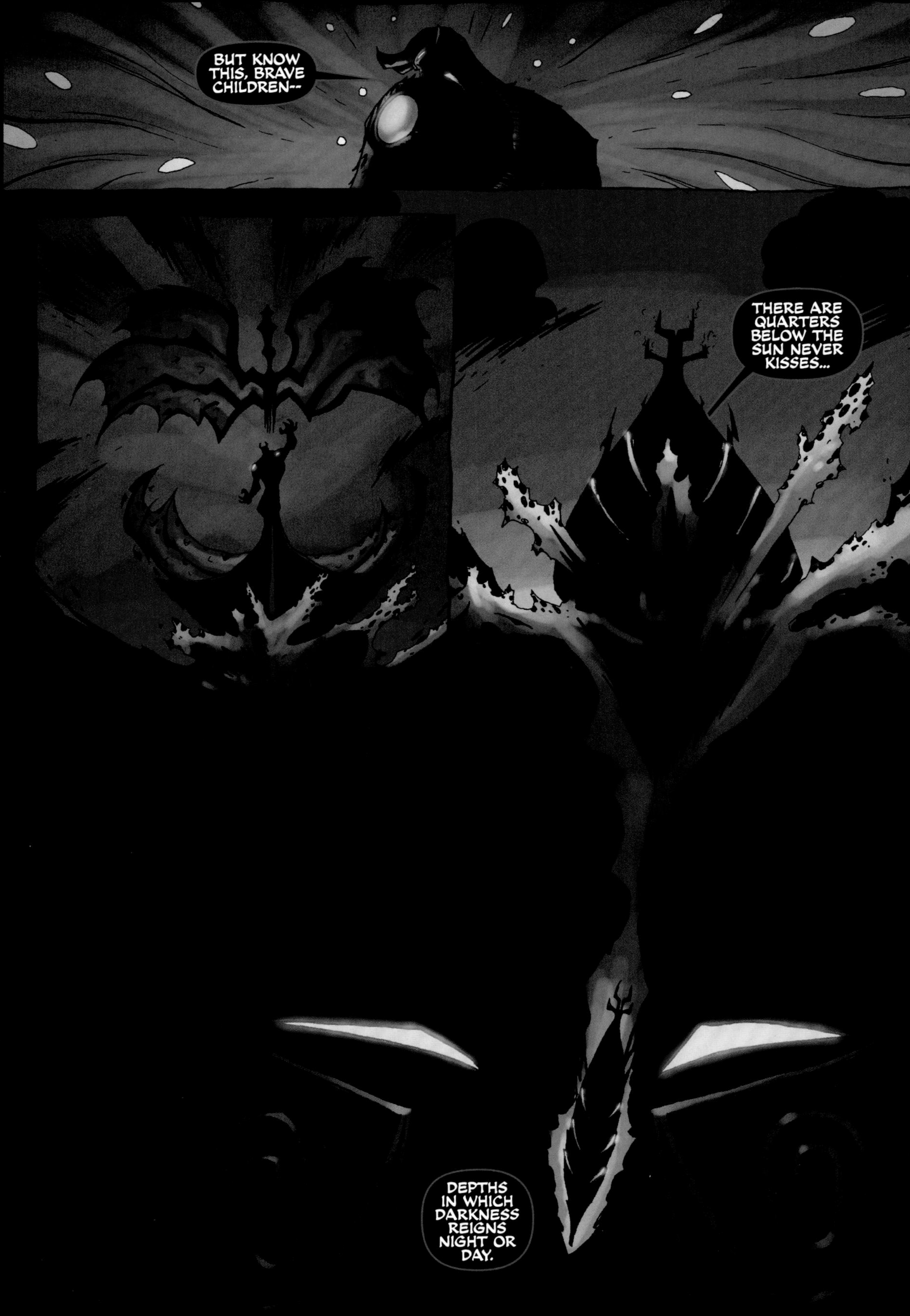
BUT KNOW THIS, BRAVE CHILDREN--
THERE ARE QUARTERS BELOW THE SUN NEVER KISSES...
DEPTHS IN WHICH DARKNESS REIGNS NIGHT OR DAY.

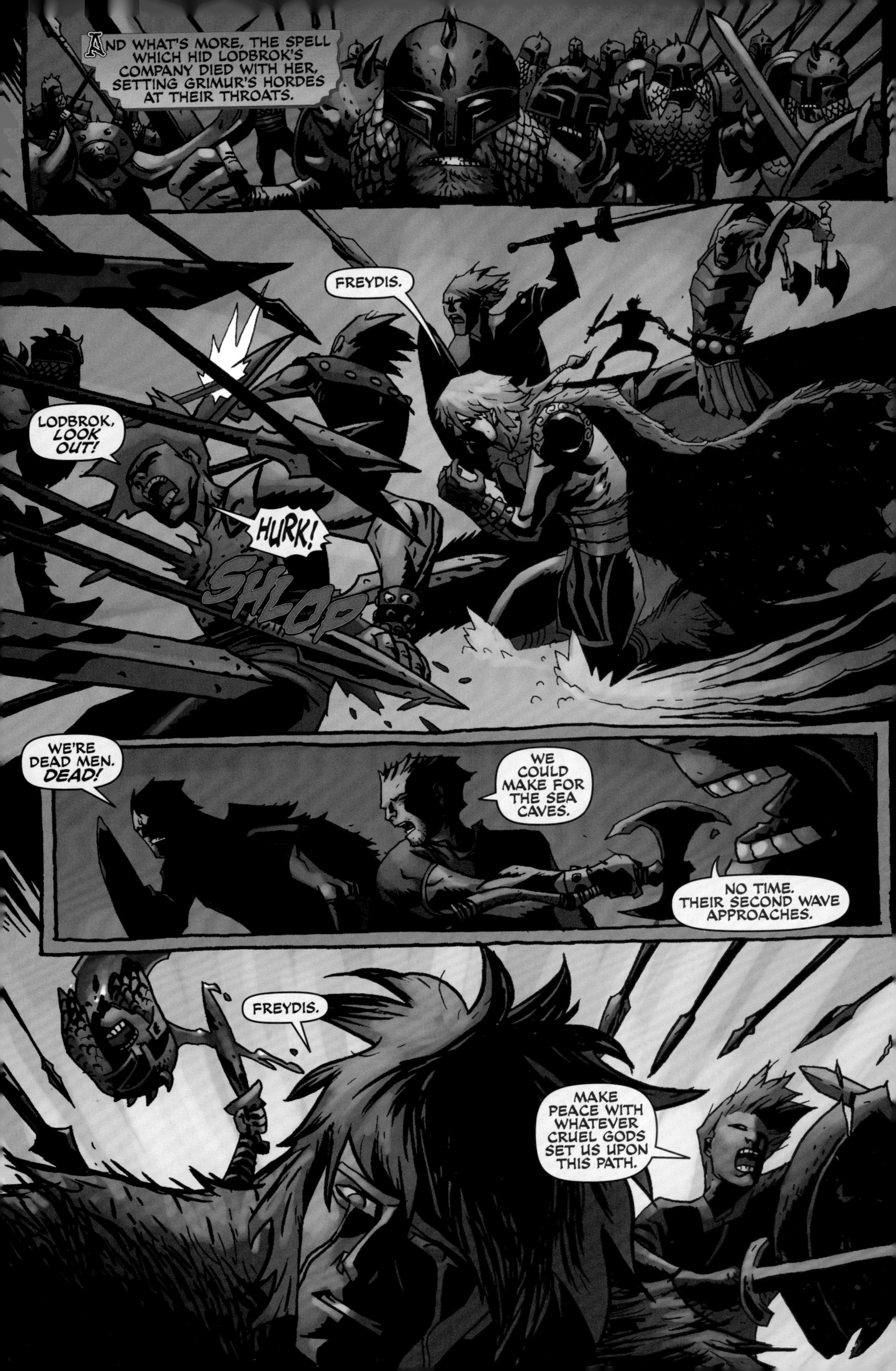
AND WHAT'S MORE, THE SPELL WHICH HID LODBROK'S COMPANY DIED WITH HER, SETTING GRIMUR'S HORDES AT THEIR THROATS.
FREYDIS.
LODBROK, LOOK OUT!
HURK!
SHLOP
WE'RE DEAD MEN. DEAD!
WE COULD MAKE FOR THE SEA CAVES.
NO TIME. THEIR SECOND WAVE APPROACHES.
FREYDIS.
MAKE PEACE WITH WHATEVER CRUEL GODS SET US UPON THIS PATH.

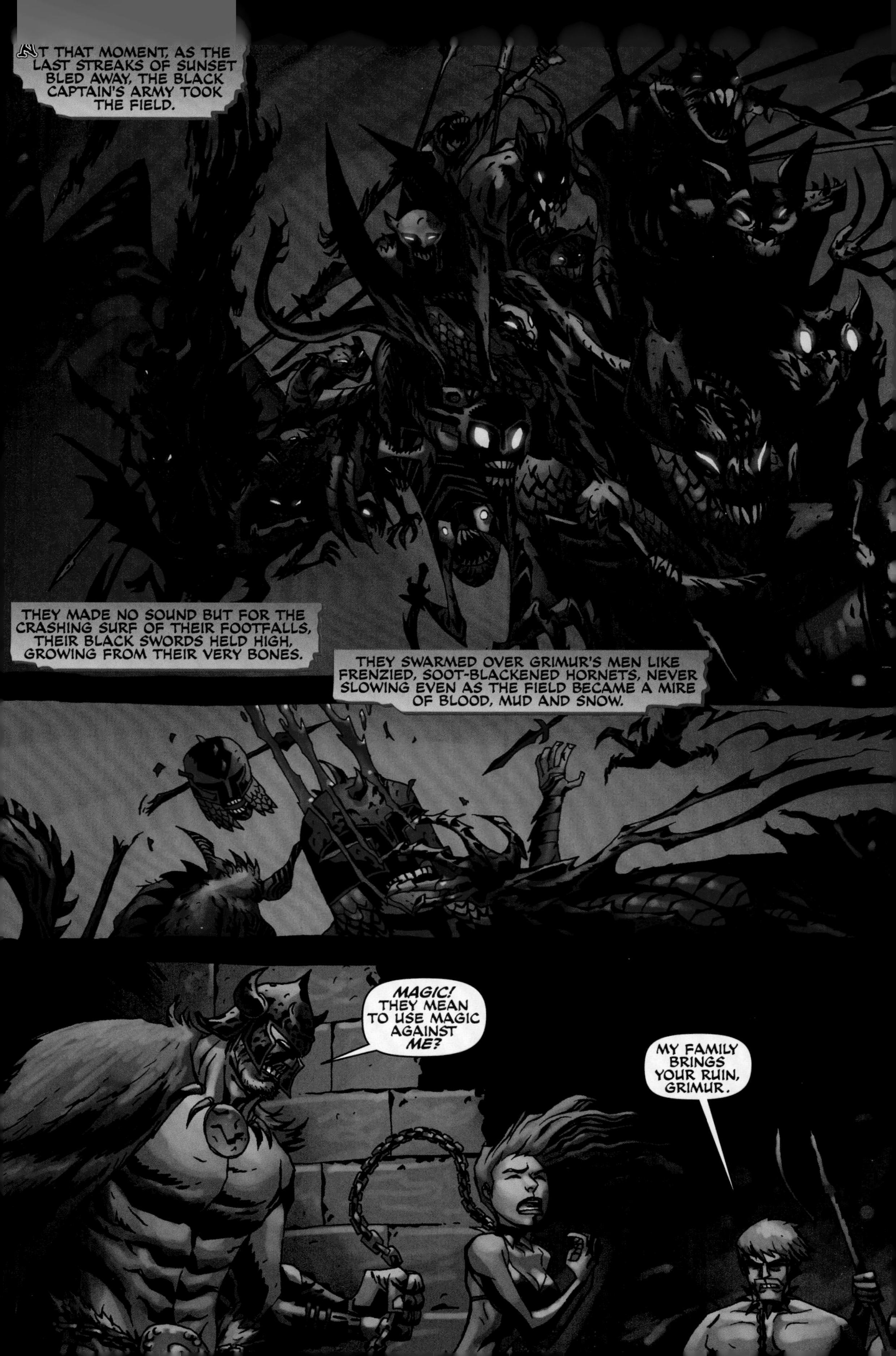
AT THAT MOMENT, AS THE LAST STREAKS OF SUNSET BLED AWAY, THE BLACK CAPTAIN'S ARMY TOOK THE FIELD.
THEY MADE NO SOUND BUT FOR THE CRASHING SURF OF THEIR FOOTFALLS, THEIR BLACK SWORDS HELD HIGH, GROWING FROM THEIR VERY BONES.
THEY SWARMED OVER GRIMUR'S MEN LIKE FRENZIED, SOOT-BLACKENED HORNETS, NEVER SLOWING EVEN AS THE FIELD BECAME A MIRE OF BLOOD, MUD AND SNOW.
MAGIC! THEY MEAN TO USE MAGIC AGAINST ME?
MY FAMILY BRINGS YOUR RUIN, GRIMUR.

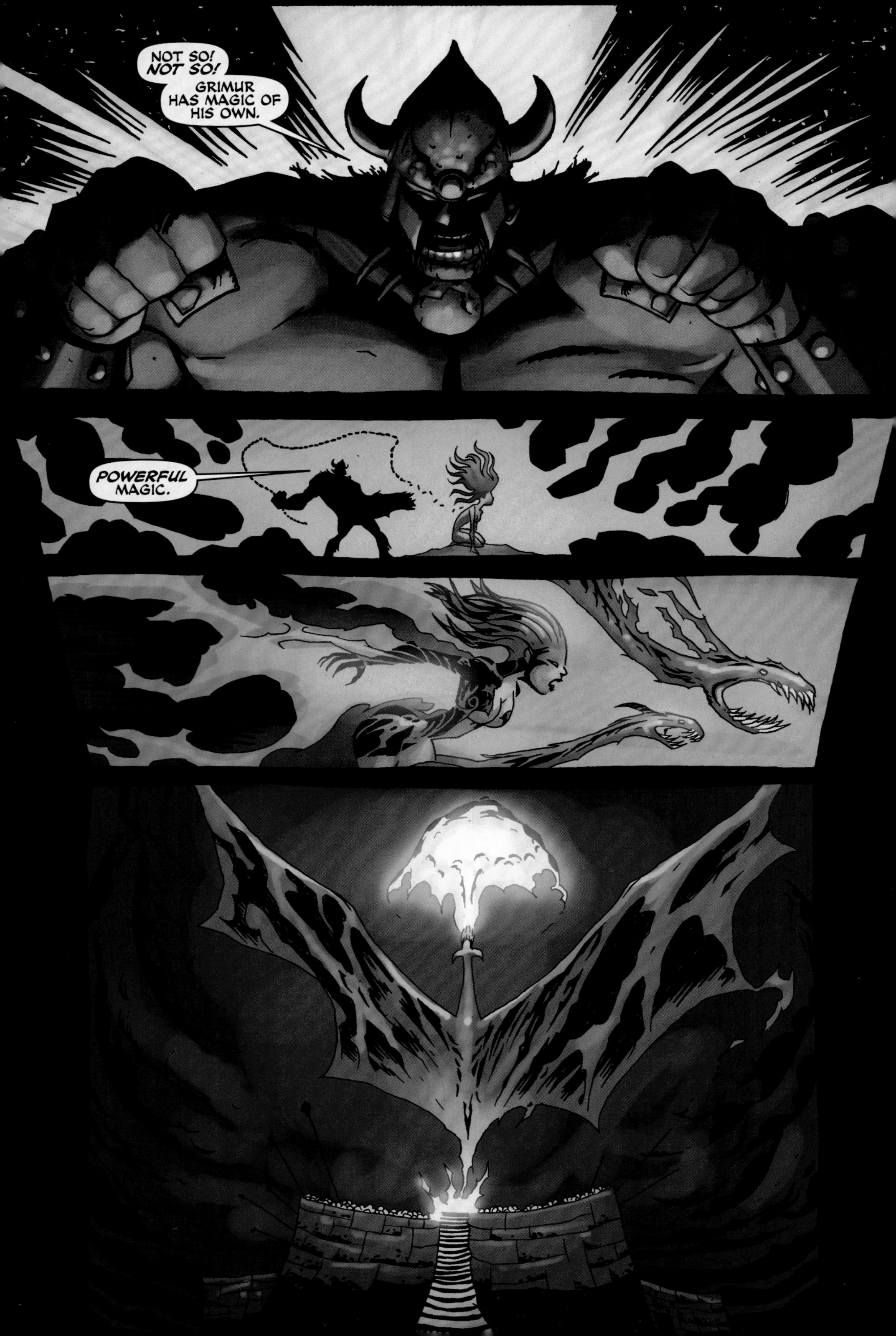
NOT SO! *NOT SO!* GRIMUR HAS MAGIC OF HIS OWN.
POWERFUL MAGIC.

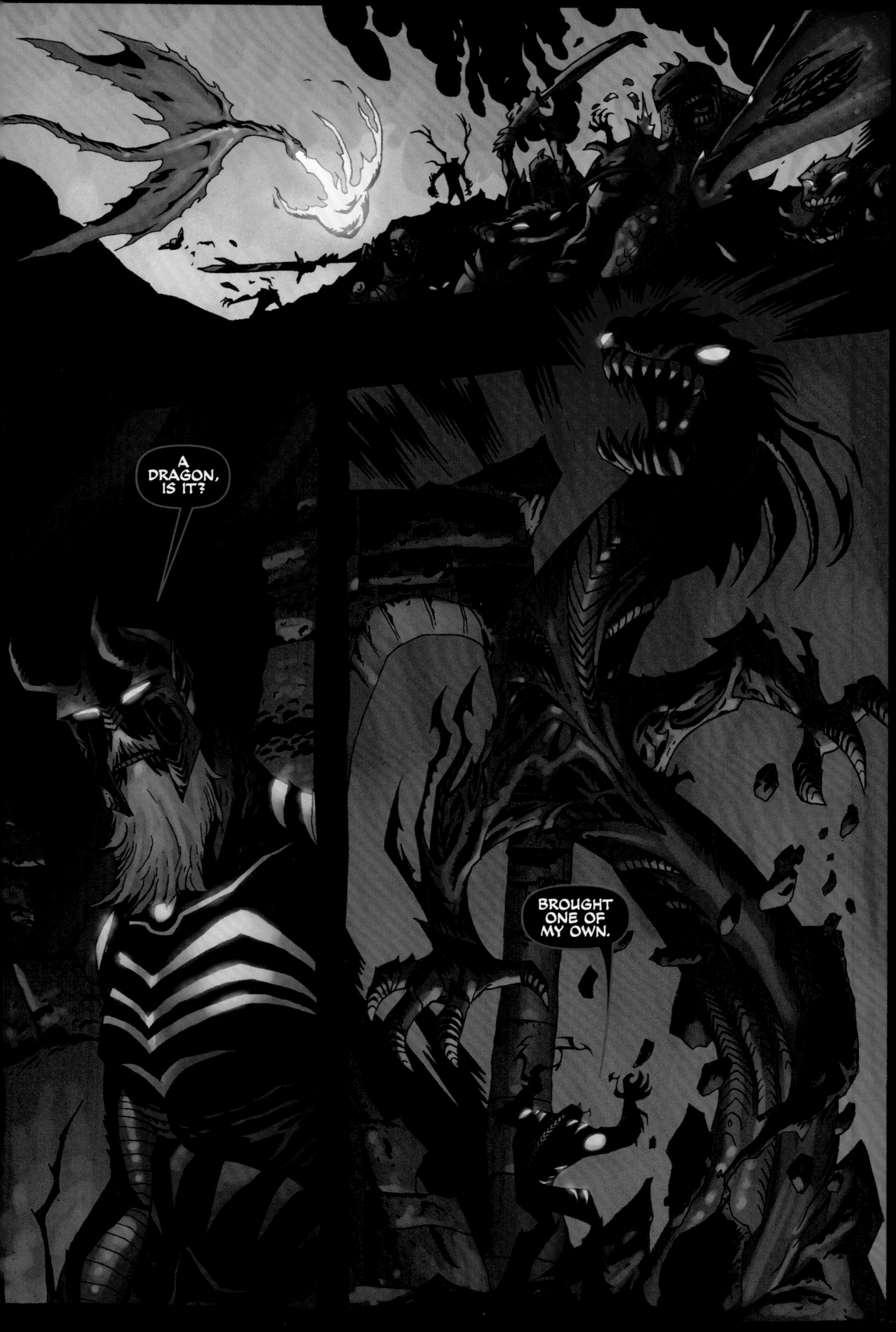
A DRAGON, IS IT?
BROUGHT ONE OF MY OWN.

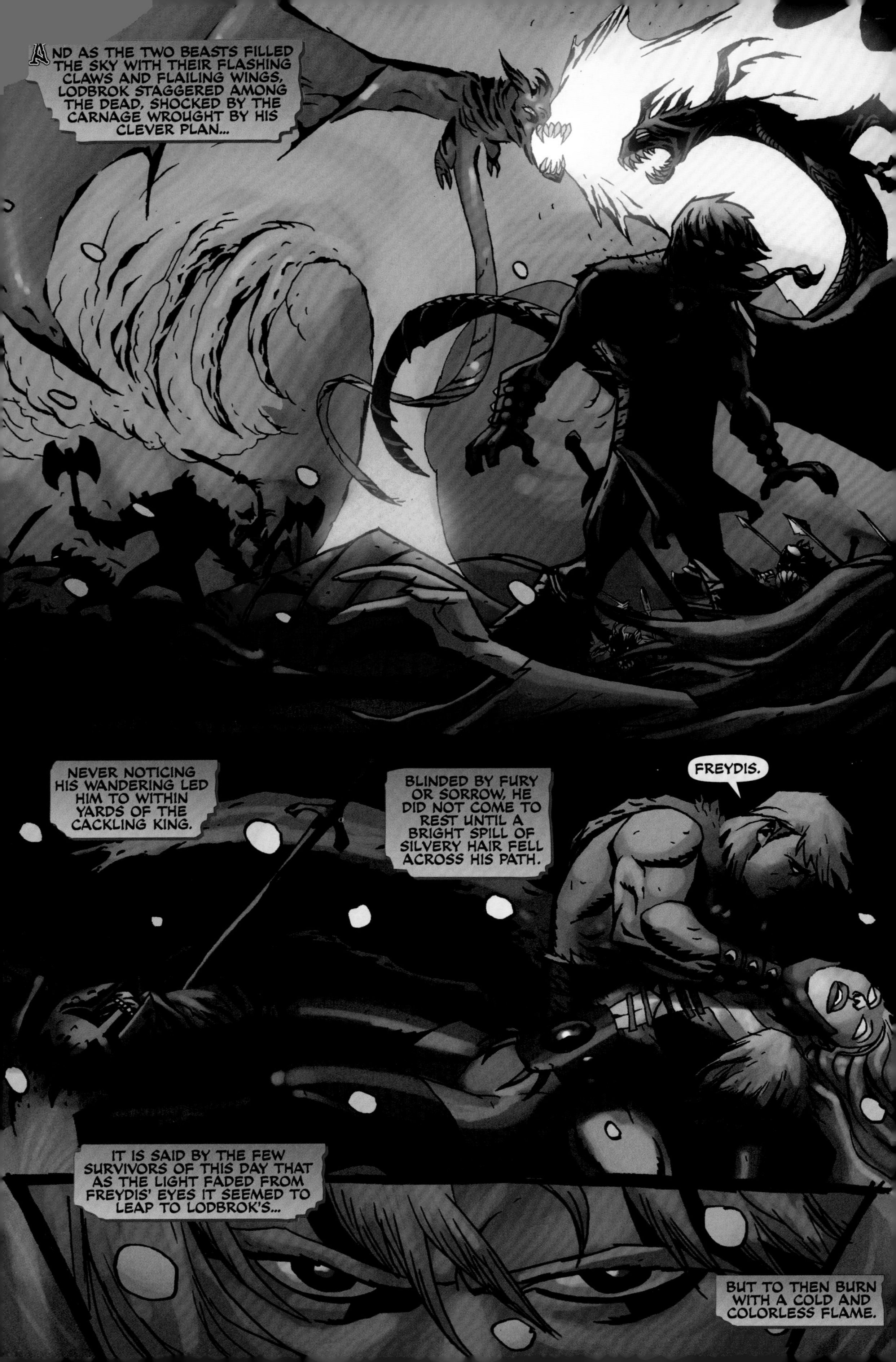
AND AS THE TWO BEASTS FILLED THE SKY WITH THEIR FLASHING CLAWS AND FLAILING WINGS, LODBROK STAGGERED AMONG THE DEAD, SHOCKED BY THE CARNAGE WROUGHT BY HIS CLEVER PLAN...
NEVER NOTICING HIS WANDERING LED HIM TO WITHIN YARDS OF THE CACKLING KING.
BLINDED BY FURY OR SORROW, HE DID NOT COME TO REST UNTIL A BRIGHT SPILL OF SILVERY HAIR FELL ACROSS HIS PATH.
FREYDIS.
IT IS SAID BY THE FEW SURVIVORS OF THIS DAY THAT AS THE LIGHT FADED FROM FREYDIS' EYES IT SEEMED TO LEAP TO LODBROK'S...
BUT TO THEN BURN WITH A COLD AND COLORLESS FLAME.

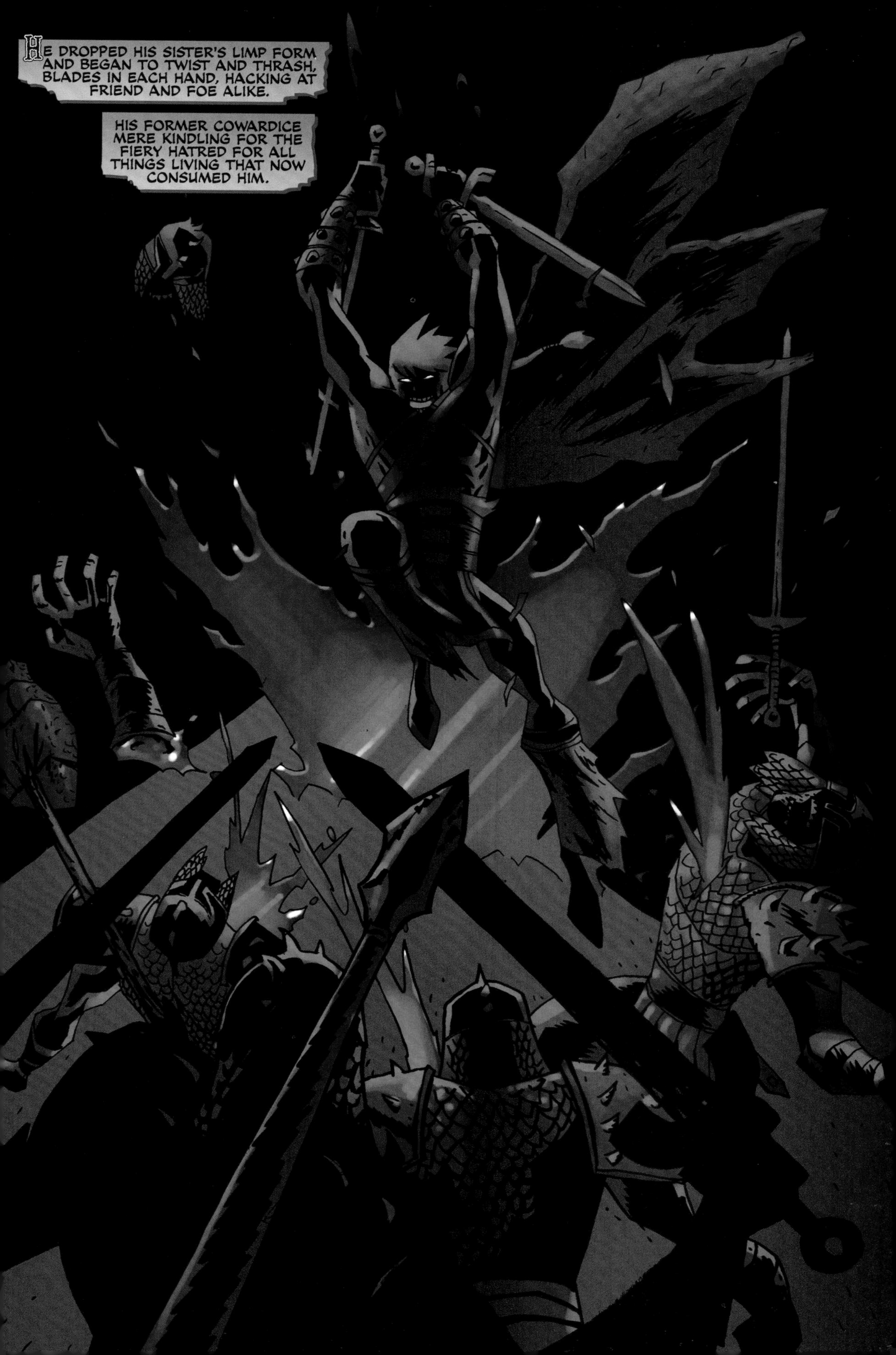
HE DROPPED HIS SISTER'S LIMP FORM AND BEGAN TO TWIST AND THRASH, BLADES IN EACH HAND, HACKING AT FRIEND AND FOE ALIKE.
HIS FORMER COWARDICE MERE KINDLING FOR THE FIERY HATRED FOR ALL THINGS LIVING THAT NOW CONSUMED HIM.

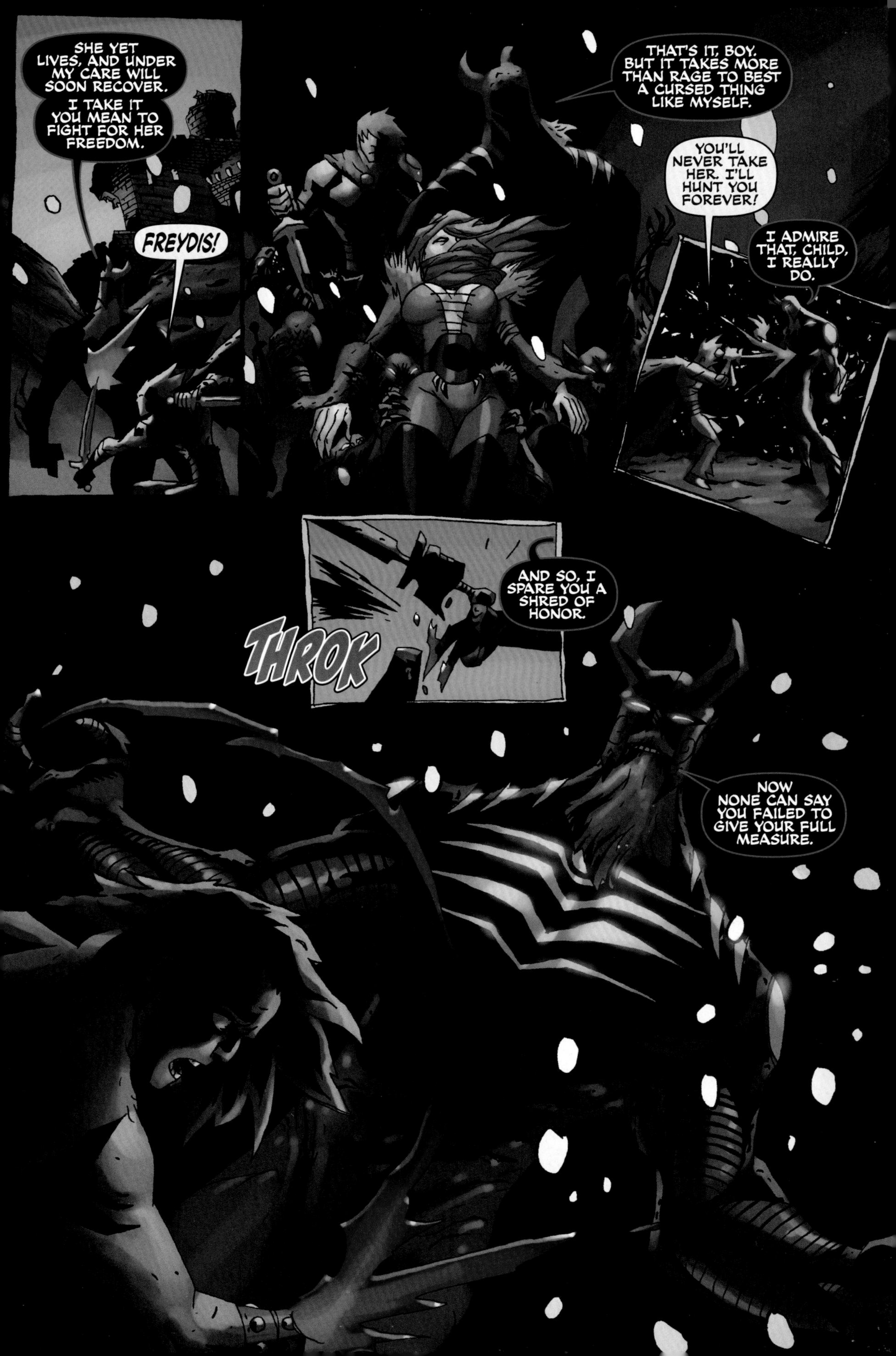
SHE YET LIVES, AND UNDER MY CARE WILL SOON RECOVER.
I TAKE IT YOU MEAN TO FIGHT FOR HER FREEDOM.
FREYDIS!
THAT'S IT, BOY. BUT IT TAKES MORE THAN RAGE TO BEST A CURSED THING LIKE MYSELF.
YOU'LL NEVER TAKE HER. I'LL HUNT YOU FOREVER!
I ADMIRE THAT, CHILD, I REALLY DO.
AND SO, I SPARE YOU A SHRED OF HONOR.
THROK
NOW NONE CAN SAY YOU FAILED TO GIVE YOUR FULL MEASURE.

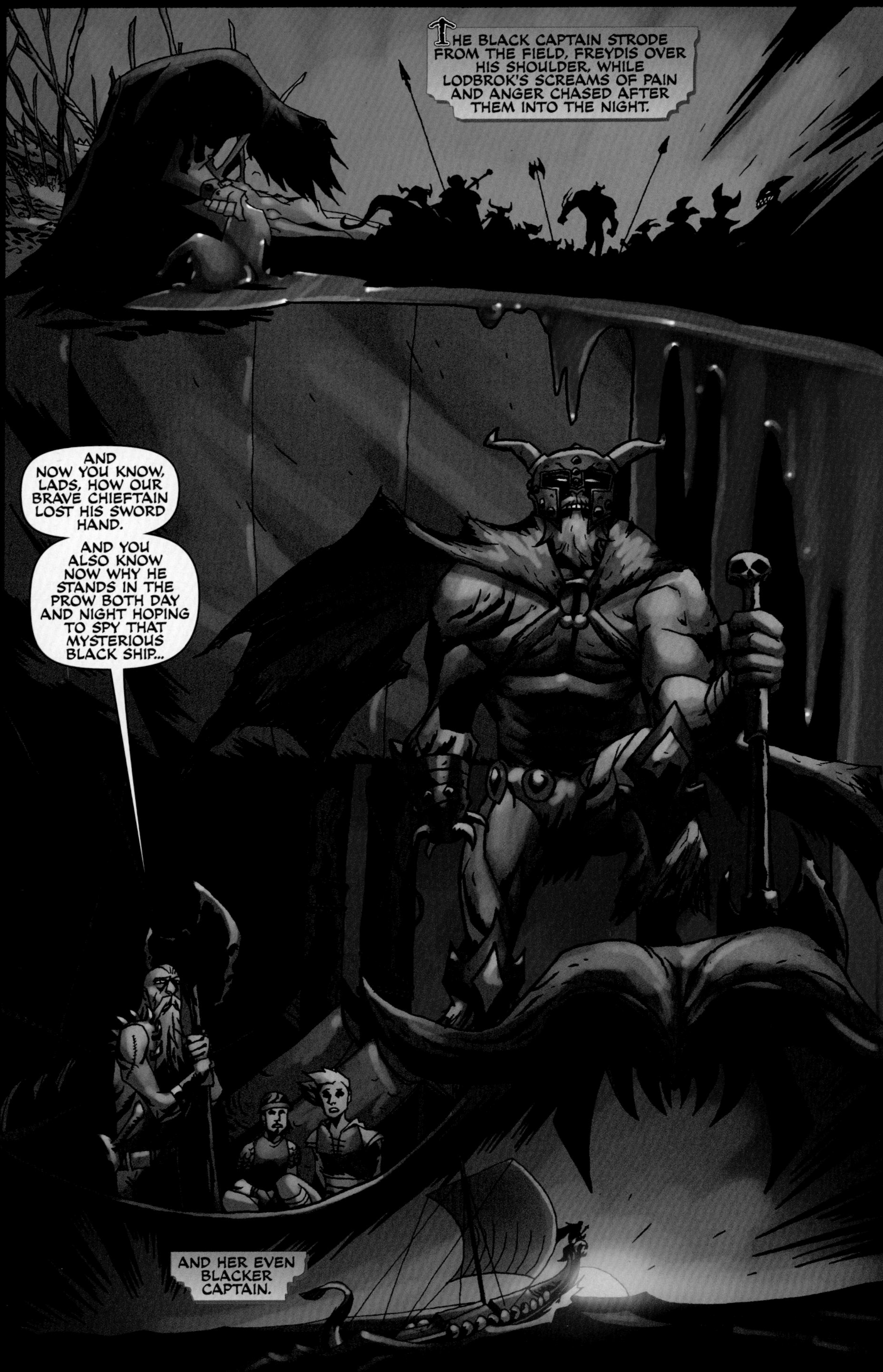
THE BLACK CAPTAIN STRODE FROM THE FIELD, FREYDIS OVER HIS SHOULDER, WHILE LODBROK'S SCREAMS OF PAIN AND ANGER CHASED AFTER THEM INTO THE NIGHT.
AND NOW YOU KNOW, LADS, HOW OUR BRAVE CHIEFTAIN LOST HIS SWORD HAND.
AND YOU ALSO KNOW NOW WHY HE STANDS IN THE PROW BOTH DAY AND NIGHT HOPING TO SPY THAT MYSTERIOUS BLACK SHIP...
AND HER EVEN BLACKER CAPTAIN.

The Darkness®
Accursed
Volume 3

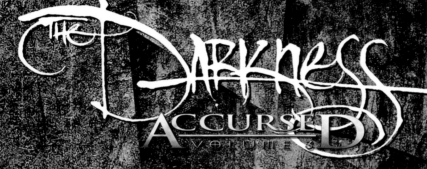

Cover Gallery

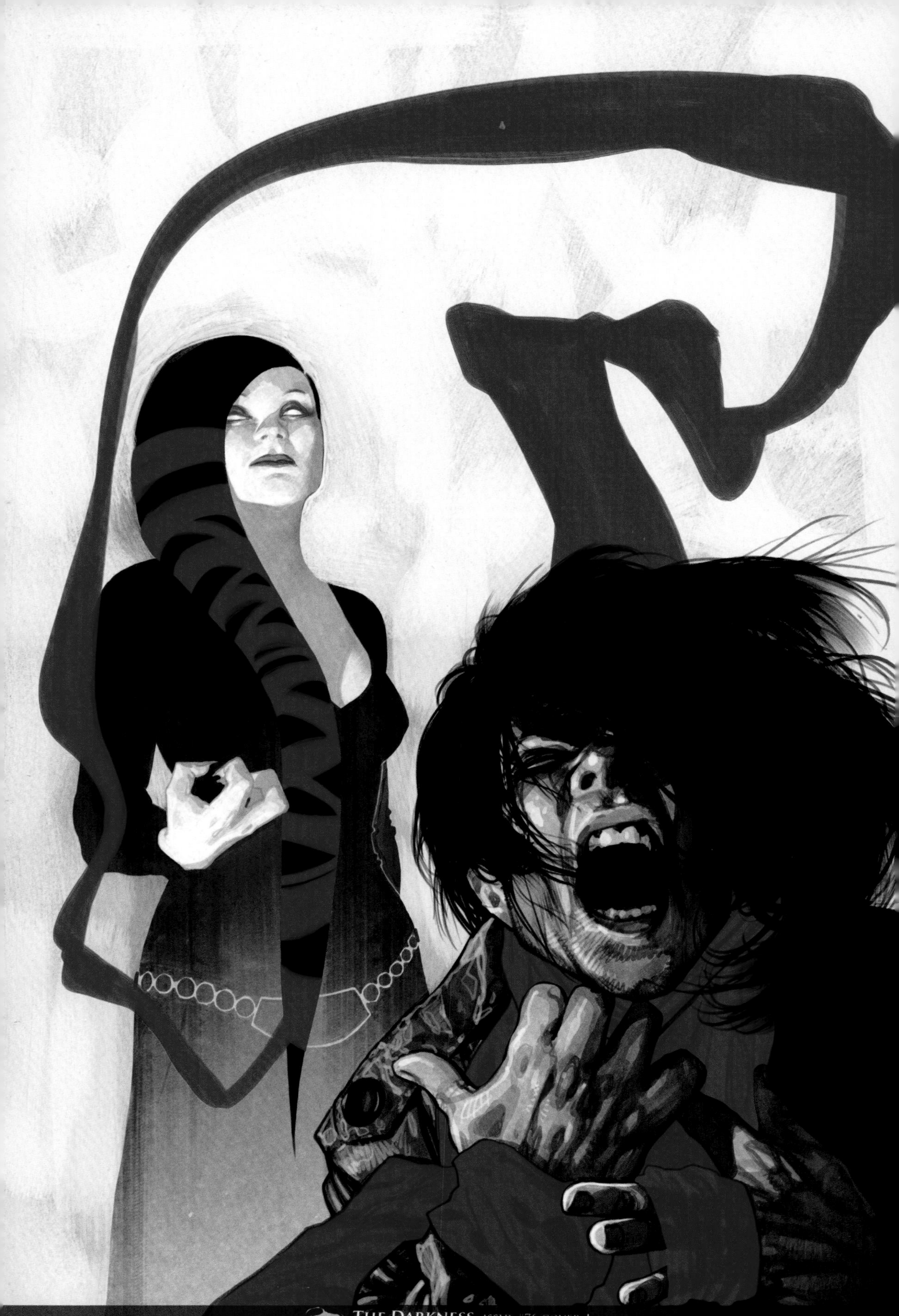

THE DARKNESS, ISSUE #76 COVER A
ART BY: FRAZIER IRVING

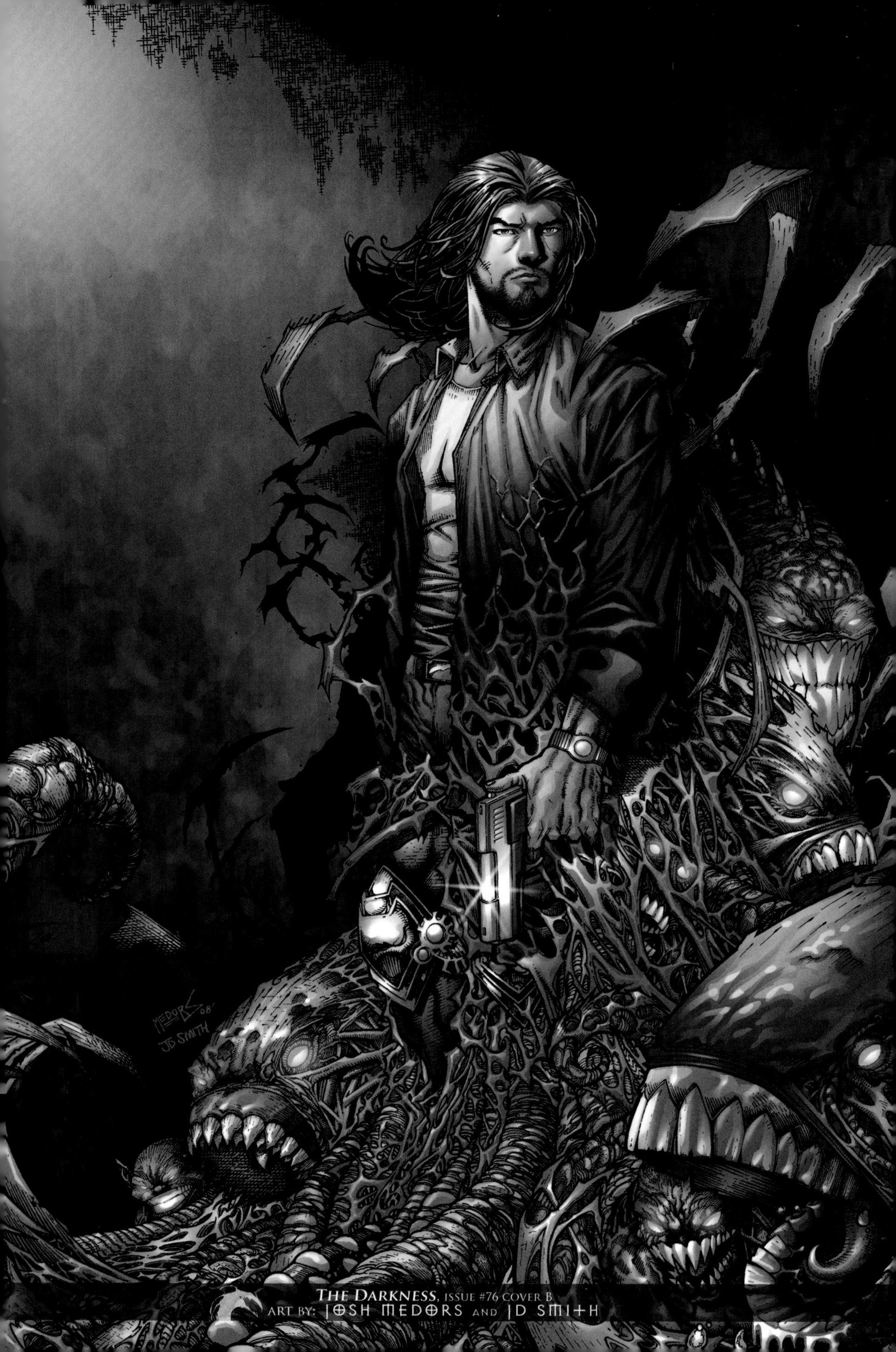
MEDORS '08
JD SMITH

THE DARKNESS, ISSUE #76 COVER B
ART BY: JOSH MEDORS AND JD SMITH

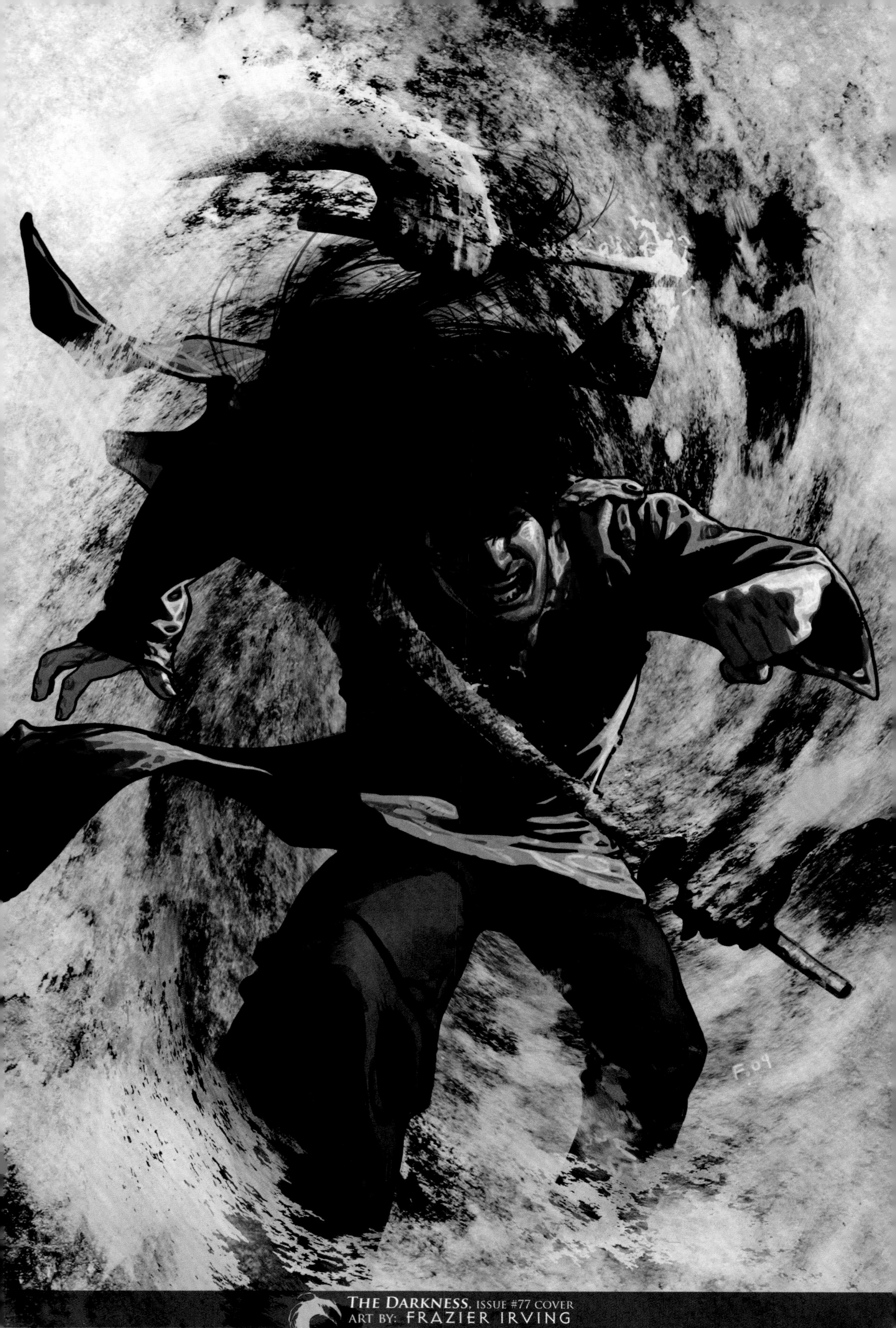
F.04

THE DARKNESS, ISSUE #77 COVER
ART BY: FRAZIER IRVING

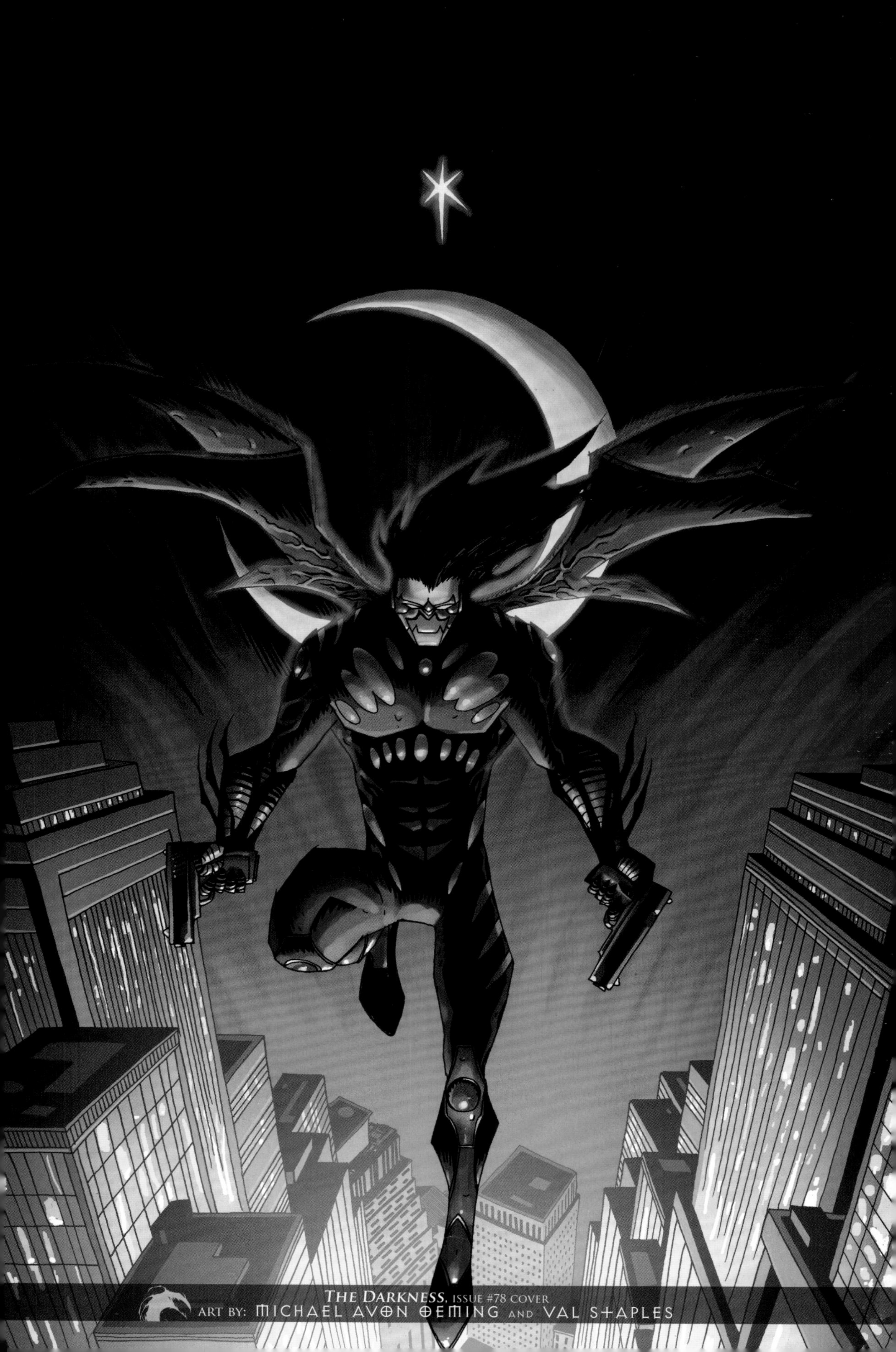

The Darkness, issue #78 cover
Art by: Michael Avon Oeming and Val Staples

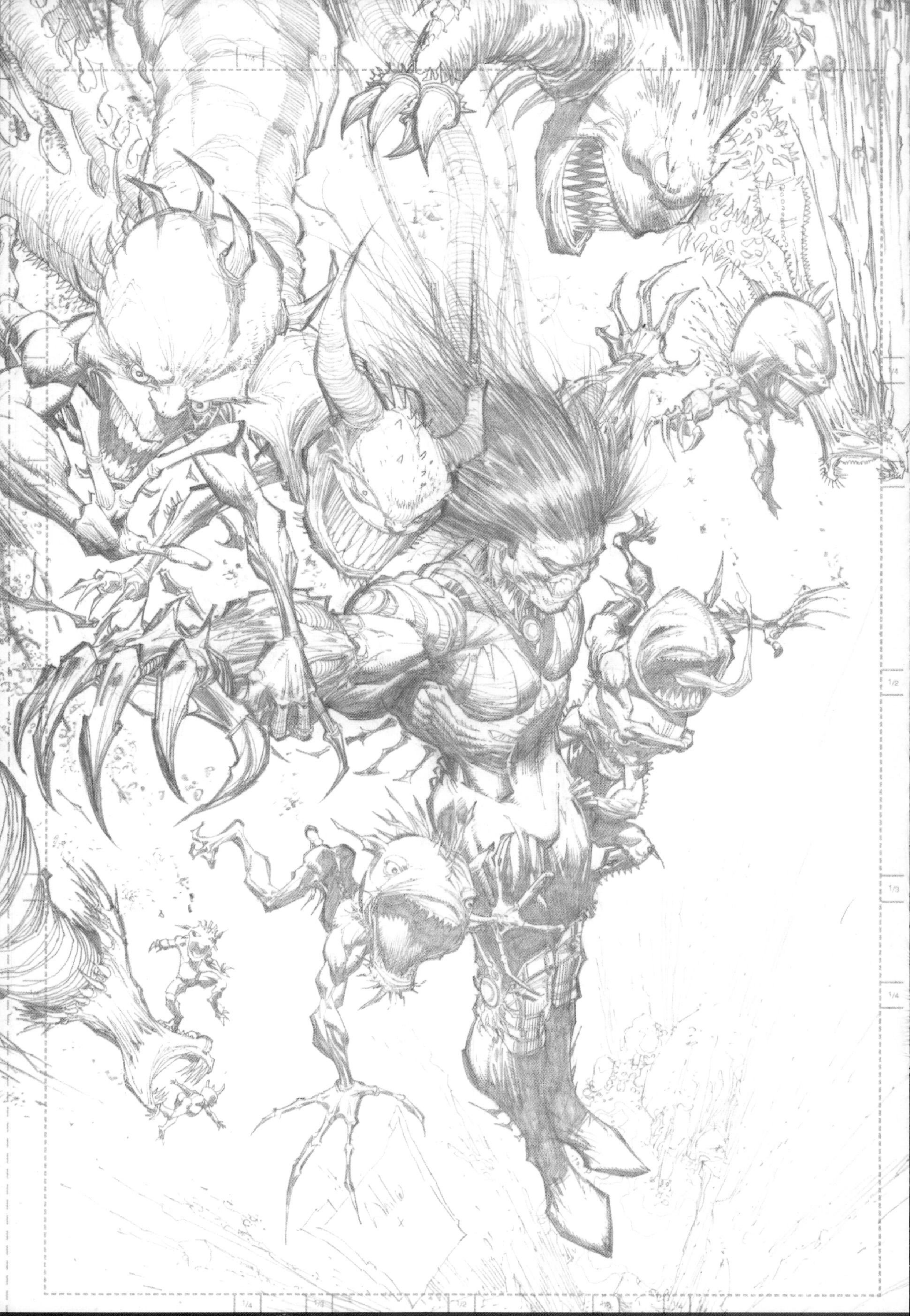

THE DARKNESS, ISSUE #79 COVER A PENCILS
ART BY: WHILCE PORTACIO

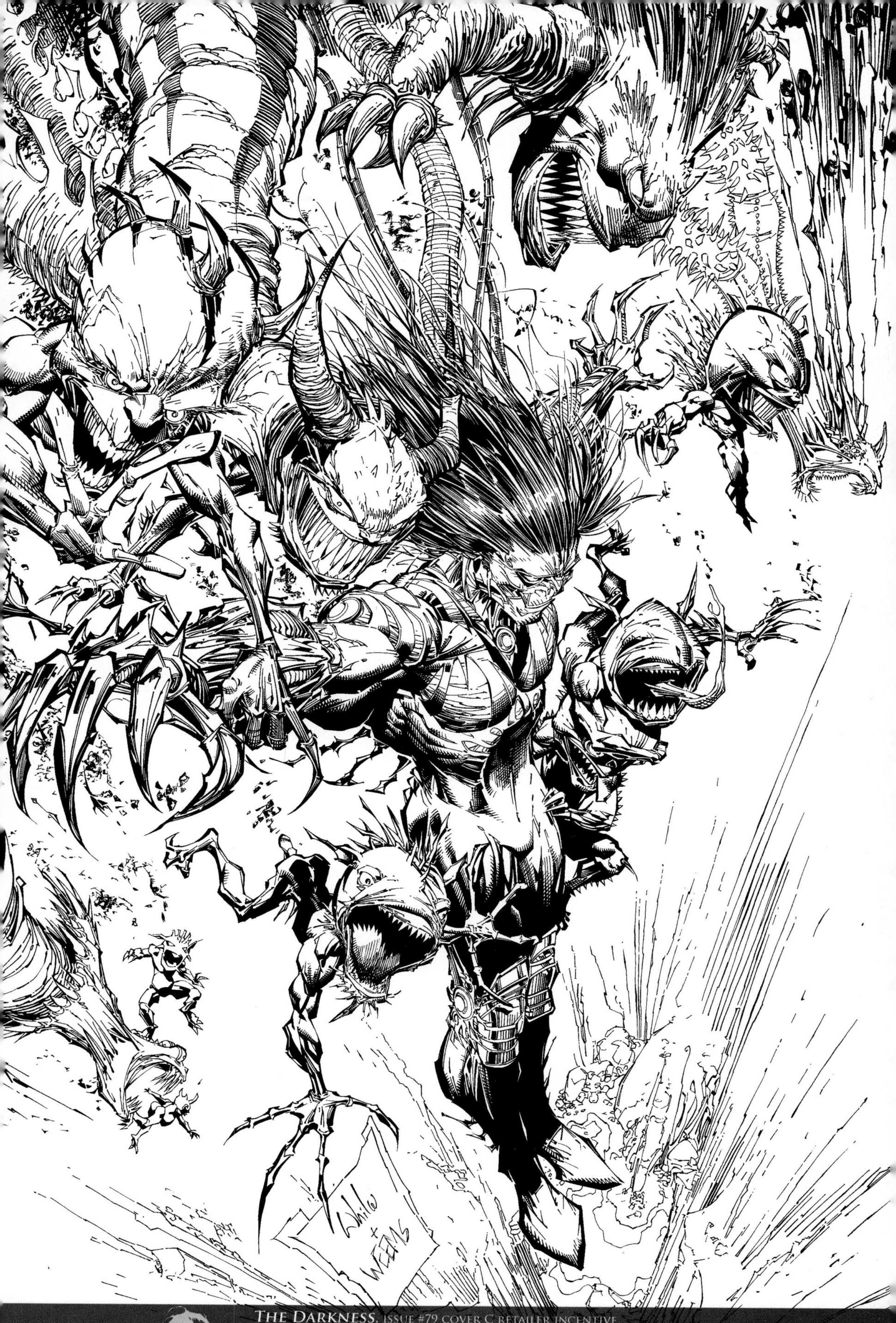
Whilce + Weems

THE DARKNESS, ISSUE #79 COVER C RETAILER INCENTIVE
ART BY: WHILCE PORTACIO AND JOE WEEMS V

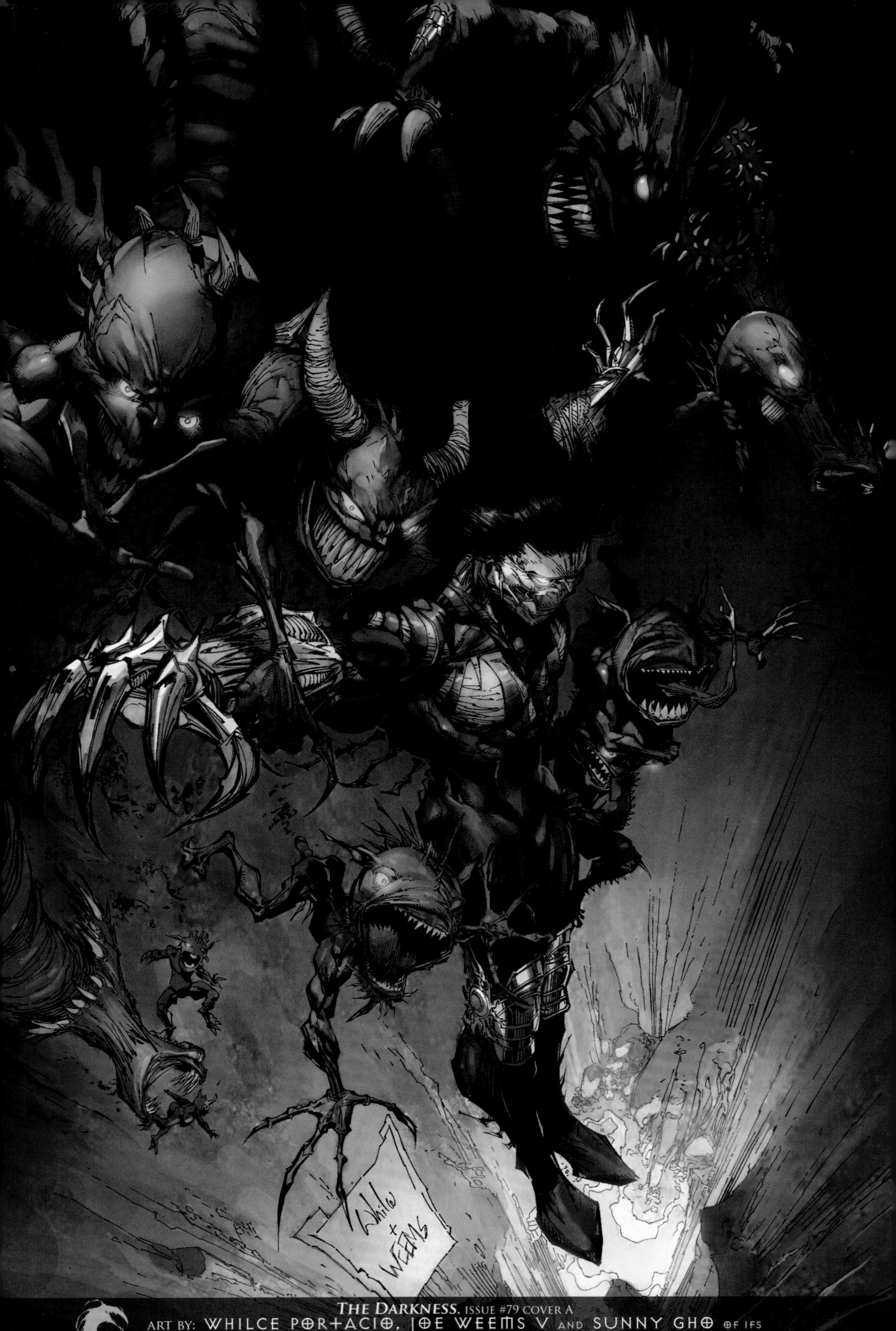
Whilce + WEEMS

THE DARKNESS, ISSUE #79 COVER A
ART BY: WHILCE PORTACIO, JOE WEEMS V AND SUNNY GHO OF IFS

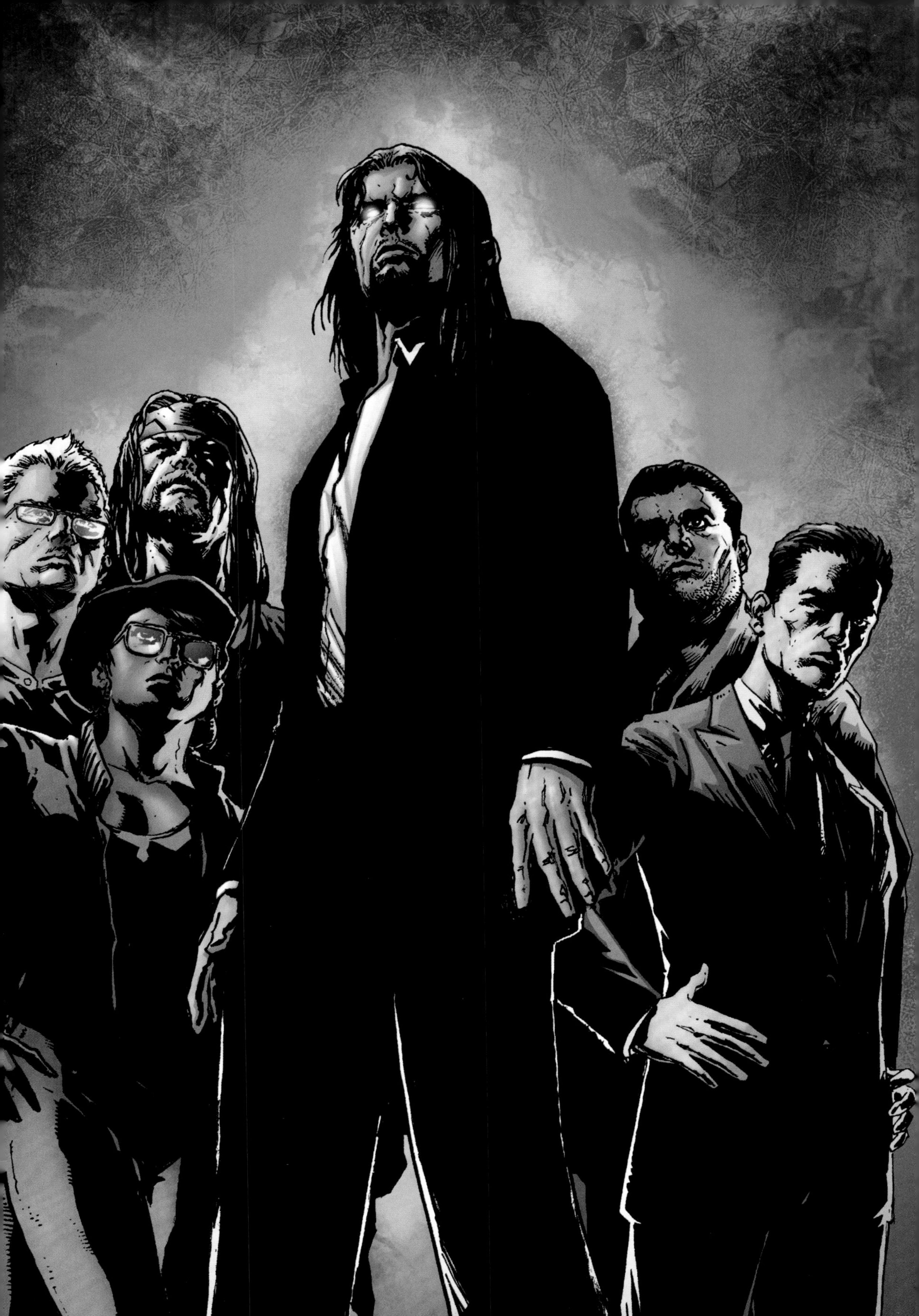

The Darkness, issue #79 cover B
ART BY: JORGE LUCAS AND FELIX SERRANO

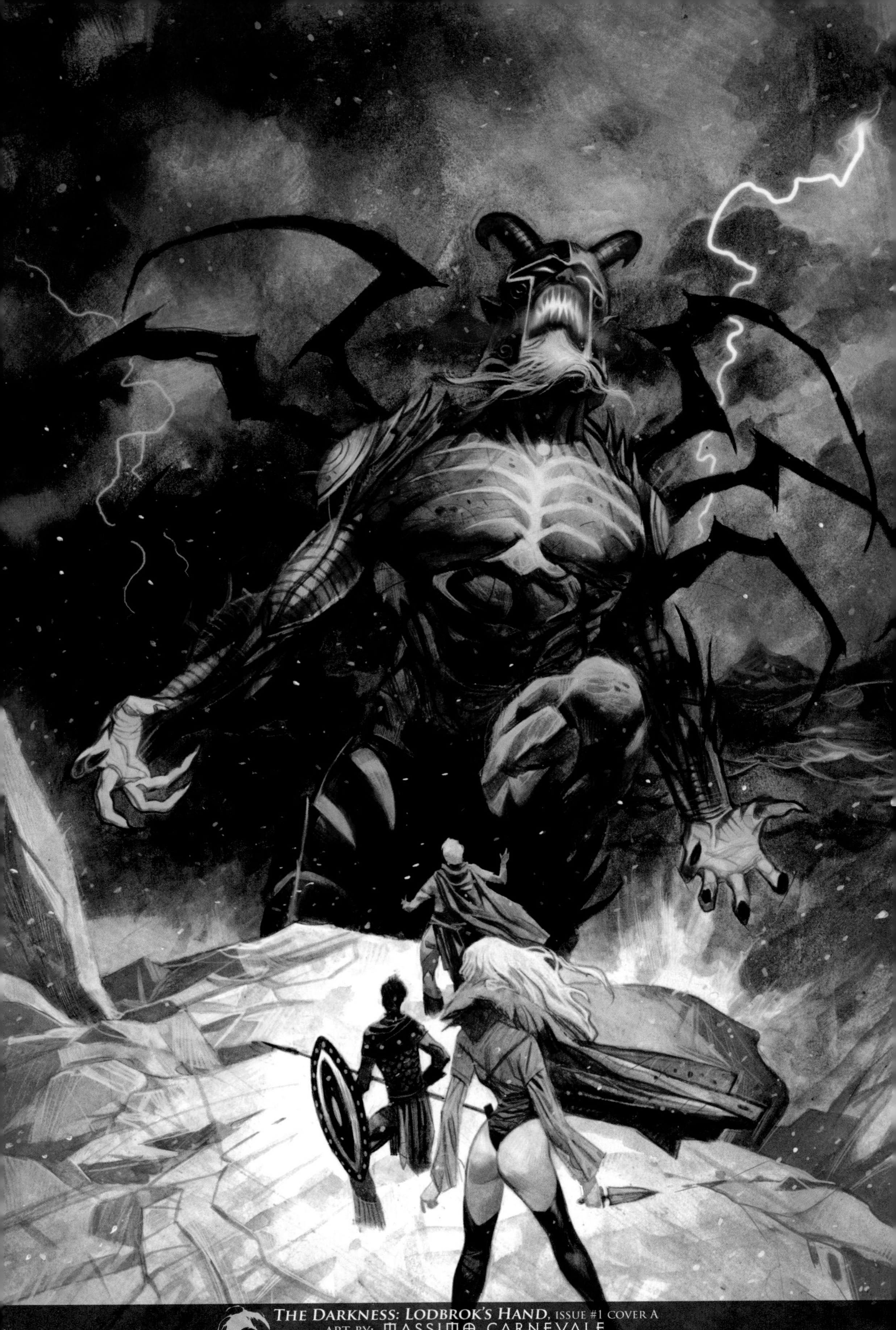

THE DARKNESS: LODBROK'S HAND, ISSUE #1 COVER A
ART BY: MASSIMO CARNEVALE

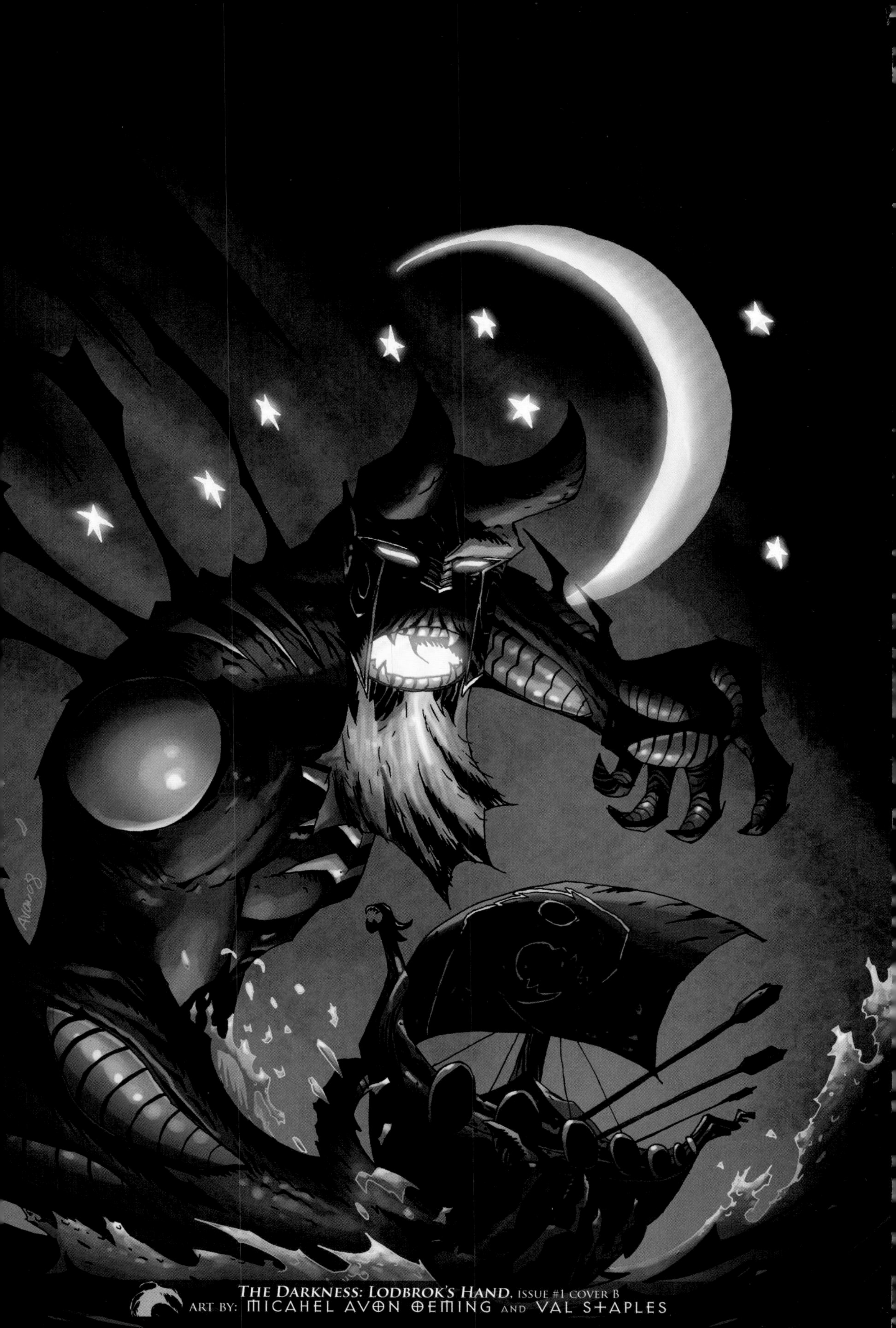

THE DARKNESS: LODBROK'S HAND, ISSUE #1 COVER B
ART BY: MICAHEL AVON OEMING AND VAL STAPLES

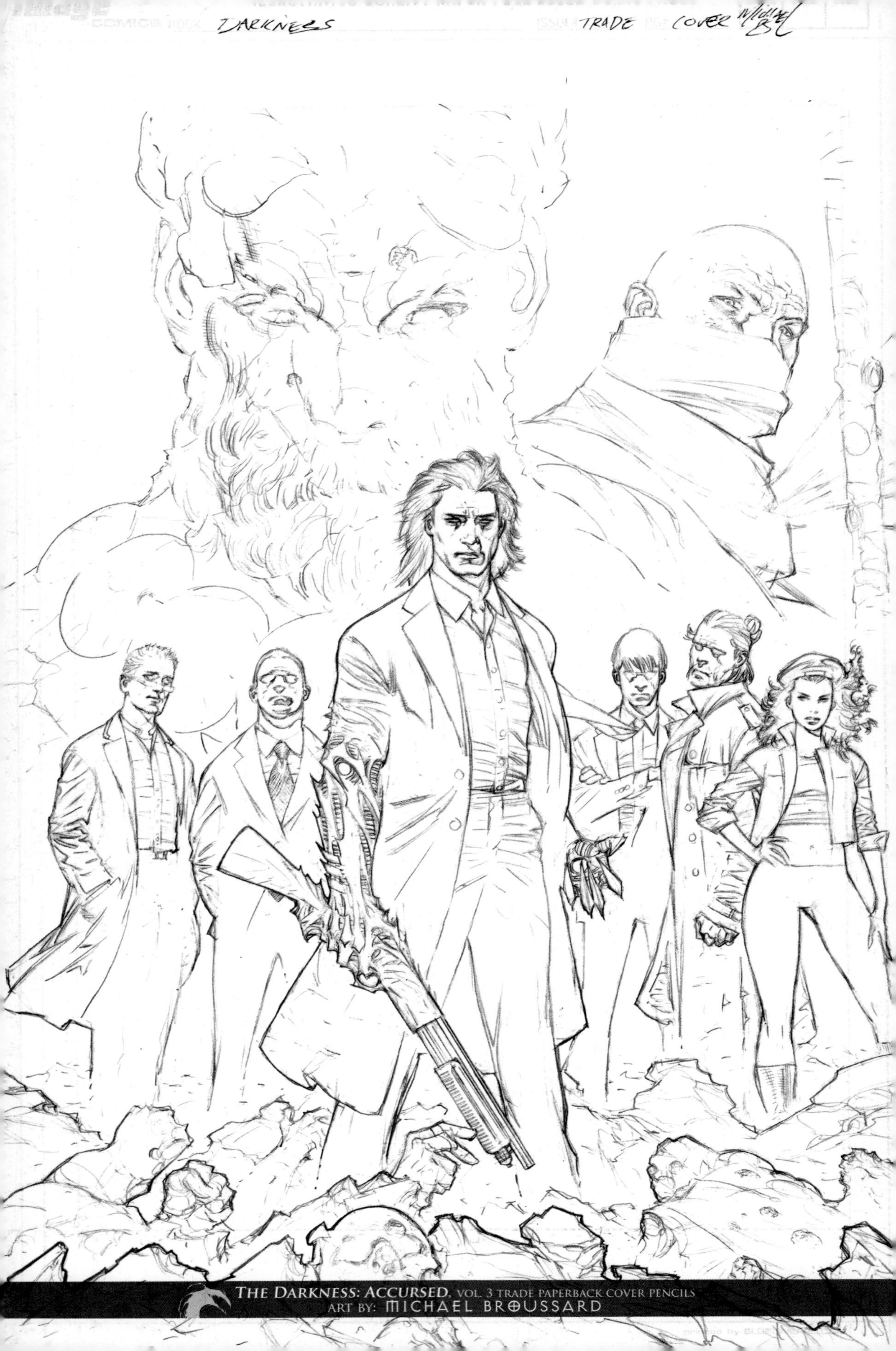
DARKNESS
TRADE COVER

THE DARKNESS: ACCURSED, VOL. 3 TRADE PAPERBACK COVER PENCILS
ART BY: MICHAEL BROUSSARD

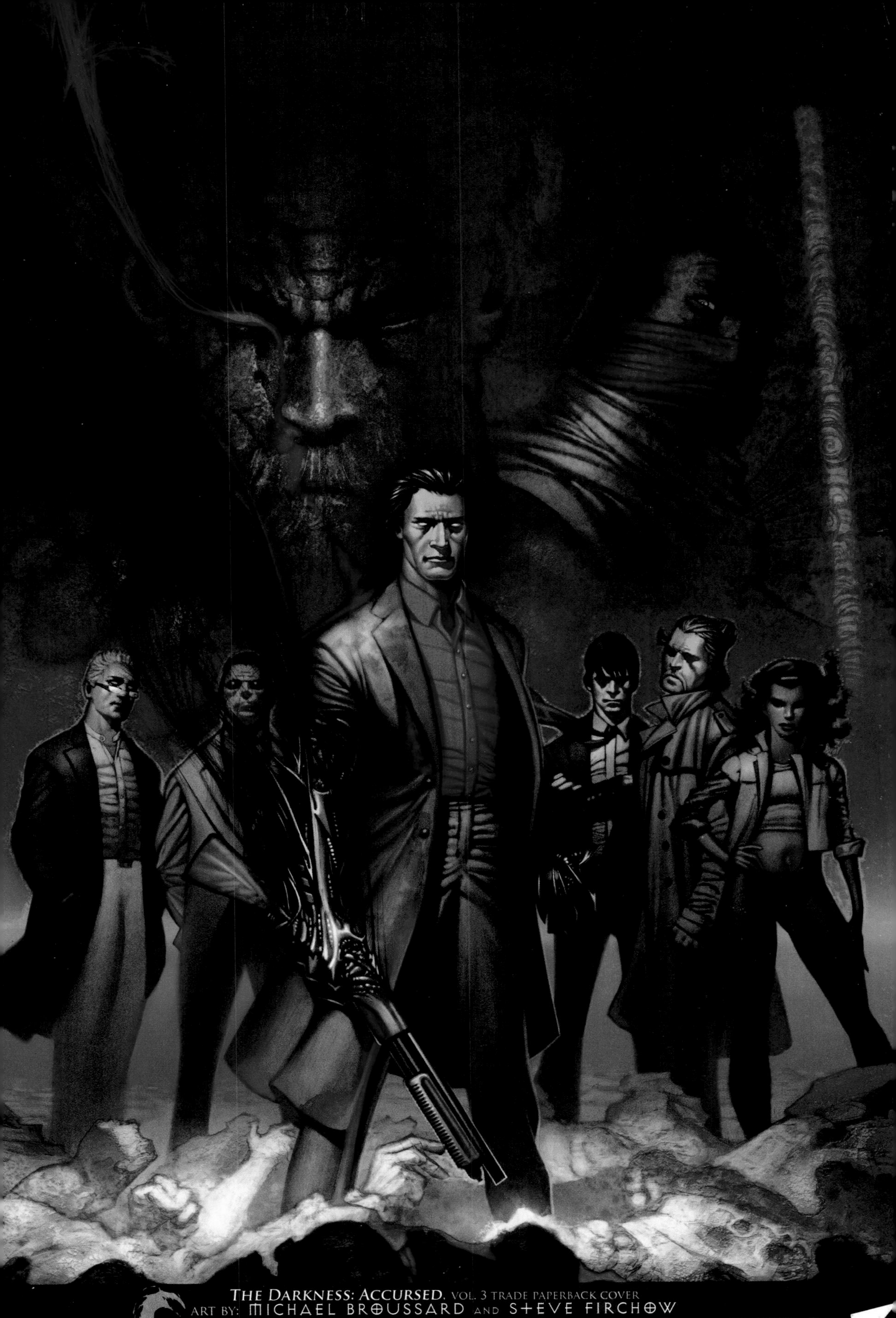

THE DARKNESS: ACCURSED, VOL. 3 TRADE PAPERBACK COVER
ART BY: MICHAEL BROUSSARD AND STEVE FIRCHOW

SCRIPT TO PAGE

On the following pages take a look at the script for *The Darkness: Lodbrok's Hand* issue #1 written by Phil Hester along with pencils and page layouts from the production process.

Original Story Outline

Lodbrok's Hand

Set in Frazetta Era- Bronze into Iron Viking age. Rookie Vikings on a primitive longboat are chatting about their grizzled captain's missing hand. An old veteran tells the tale. Lodbrok is a young warrior in a decimated farming village. Their population has been bled away by an evil warrior king who demands tribute in the form of the village's strongest laborers to build a vainglorious temple to some forgotten god. This mad king has destroyed his subjects' communities, enslaving all the able bodied men who would otherwise be farming, fishing, or raiding. Lodbrok is the leader of his village by default, all the "real" warriors being enslaved. His village was punished for their defiance by the mad king's secret weapon- a dragon (the same type of dragon- or maybe even the same one in an earlier incarnation- we see in Broken Trinity). The dragon killed Lodbrok's father and burned their longships, stealing away his older brother. The king's raiders will be coming soon to further gut the village, and Lodbrok, now a man, has decided to stage a desperate resistance.

He decides, against the counsel of his wise and beautiful sister Freydis (with some witchy magic powers), to find and blow a fabled horn found in a treacherous fjord that will call a legendary Black Captain to their shores. The legend states that the Black Captain is an immensely powerful spirit who rules the night and will grant a boon to anyone brave enough to find and blow the horn that calls him, but always exacts a terrible price. Lodbrok figures- what do we have to lose? With the aid of his sister he finds and blows the horn. The Black Captain (the Viking Darkness wielder of Mike's design) glides into the fjord on a warship that looks to be built from the Darkness itself. Lodbrok pleads his case and the Captain agrees to destroy the mad king's army, then names his price- Whereas the mad king would take all the village's bravest warriors, the captain will take but one- the bravest- as his crewman for eternity. Lodbrok swallows hard. He's basically selling his soul to the devil for his people, but his courage wins out and he agrees. Lodbrok and Freydis are taken on board the Black Captain's fantastic ship, oars manned by Darklings, and they return to the village to pick up the rest of the rebel warriors. They're taking the fight to the mad king. All the young warriors agree to be cast into the lottery, even knowing the very bravest among them will become The Black Captain's slave, and knowing the upcoming battle with the mad king will prove incontrovertibly just who that is to all.

Dawn begins to break on the sailing Darkness ship, but The Black Captain merely gestures and the ship's hull grows up and over the deck forming an ersatz submarine which plunges into the safety of the darkened ocean depths. They emerge in a dark cave in the harbor of the mad king's city. The Black Captain cannot attack until nightfall. The human warriors reconnoiter and witness the mad king's massive temple. A feast is under way. The mad king has Lodbrok's older brother trussed up for sacrifice. He had been leading a revolt among the slaves. Freydis cannot bear to see this and actually attacks the feast party with all her witchy powers in full effect. Lodbrok argues to wait for The Black Captain, but Freydis cannot be restrained and winds up being swarmed under by the mad king's hordes. Lodbrok's party is now under attack and it looks bad, until night falls and an army of Darklings crest the hill, slaying the hordes. The mad king calls up his dragon and The Black Captain responds by conjuring a Darkness-formed beast (I brought one, too). Lodbrok finds his dying sister in the carnage and his anger sends him into a berserker rage that ends with his slaying the mad king. The dragon is now free of the king's spell and flies off after a few words for The Black Captain.

Lodbrok is pretty disillusioned at this point. Most of his friends he sought to save are dead, his sister is dying. He's free but the cost has been terrible, and now he's got to pay the price and go sail with The Black Captain forever. He kneels before the Darkness wielder who merely laughs. "I said I would take the bravest among you," and gestures to the bloodied Freydis. Darkness goo forms around her wounds and binds them. Darklings raise her up and bring her to the Captain. Lodbrok protests and attacks. It's useless. The Darkness wielder offers Lodbrok some small measure of honor by cutting off Lodbrok's hand to end the attack, then sails into the night with Freydis over his shoulder. Lodbrok vows to find her and free her.

Cut back to the longship. The rookies stare at Lodbrok. Now they know why their captain spends every waking our in the prow of the ship scouring every fjord for some darkened cave capable of containing a mysterious black ship, and her even blacker captain.

DARKNESS- Lodbrok's Hand

Mike- This is set in some kind of kick-ass imaginary Frazetta Era- Bronze into Iron Viking age, so don't get hung up on historical accuracy. We want this airbrushed on the side of a van, not debated in a Norse historical society meeting. Have fun! -P

DARKNESS- LODBROK'S HAND
PAGE 1

P1- Big panel. we're in front of a Viking long ship at night. The men rest on their benches next to their oars. Two younger fellows are questioned by an old, grizzled Viking on the center deck. In the FG, and the real focus of the panel, is Lodbrok, a bearded Viking chieftain with one foot up on the prow of his ship as he stares out into the twilight. NOTE: His right hand is missing and covered by some kind of metal bands.

OLD VIKING: What are you two on about?

YOUNGSTER ONE: The captain. Does he never sleep?

P2- Horizontal panel. Reverse shot so now the trio is in FG and Lodbrok is in BG. The kids are joking around and the old guy doesn't appreciate it.

OLD VIKING: I've been in his service near twenty years and I've never seen it. Night or day he's in the prow, eyes fixed on the horizon.

YOUNGSTER ONE: That's how he lost his hand, then. It wanted some rest and finally ran off on its own.

YOUNGSTER TWO: Or perhaps he stood so long in the bow the salty spray rusted it away.

P3- Closer on Old Viking as he spins his yarn.

OLD VIKING: Laugh if you will, boys, but the truth of the matter is stranger than your farces.

OLD VIKING: Long ago, when good Lodbrok there was younger than even you two, his village was raided by the mad king Grimur.

OLD VIKING: His father, his older brother, every able warrior, farmer or fisherman was pressed into service in the mad king's army.

P4- Long shot of the boat on calm seas under the stars.

OLD VIKING: Only Lodbrok's youth saved him from the same fate, but even though his chin was clean of whiskers and his blade clean of blood, his heart was brave.

OLD VIKING: He rallied the young warriors of his village and set out to free their families from Grimur's thrall.

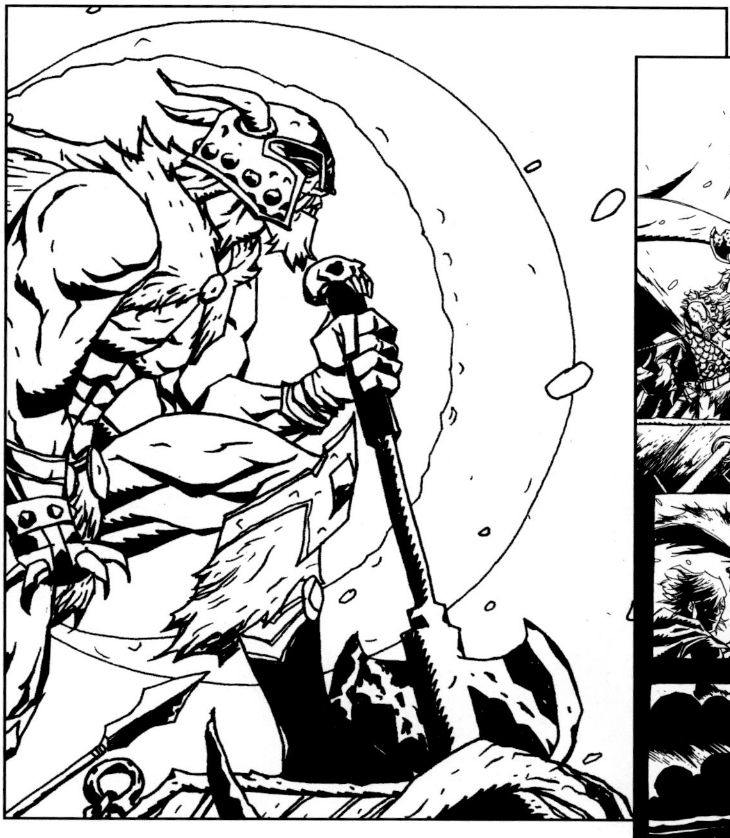

page 1, lineart detail

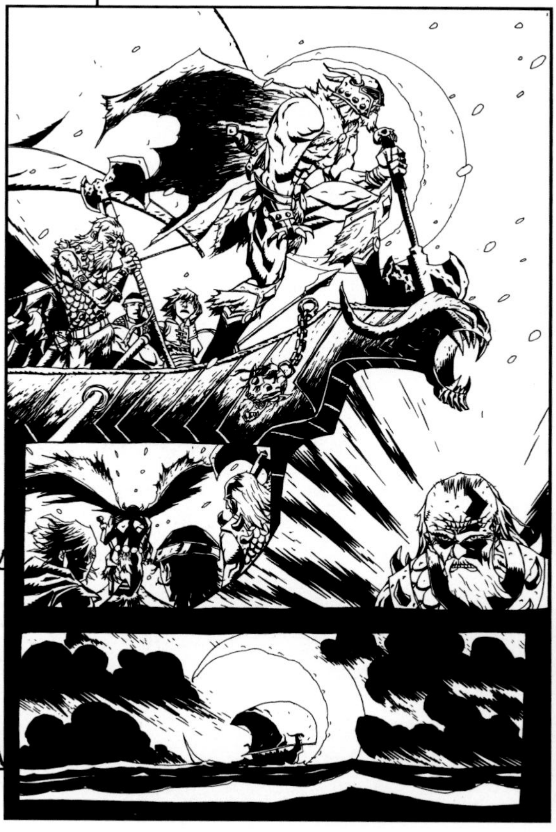

page 1, lineart

P1- OTS past Old Viking to the youngsters who now laugh openly.

OLD VIKING: Now, this in itself was an act of heroic courage, for every town who dared rise up against Grimur met its end at the claws of a fiery dragon bound to his service.

YOUNGSTER ONE: A dragon? Is this a bedtime story, then?

P2- Big panel. Close profile of Old Viking bleeds into a flashback panel. Perhaps the white of his hair and beard become the white snow in the flashback? We see a line of very young Viking warriors (like 14-18 years old) struggling to march through a raging snowstorm, maybe 12 of them, but we need not see them all. Lodbrok is out of sight in this shot, but we see his beautiful sister Freydis at the head of the column with her silvery hair tossed in the blizzard.

OLD VIKING NARRATION: Mock me, boys. It matters not.

OLD VIKING NARRATION: Magic flowed more freely in the years before your birth. In fact, Lodbrok's sister Freydis, though young and fair, had the ken of the ancient witches, and their forgotten fire burned blue in her veins.

OLD VIKING NARRATION: As she walked at the head of Lodbrok's band her hair flashed like steel and the images of her village's demise danced in her locks, filling those who followed with dread.

P3- Freydis in FG, panel right. The young vikings behind her shout complaints.

VIKING ONE: This is madness!

VIKING TWO: Let us turn back. The storm grows worse.

FREYDIS: The fjord is ahead, as I divined. My brother will sound the forbidden horn.

P4- Long shot of the scene. The line has stopped to argue. The snow is really blinding.

VIKING ONE: Good for him!

VIKING THREE: We should be marching on Grimur's keep, not chasing after some old wives' tale.

FREYDIS: Our strength wouldn't prevail over the king's weakest guard post. We need the boon of the horn.

VIKING ONE: I still say-

LODBROK OFF PANEL: I found it!

P5- We're overhead. Lodbrok, now about 17 and slimmer, has already begun to clamber down the cliff wall of a steep fjord, the bottom lost in the snowstorm. The others stand around the lip of the cliff.

LODBROK: Well, the fjord, anyway. You all stay here. I'll make my way down and-

VIKING ONE: Be careful, Lodbrok. Those rocks would be slippery in the heat of summer.

OLD VIKING NARRATION: Although none could see the breakers in the gloom below, the unseen surf sounded as if the whole of the sea sloshed through the devil's lips to crash against his jagged teeth.

page 2, lineart detail

page 2, lineart

P1- Reverse shot. We're below Lodbrok as he slips and falls away from the rock face. If we can see his sister and party above they look frightened.

LODBROK: I can't wait, Hemrir. The horn must be blown in the first hour of dusk, before high tide.

LODBROK: Don't worry, this is nothing compared to the walls I've scaled back in-

FREYDIS: Lodbrok!

P2- Freydis gestures and a shimmering net of golden energy leaps from her hand and toward the camera.

FREYDIS: Lodbrok!

P3- Side view of Lodbrok falling through the broken energy net and into the snowstorm.

OLD VIKING NARRATION: Lodbrok tumbled through the snow. His sister's gossamer web only just slowing him as he fell into the darkness.

P4- At the top of the cliff Freydis hangs her head in sorrow, The rest of the party looks resigned to defeat.

FREYDIS: Lodbrok.

VIKING ONE: Well, there's naught to do but make camp. We'll look for his body in the morning light.

LODBROK: Hello! Hello up there!

P5- Close on the party and Freydis as the lean to the very edge of the cliff to shout down at Lodbrok in happy surprise .

FREYDIS: Lodbrok! You're alive! Are you unhurt?

LODBROK OP: Yes, and what's more...

P6- Biggest panel. Down-shot. We see Lodbrok sort of sprawled out, up on his elbows on a huge (like 10 feet long) black hunting horn carved out of the black rock all around. The sea crashes around him. He smiles.

LODBROK: I've found the horn.

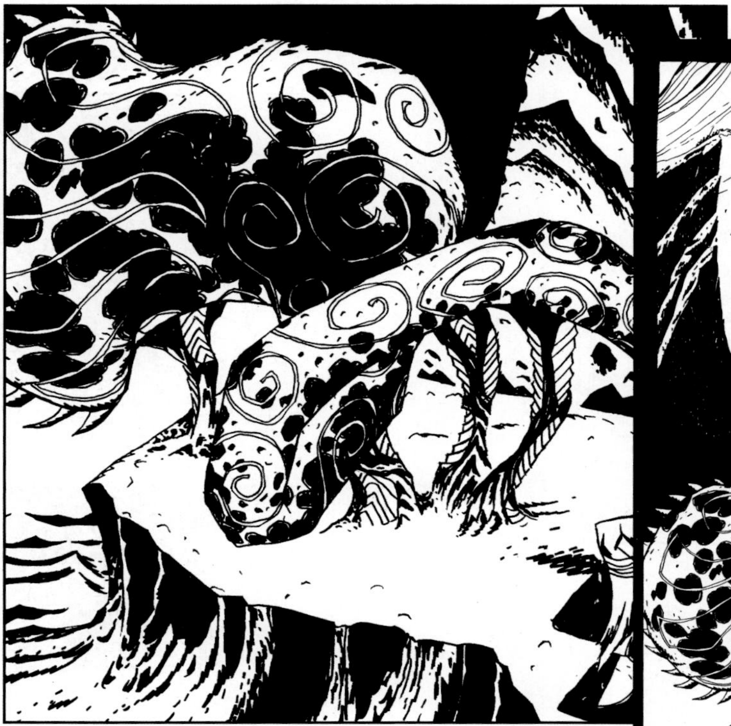

page 3, lineart detail

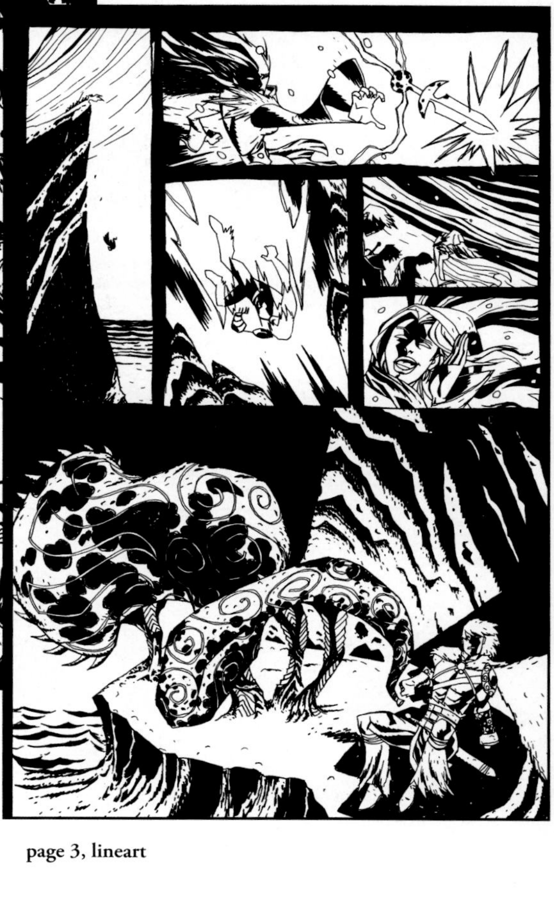

page 3, lineart

P1- Big panel. The group stands around Lodbrok as he steps up a natural dais toward the big horn. Nice perspective shot from in front of the horn.

OLD VIKING NARRATION: Soon his meager but valiant band gathered around him and the terrible black horn that seemed built to hang from the belt of a long-dead giant.

P2- 2 shot of worried Freydis calling up to determined, but nervous Lodbrok.

FREYDIS: Brother, I beg you one last time. Reconsider your plan.

LODBROK: There's nothing else to weigh. We are at Grimur's mercy. We need an ally that can match his power.

P3- Close of wise, worried, beautiful Freydis.

FREYDIS: And that is what frightens me, Lodbrok. I walk in the witching world. The power you seek to call may be darker, more dangerous, than Grimur himself.

P4- CU Lodbrok trying to screw up his courage.

LODBROK: Freydis-

FREYDIS: The Black Captain will aid you, that much I believe is true, but his boon may come at too terrible a price.

P5- Profile shot of Lodbrok putting his lips to the horn.

OLD VIKING NARRATION: Lodbrok reddened at his sister's warning, but drew himself up to the horn and blew without hesitation.

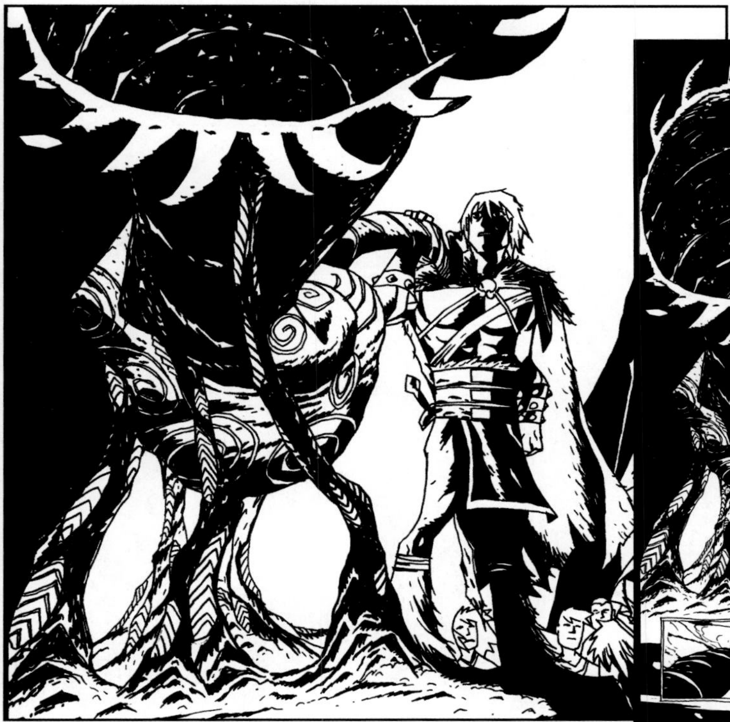

page 4, lineart detail

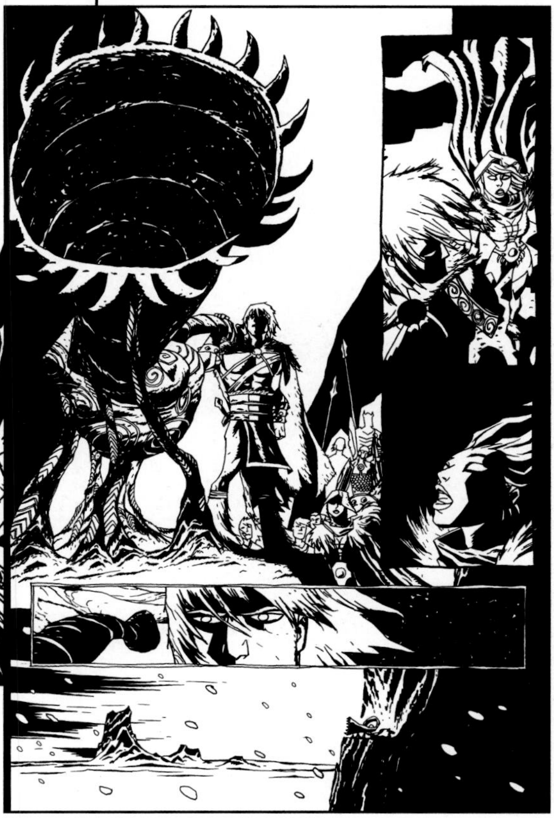

page 4, lineart

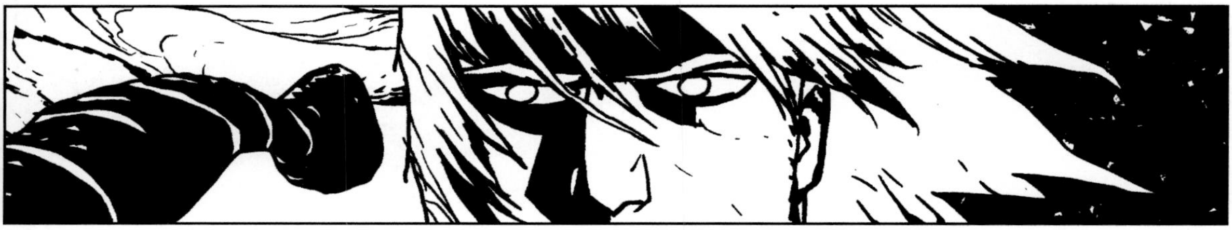

page 4, lineart detail

DARKNESS- LODBROK'S HAND, PAGE 5

P1- Similar to P1 of Page 4, but smaller. They all stand around quizzically, Lodbrok tilting his head away from the horn to look out into the bay.

VIKING ONE: That's it?

VIKING TWO: I didn't hear anything.

FREYDIS: Perhaps you should do it aga-

P2- Wide shot of the bay. The water is glassy and calm as a viking ship glides into the sheltered fjord. The ship is like any other Viking ship, but built out of Darkness matter, so it's oily and black with gold and green detail. It should look like a death ship. Oars poke out of the side like blackened spines.

OLD VIKING NARRATION: Before Lodbrok could draw another breath the frothing sea suddenly flattened, like a banner blown stiff by the wind.

OLD VIKING NARRATION: A black long-ship, like none seen before or since, glided silently into the fjord like whale oil over ice.

OLD VIKING NARRATION: Its cankerous oars slid in and out of the polished water as effortlessly as a dagger scoring bare flesh.

P3- OTS past the company on the shore as the ship pulls up right in front of them, beaching.

OLD VIKING NARRATION: The company's eyes raced over the floating abomination, desperate for evidence of an earthly maker, and found none.

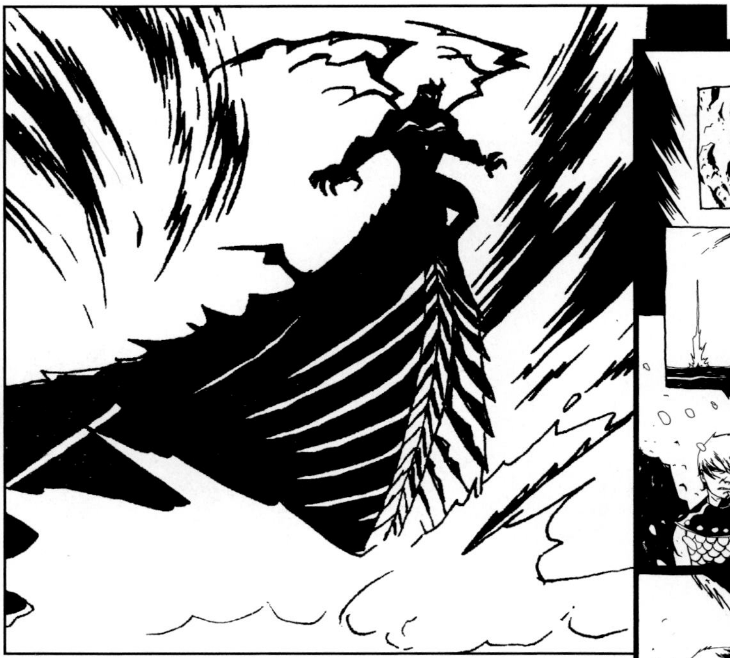

page 5, lineart detail

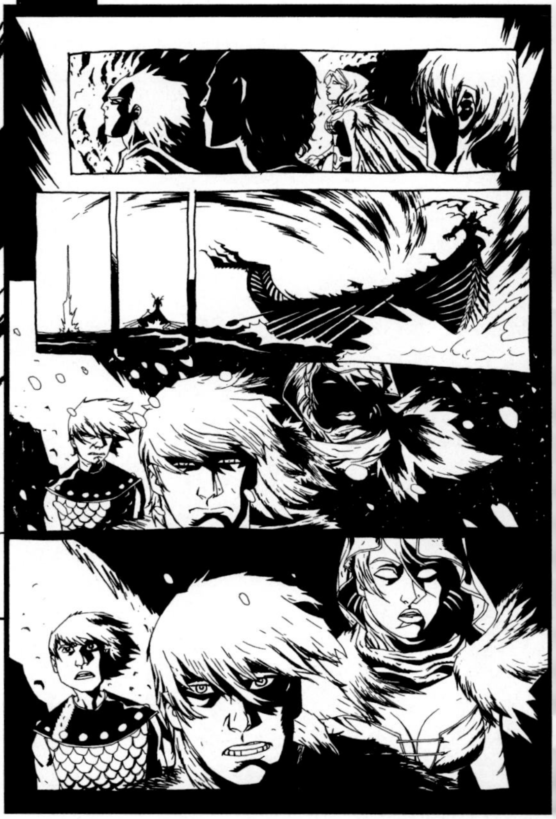

page 5, lineart

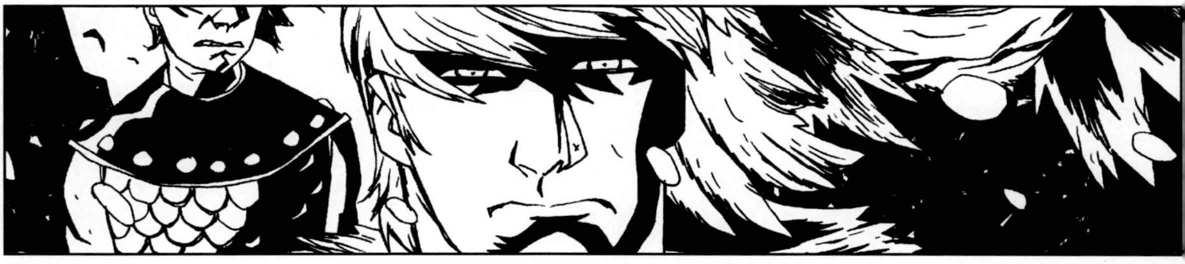

page 5, lineart detail

P1- Big, money shot of the Viking Darkness wielder- The Black Captain standing at the front of his boat. He looks completely badass.

OLD VIKING NARRATION: And even less in the face of her captain.

BLACK CAPTAIN: Who calls?

P2- Meek Lodbrok looks up at Black Captain unsure of himself.

LODBROK: L- Lodbrok of Skaarstad. I- I beg the Black Captain grant my company a boon.

LODBROK: Our humble village stands in ruin at the hand of the mad king Grimur and we seek-

P3- CU B.C. looking down at the humans with disdain. Lots of balloon space!

BLACK CAPTAIN: I know your plight. I know your goal. Grimur harvests the strongest backs from every end of his kingdom and wastes their vigor building a vainglorious monument to a dead god.

BLACK CAPTAIN: Mourning the loss of your fathers and fearful of sharing their fates, you children have decided to cast your lot with me, an enemy of all men, knowing I will ask an unthinkable wage for my services.

P4- Down-shot of the scene. All are tiny figures.

BLACK CAPTAIN: Very brave little things you are.

P5- MCU BC spreading his arms wide, making his offer.

BLACK CAPTAIN: Very well, I will dethrone this pretender Grimur and free your countrymen. And while the mad king demands the servitude of all your brave warriors, I ask for but one.

BLACK CAPTAIN: Here is my fee, children; At the completion of my task I will take the bravest among you as my shipmate to sail with me under the stars until the last of them fall from the sky.

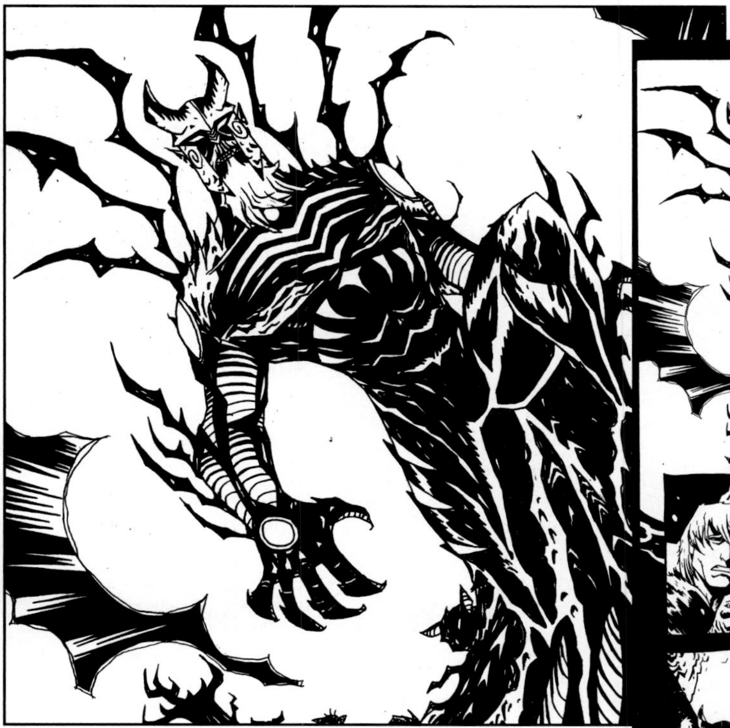

page 6, lineart detail

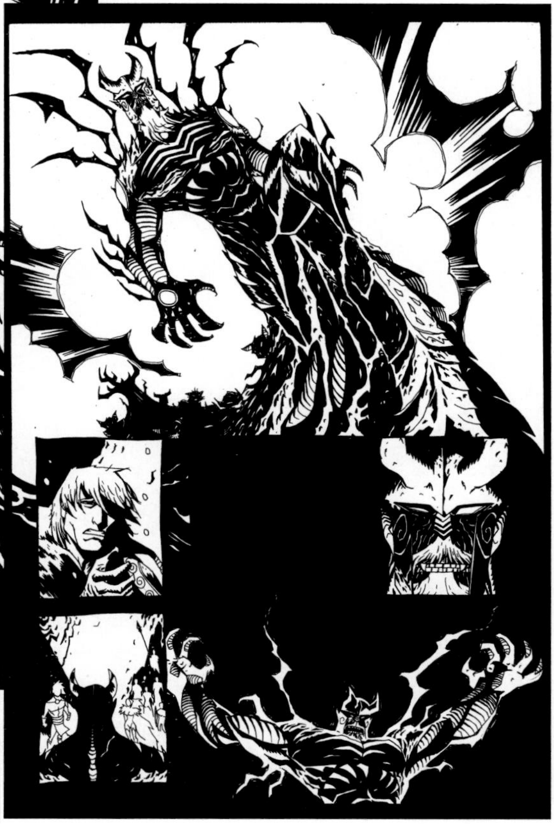

page 6, lineart

P1- The humans stand in the center deck of the long ship. We see the Darklings in the oar wells glaring up at them. BC standing at the mast.

OLD VIKING NARRATION: To a soul they agreed and boarded the Black Captain's unearthly vessel, each of them knowing the battle to come would reveal the true depth of their valor.

OLD VIKING NARRATION: Each of them knowing their courage might warrant their damnation.

P2- Med shot of a group of Darklings. Their weird arms grow right into the oars because they are "grown" from the same Darkness matter. They glare at the camera.

OLD VIKING NARRATION: The oarsmen, whose bodies resembled nothing so much as a twisted heap of bruise colored scars, glared at the passengers for a brief moment before silently returning to their toil.

P3- Long shot of the black ship crashing through the waves and into the open sea. The snow still swirls around them.

OLD VIKING NARRATION: They kept a pace that would splinter a human rower's bones, their limbs seemingly grown backwards from the oars themselves.

OLD VIKING NARRATION: Lodbrok swore later that the black ship sailed so fast that the stars seemed to blur and the human company fell to the deck and squeezed shut their eyes lest they take leave of their senses.

P4- Freydis is clinging to the floor of the deck and looking over at a panicked Lodbrok doing the same.

FREYDIS: Lodbrok, the dawn is upon us. Legend tells the Black Captain's ship can only sail by night- that the light of the sun burns his works away like the morning frost.

P5- Wide shot. BC calmly stares out ahead in FG. The human crew manages to stand and look out at the greying pre-dawn sky behind them. They are freaking out.

VIKING ONE: There's no shore in sight. We'll be drowned!

LODBROK: This- this can't be true.

BLACK CAPTAIN: Your sister knows her fey lore well.

BLACK CAPTAIN: The sun chases me across the sea, her light melting the fruits of my labor into nothing more than a forgotten dream.

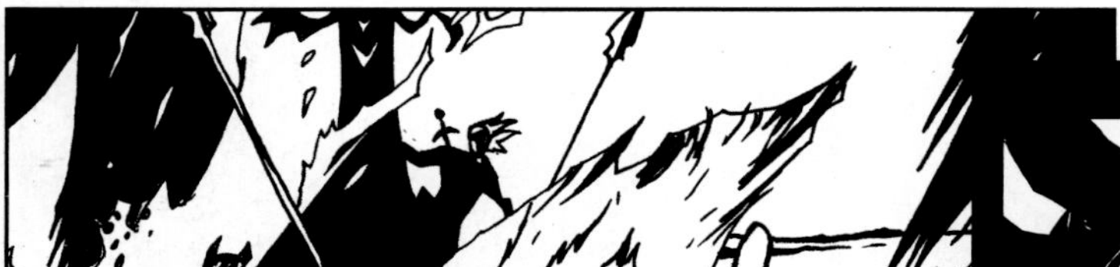

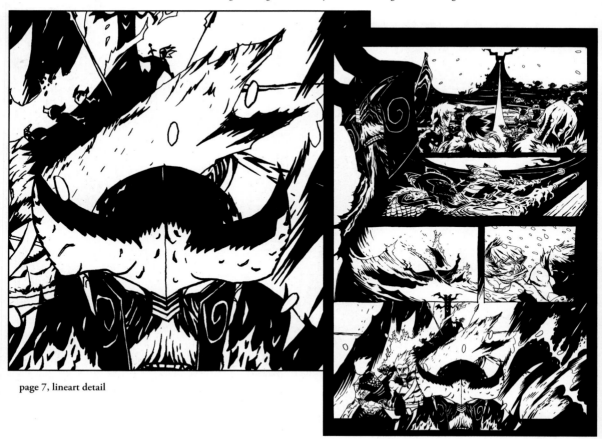

page 7, lineart detail

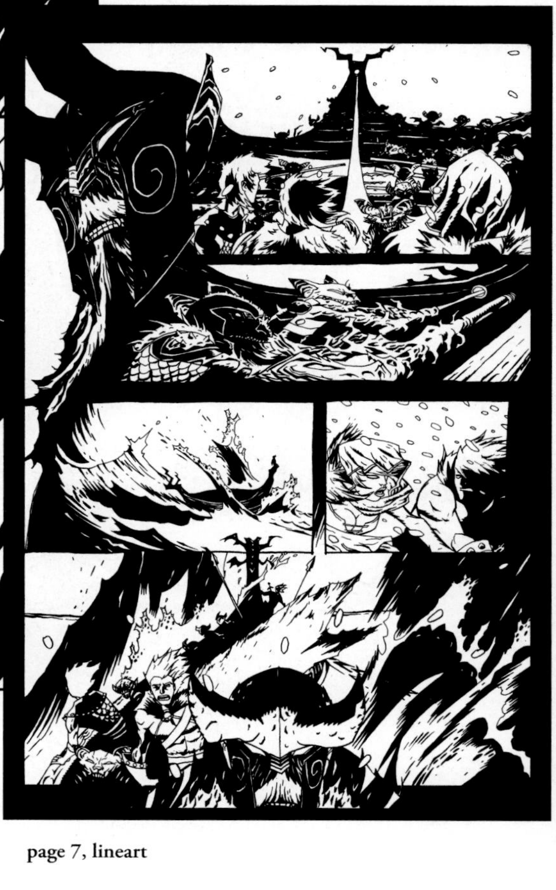

page 7, lineart

P1- CU BC turning to look back at his passengers.

BLACK CAPTAIN: But know this, brave children-

P2- Wide shot he raises his arms and a canopy of Darkness material begins to form above them like the ribs of a great beast.

P3- Repeat P2, but now a membrane grows between the ribs, making the ship essentially a submarine.

BLACK CAPTAIN: There are quarters below the sun never kisses...

P4- From below the surface of the sea as the black sub dives into the murky depths.

BLACK CAPTAIN FROM INT. SHIP: Depths in which darkness reigns night or day.

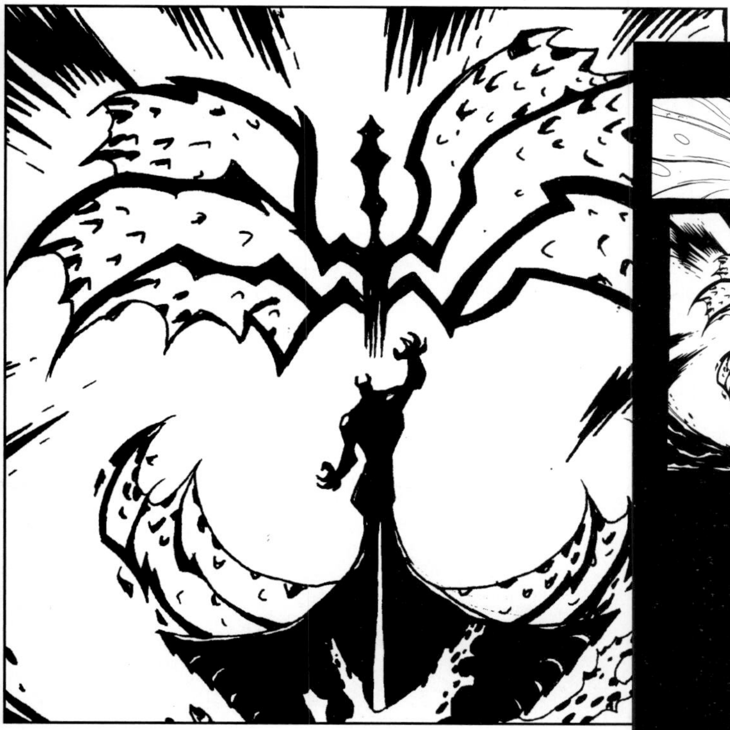

page 8, lineart detail

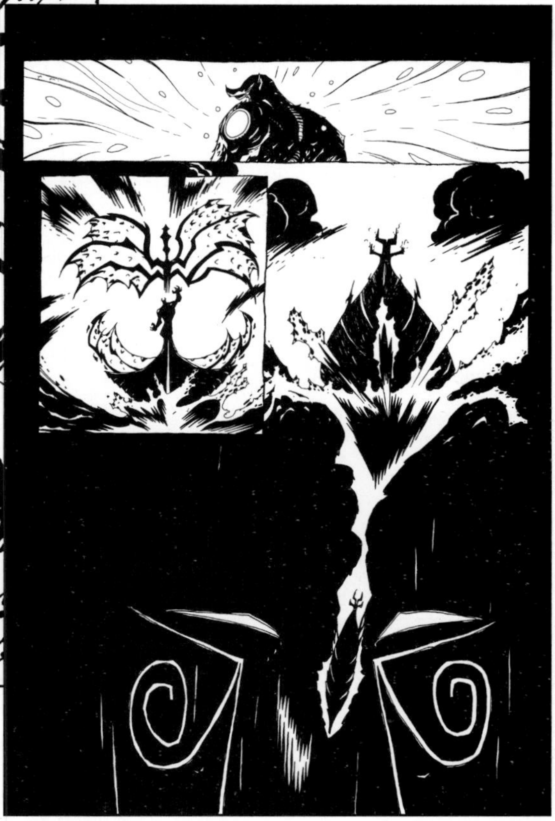

page 8, lineart

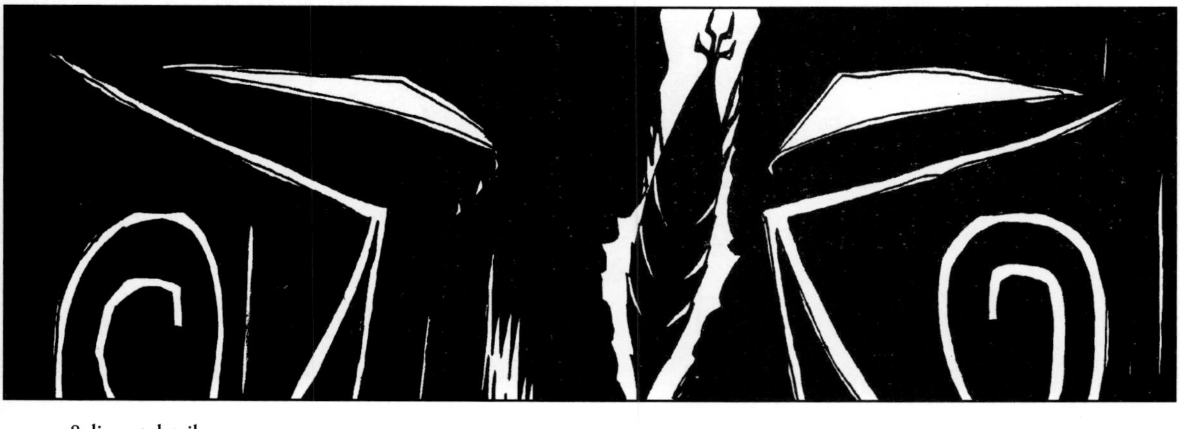

page 8, lineart detail

DARKNESS- LODBROK'S HAND, PAGE 9

P1- We're now in a sea cave. The black ship is back to normal and green lights (Darkness jewel-like things) glow at the prow and aft, giving a dim illumination to the scene.

OLD VIKING NARRATION: How long they traveled like this none can know, but when they emerged they were berthed in a gloomy cave near Grimur's castle.

P2- The humans face the BC, asking for action. He is still, maybe now sitting on a kind of Darkness-grown throne.

LODBROK: What is your plan, Captain?

LODBROK: We bob here like lost fishermen while Grimur's armies march overhead.

BLACK CAPTAIN: Eager for war as only a young man can be. Have patience. My armies march only by night.

P3- MCU dismissive BC.

BLACK CAPTAIN: By dawn Grimur's throne will be split like so much kindling and his works will lie ruined around his corpse. But not until nightfall.

VIKING ONE OP: And what of us? Are we to simply wait while Grimur works our fathers and brothers to death mere yards away?

BLACK CAPTAIN: Do as you will, children. This one waits.

P4- Wider shot of the humans with Lodbrok in front looking around, unsure of himself. The others raise their weapons in eagerness for battle. Freydis in BG looks at the Viking youths warily.

VIKING ONE: What say you, Lodbrok?

VIKING THREE: Lead us, Lodbrok!

LODBROK: I-

P5- CU Freydis offering a solution to crowd. We see Lodbrok catching on in BG.

FREYDIS: It can't hurt to scout Grimur's keep. I'll cast a spell to cloak our presence. Our observations may serve the captain's plan of attack.

LODBROK: Yes.

LODBROK: Yes! Our eyes will be the key to Grimur's defeat.

P6- A wide panel of the Vikings marching off the gangplank and on to the rocky shore of the cave, Lodbrok at the front. Freydis at the rear looks back at BC in who addresses her.

LODBROK: Onward!

VIKINGS: Lodbrok!

VIKINGS: Lodbrok!

BLACK CAPTAIN: Well said, little witch.

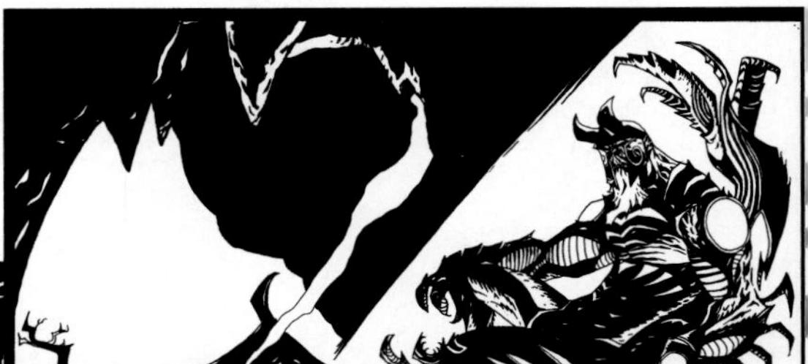

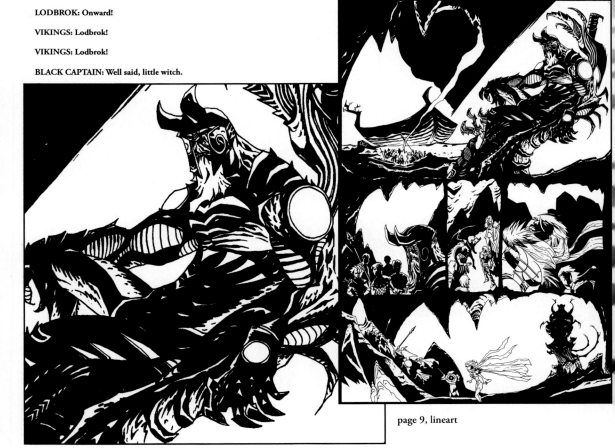

page 9, lineart

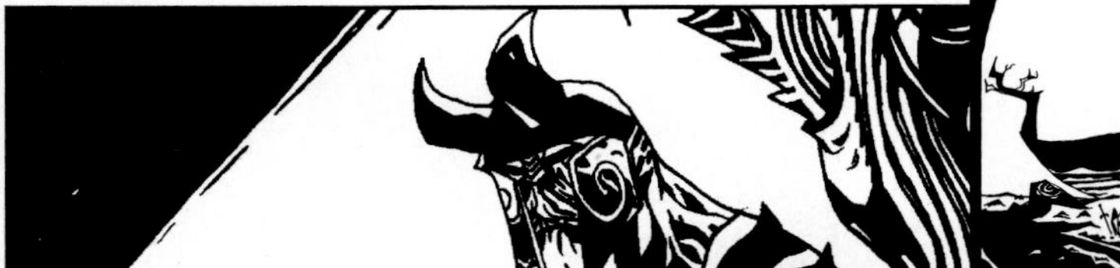

page 9, lineart detail

P1- Huge panel. Hang on lots to cram in here. We're at the top of a wide ziggurat of your kick-ass design. Grimur has a throne on the top plateau about 20 feet up. At his side is a beautiful lava-haired woman in chains who resembles the woman in the attachment. Dozens of warriors watch from the steps below as bound slaves are sacrificed at Grimur's feet. Their bodies pile on the steps below the plateau and their blood coats the outside of the ziggurat. Sword wielding priests do the deed. In far BG we might see our human heroes on a nearby snow-covered cliff watching in horror (though we're too far away to see that).

OLD VIKING NARRATION: It was but a short march from the sea caves to the curiously open border of Grimur's temple, but none among them were prepared for the spectacle that spread before them.

OLD VIKING NARRATION: They had come on a holiday.

OLD VIKING NARRATION: A day of feasting. A day of song.

OLD VIKING NARRATION: And a day of sacrifice.

P2- Close on the good guys all in disgusted disbelief. The people they came to rescue are being slaughtered!

VIKING ONE: Gods below. What are they doing?

FREYDIS: He's mad. He's truly mad. Grimur works new magic, brutal magic.

LODBROK: What is it, Freydis?

P3- Another shot of the blood cascading down the stone walls of the temple. Another bound slave is brought to the priests- It's Freydis & Lodbrok's older brother, beaten and resigned.

FREYDIS: He means to consecrate his temple by sacrificing those who built it. He'll paint the temple walls with their blood.

VIKING TWO: Lodbrok, look! At the head of the column. It's your brother!

P4- CU Lodbrok in shocked denial.

LODBROK: No.

LODBROK: No. Not when we're so close.

page 10, lineart detail

page 10, lineart

P1- Freydis breaks away from the troop and runs down a snowy slope toward temple. Lodbrok call after her. Other Vikings look around timidly.

LODBROK: Freydis, what are you doing?

FREYDIS: I'm going to our brother, Lodbrok. I'll not watch him die without spending the last ember of my power to free him.

P2- OTS past Lodbrok reaching out for Freydis as she approaches the temple. The guards on the periphery turn and notice her.

LODBROK: Freydis, wait- it's hopeless! Wait for the Black Captain!

LODBROK: Freydis!

P3- Money shot of Freydis wading into the throng of soldiers and casting whatever kind of cool magical blasts you want to draw, Mike. She's wasting them.

OLD VIKING NARRATION: And like a candle set in a woven leaf boat she flickered with eldritch power as she waded into the center of Grimur's army, sending the bodies of the first to meet her flying like so much chaff.

P4- Close up of several of Grimur's men's upraised swords.

OLD VIKING NARRATION: But Grimur's army was large, and like all candles Freydis eventually guttered out beneath the draught of their bloody blades.

P5- XCU sad and shocked Lodbrok.

LODBROK: Freydis.

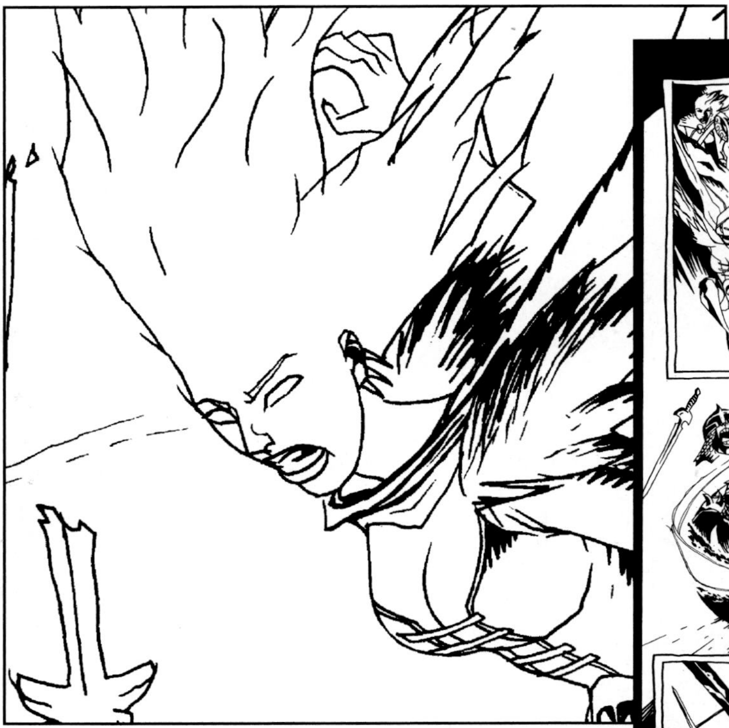

page 11, lineart detail

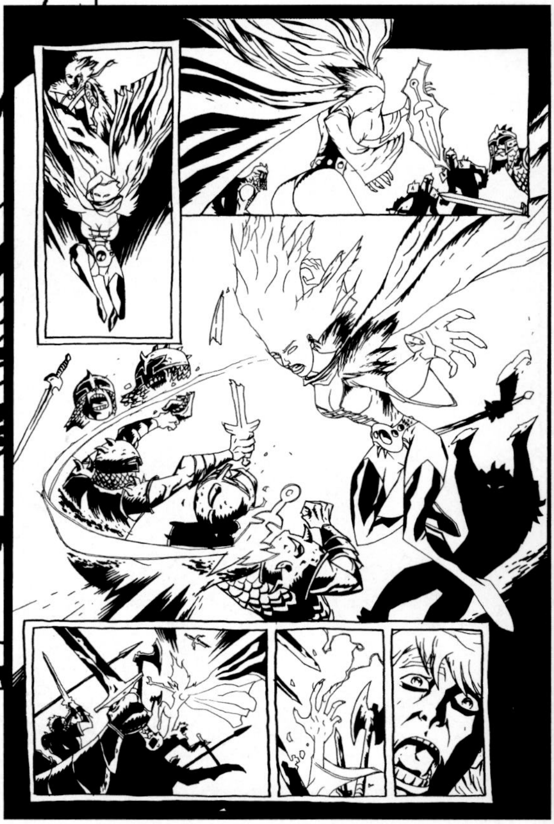

page 11, lineart

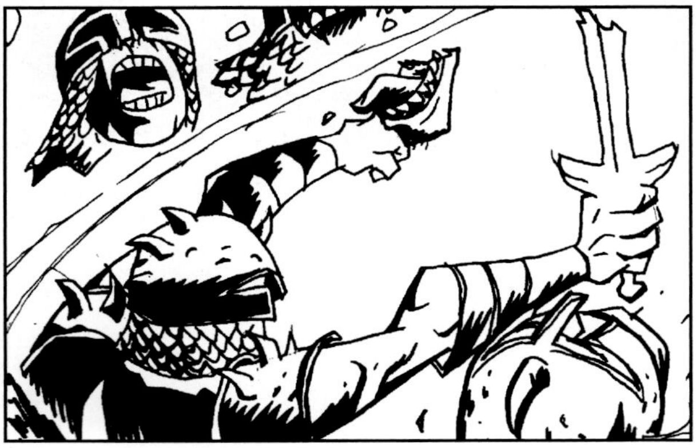

page 11, lineart detail

P1- Wide shot of Grimur's men charging at Lodbrok's crew in XFG.

OLD VIKING NARRATION: And what's more, the spell which hid Lodbrok's company died with her, setting Grimur's hordes at their throats.

P2- The shellshocked Lodbrok kneels in the snow, useless. His men attempt to defend him and are cut down.

LODBROK: Freydis.

VIKING ONE: Lodbrok, look out!

VIKING ONE: Hurk!

SFX: Shlop!

P3- Closer on the Vikings shouting to one another as they fight to survive.

VIKING TWO: We're dead men. Dead!

VIKING THREE: We could make for the sea caves.

VIKING FOUR: No time. Their second wave approaches.

P4- Lodbrok looks forlorn in FG as his companions fight fiercely in BG. More of Grimur's hordes approach in BG.

LODBROK: Freydis.

VIKING FOUR: Make peace with whatever cruel gods set us upon this path.

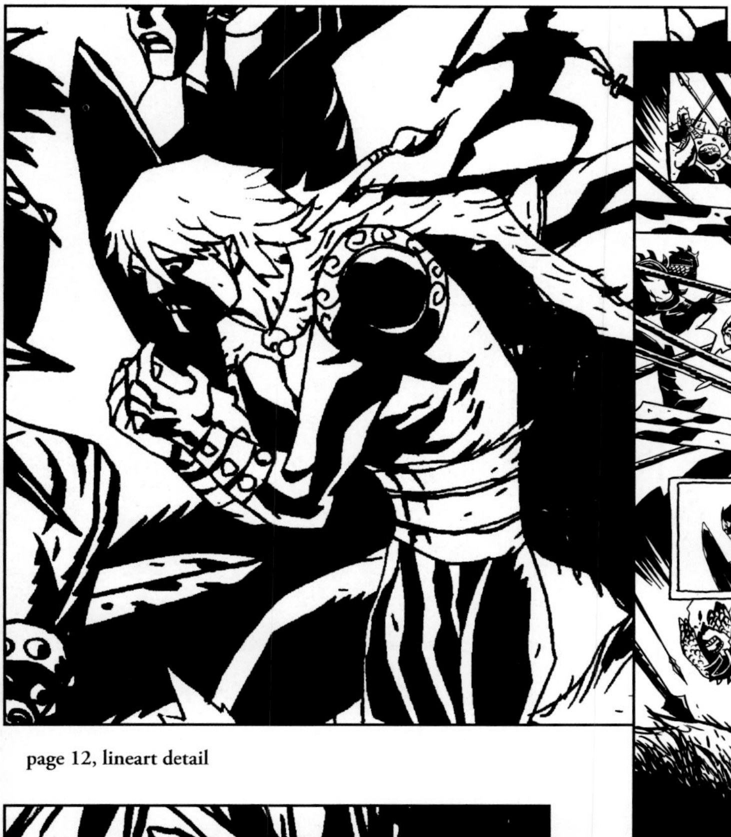

page 12, lineart detail

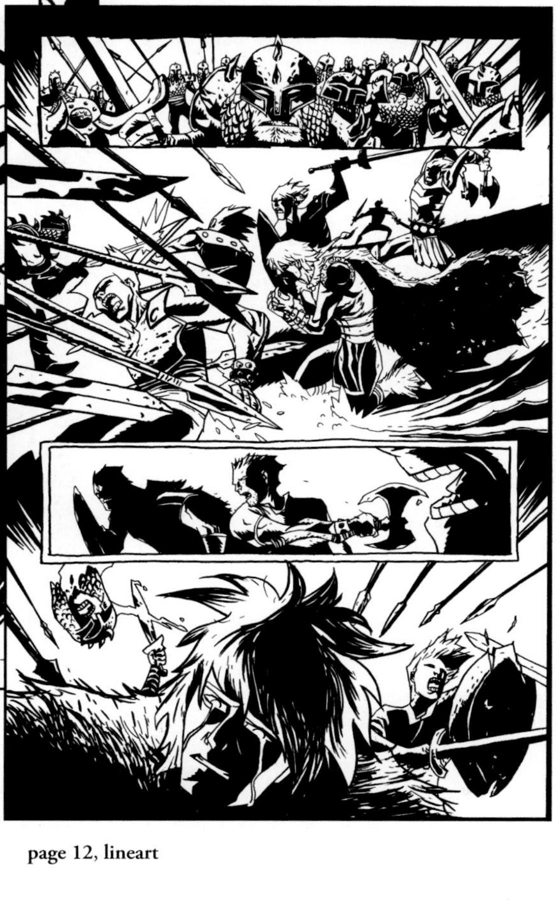

page 12, lineart

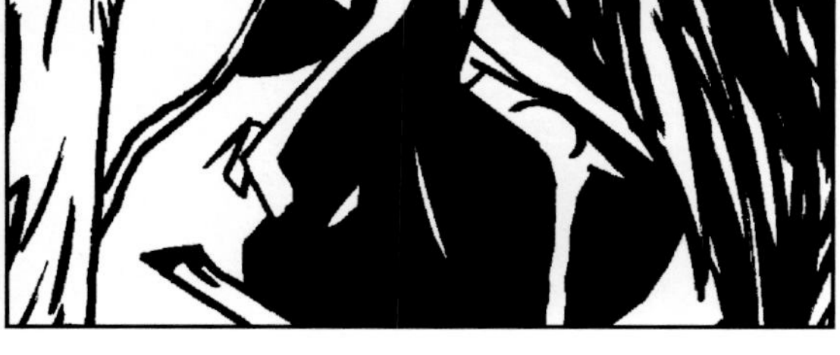

page 12, lineart detail

P1- Money shot of an ARMY of Darklings with swords and spears growing like appendages in place of their hands thundering over the snowy ridge.

OLD VIKING NARRATION: At that moment, as the last streaks of sunset bled away, the Black Captain's army took the field.

OLD VIKING NARRATION: They made no sound but for the crashing surf of their footfalls, their black swords held high, growing from their very bones.

P2- Closer on the two armies clashing. The Darklings are just whipping Grimur's army.

OLD VIKING NARRATION: They swarmed over Grimur's men like frenzied, soot-blackened hornets, never slowing even as the field became a mire of blood, mud and snow.

P3- Back atop the ziggurat, a bloodied, but smiling Lodbrok's brother looks out at the battle. Shocked Grimur rises to his feet, yanking the chain of the lava girl. She looks resentful, but resigned.

GRIMUR: Magic! They mean to use magic against me?

LODBROK'S BROTHER: My family brings your ruin, Grimur.

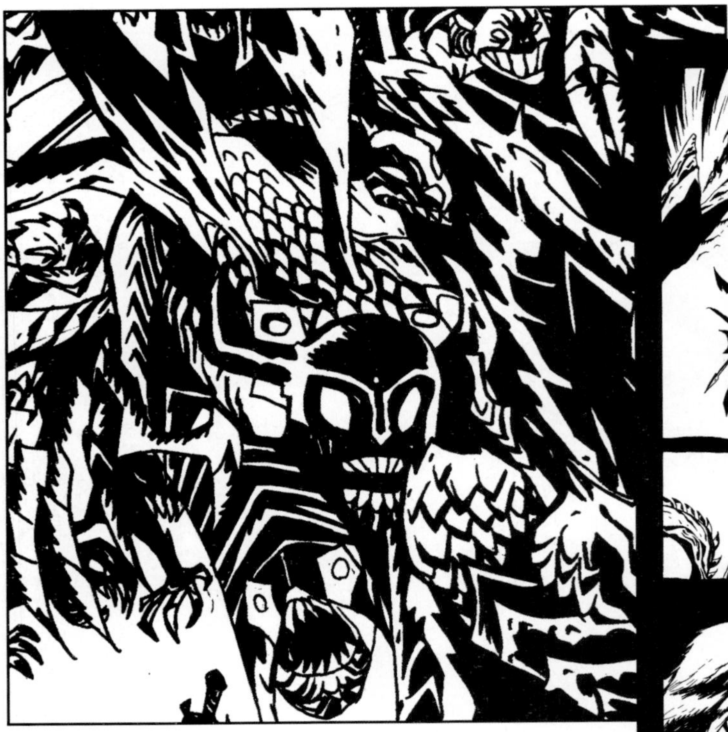

page 13, lineart detail

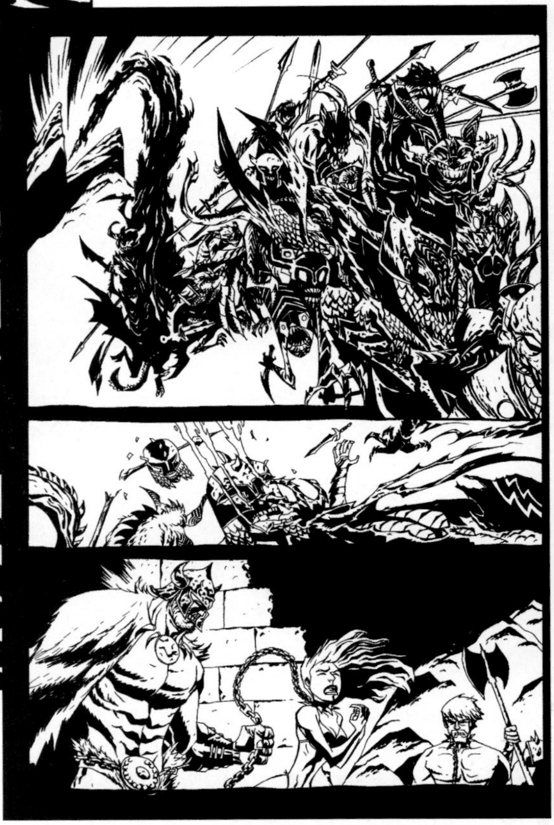

page 13, lineart

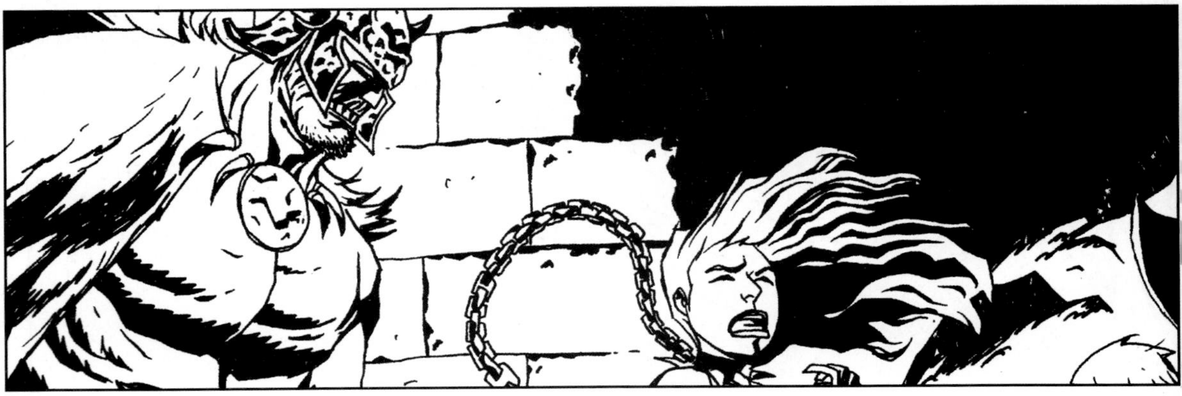

page 13, lineart detail

P1- CU mad Grimur, spittle flying.

GRIMUR: Not so! Not so!

GRIMUR: Grimur has magic of his own.

P2- Grimur unlocks the collar on the lava girl.

GRIMUR: Powerful magic.

P3- Lava girl spreads her arms and fiery wings seem to form around her.

P4- Now transformed into a lava-fiery dragon, she takes flight above the ziggurat.

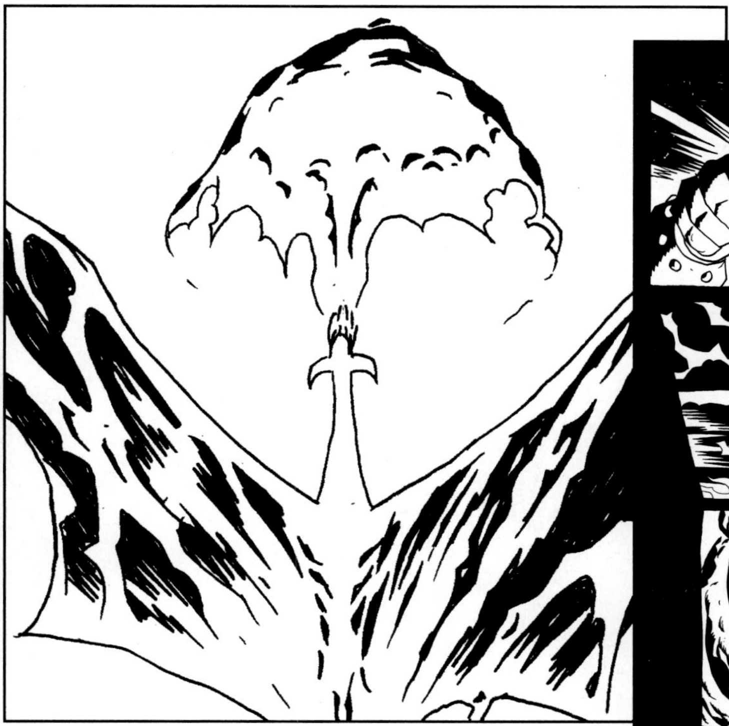

page 14, lineart detail

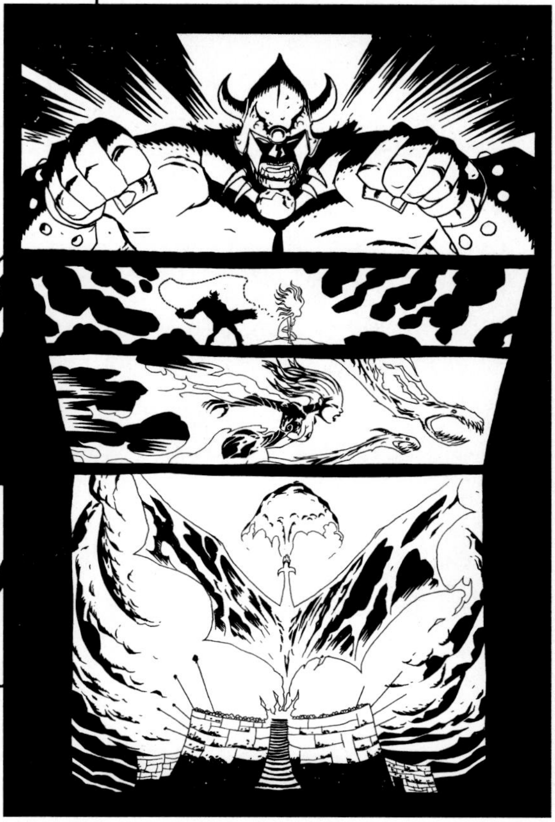

page 14, lineart

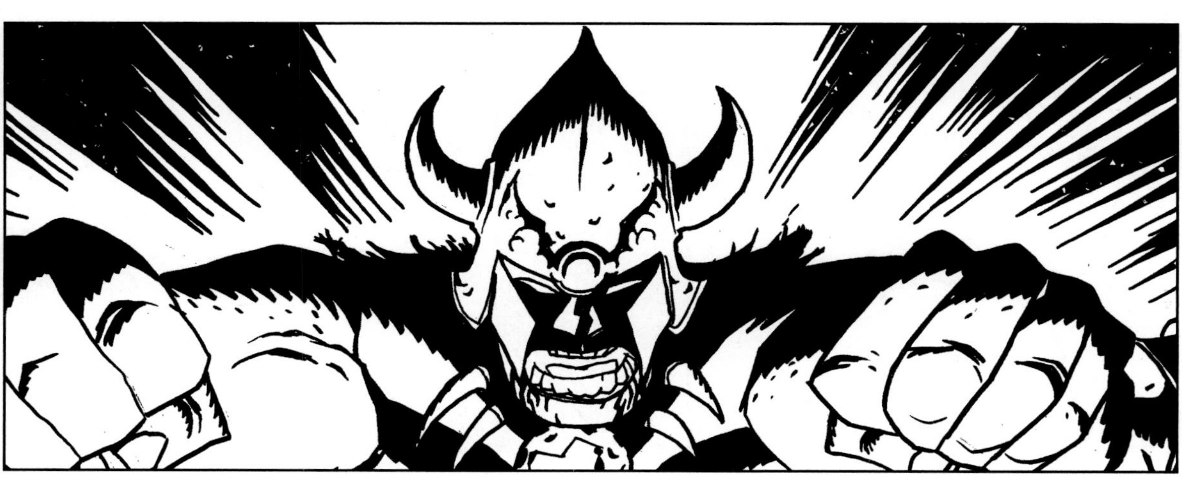

page 14, lineart detail

DARKNESS- LODBROK'S HAND, PAGE 15

P1- Wide panel. The dragon swoops down at the Black Captain and his army.

P2- CU BC looking up at the dragon. Unperturbed.

BLACK CAPTAIN: A dragon, is it?

P3- Big panel. BC gestures and a Darkness-borne dragon rises from the earth and roars skyward. This one should look more snake-like and solid than the fire dragon.

BLACK CAPTAIN: Brought one of my own.

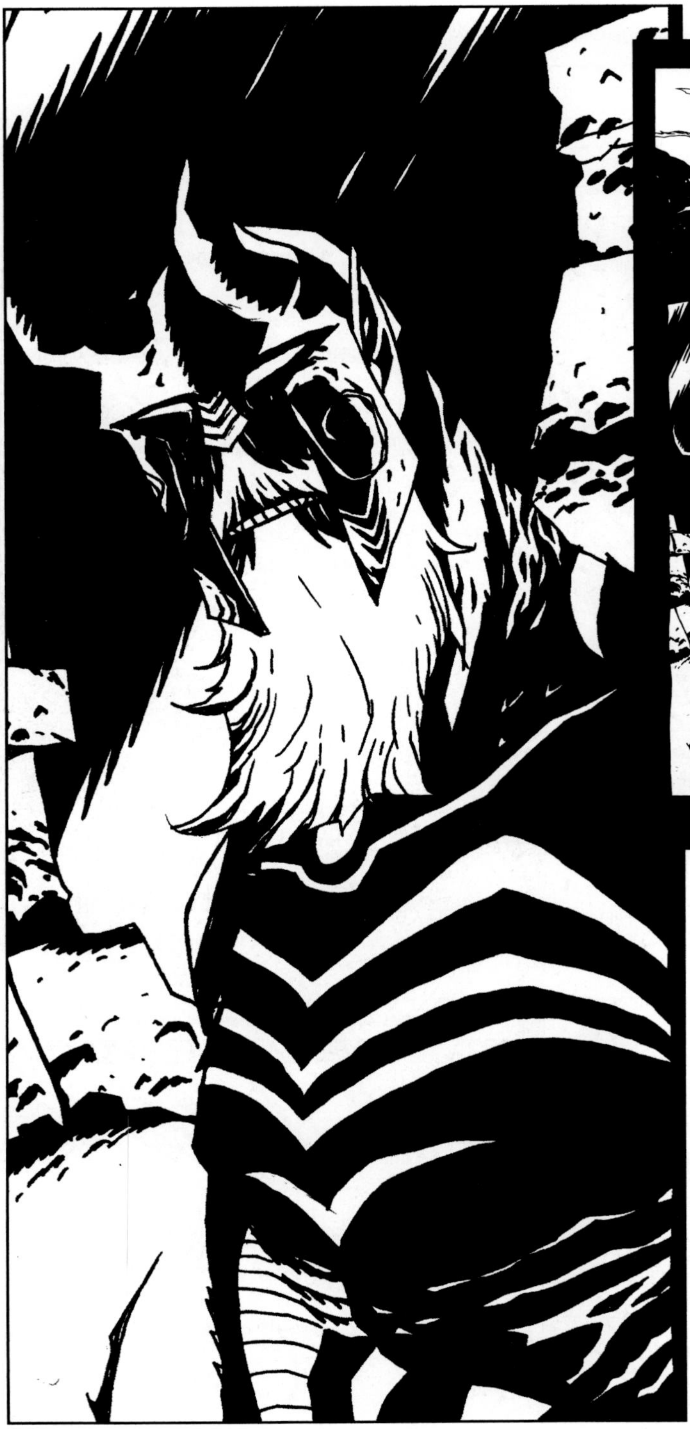

page 15, lineart detail

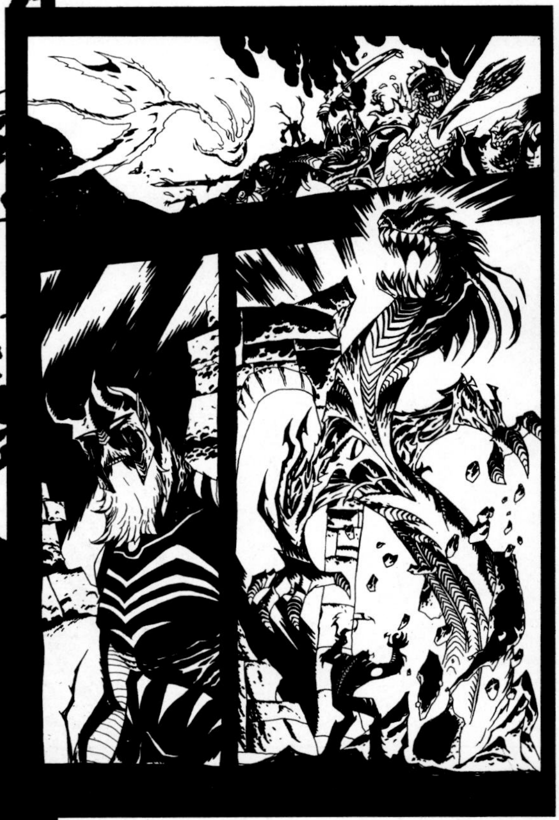

page 15, lineart

P1- Half splash of the dragons tearing at each other in the sky. Below, in either the FG or BG (depending on how you stage this, Mike), Lodbrok staggers amidst the carnage. A few battle still rage around him, but about 75% of the combatants are dead.

OLD VIKING NARRATION: And as the two beasts filled the sky with their flashing claws and flailing wings, Lodbrok staggered among the dead, shocked by the carnage wrought by his clever plan...

P2- Worms-eye, in FG we see a lock of Freydis' long hair spilling out across the bloody ground. Lodbrok staggers toward it, hands outstretched.

OLD VIKING NARRATION: Never noticing his wandering led him to within yards of the cackling king.

OLD VIKING NARRATION: Blinded by fury or sorrow, he did not come to rest until a bright spill of silvery hair fell across his path.

LODBROK: Freydis.

P3- Down-shot of Lodbrok holding Freydis' bloody form. She's been stabbed multiple times in abdomen and legs.

OLD VIKING NARRATION: It is said by the few survivors of this day that as the light faded from Freydis' eyes it seemed to leap to Lodbrok's...

P4- Wide, shallow panel. XCU Lodbrok's dead, angry eyes.

OLD VIKING NARRATION: But to then burn with a cold and colorless flame.

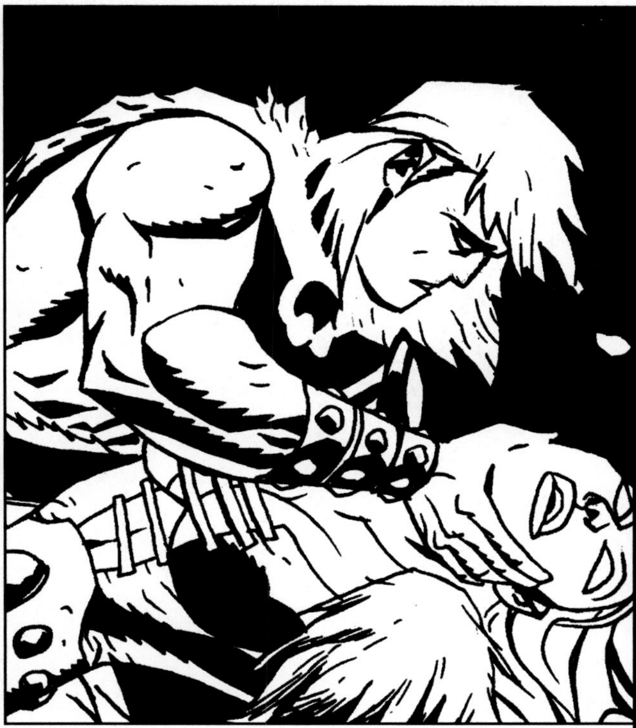

page 16, lineart detail

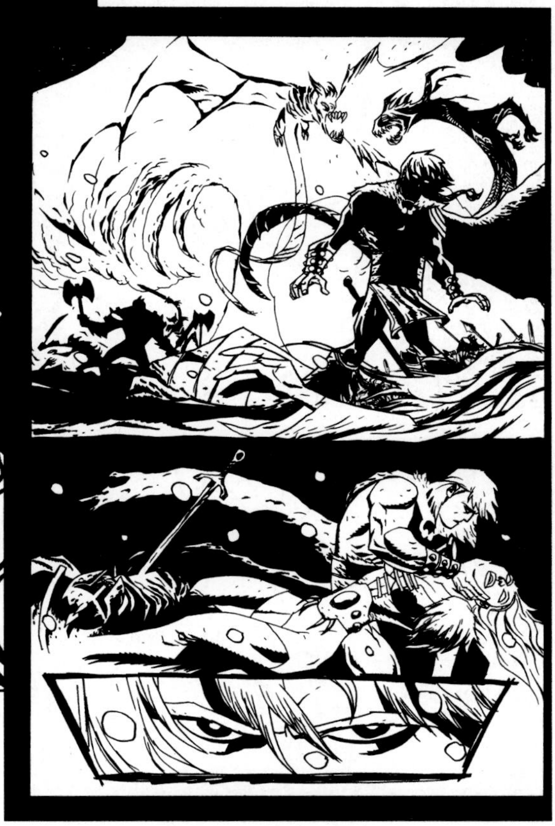

page 16, lineart

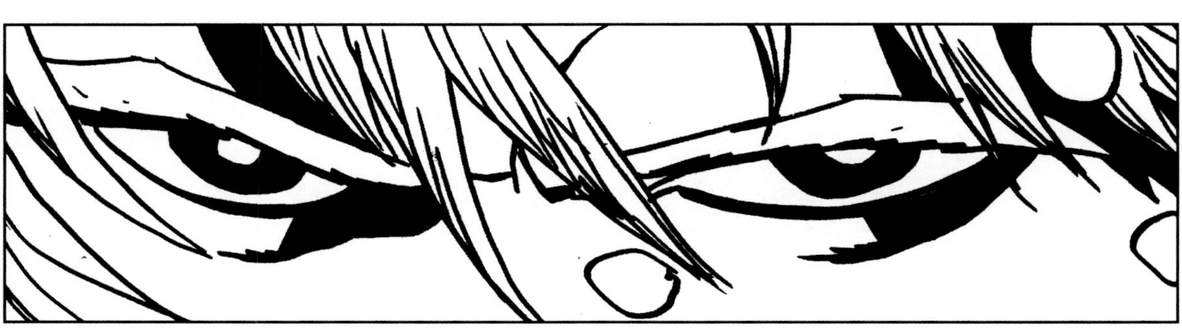

page 16, lineart detail

P1- Splash. Frazetta throws down his brush in defeat when he sees Mike Oeming show him how it's done these days. This is just an awesome shot of young Lodbrok gone all berserker. He's a whirling dervish of swords, chopping all in his way! Freydis' beautiful corpse lay at the pile of dead and wounded of his making.

OLD VIKING NARRATION: He dropped his sister's limp form and began to twist and thrash, blades in each hand, hacking at friend and foe alike.

OLD VIKING NARRATION: His former cowardice mere kindling for the fiery hatred for all things living that now consumed him.

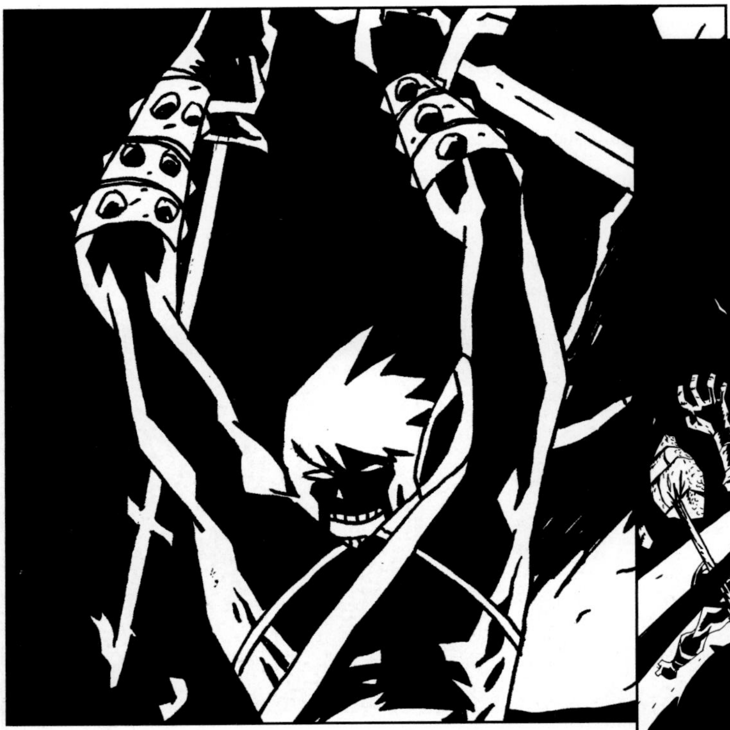

page 17, lineart detail

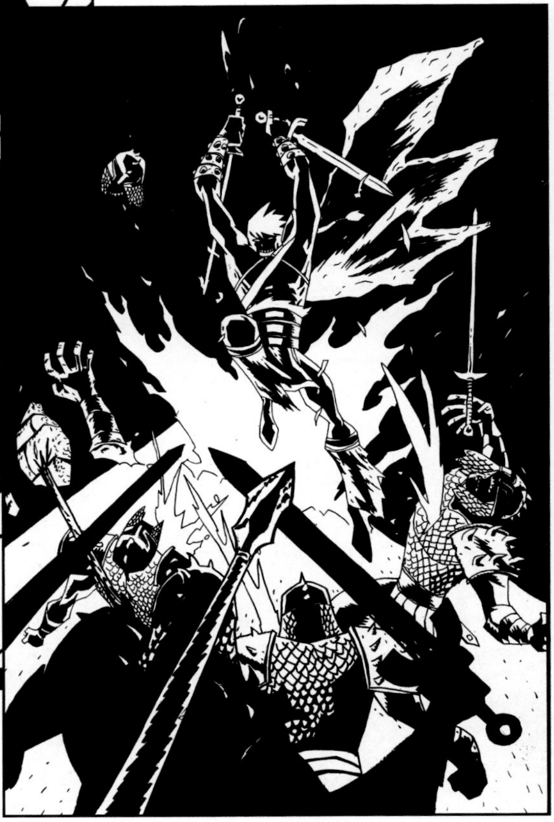

page 17, lineart

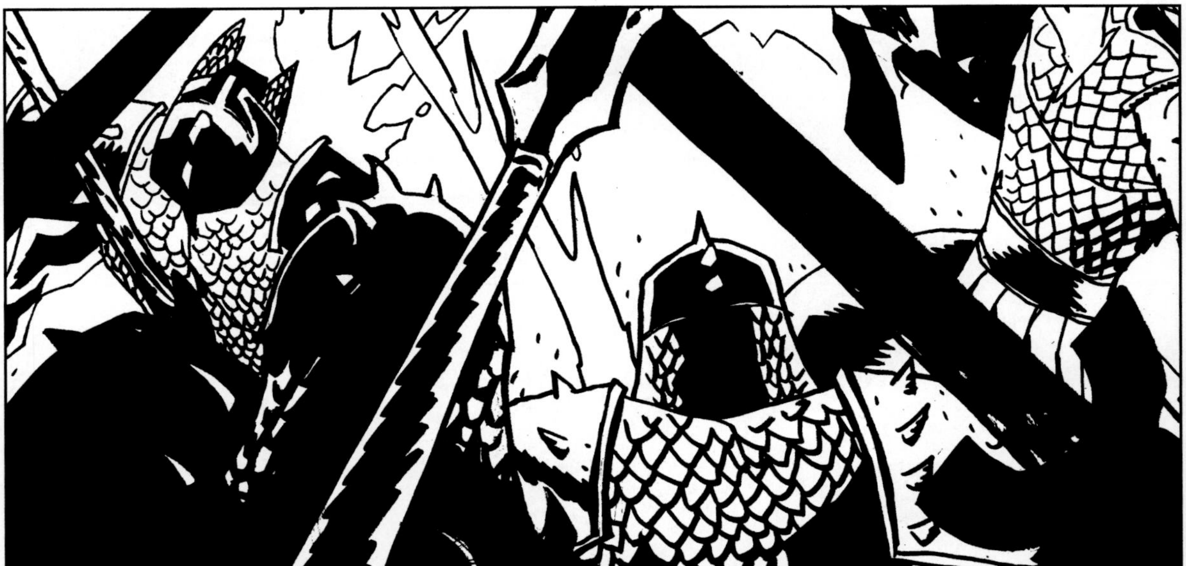

page 17, lineart detail

P1- Blood coated Lodbrok now stands at the foot of the ziggurat and looks up at Grimur cowering at top step (maybe 20 feet above).

OLD VIKING NARRATION: And of all those who lived he hated none more than the Mad King, Grimur.

P2- Lodbrok ascends the top step and begins to march toward Grimur in FG holding a dagger to Lodbrok's brother's throat (he's still bound).

GRIMUR: Stay your hand or your brother dies!

P3- With one deft thrust Lodbrok guts Grimur who drops his dagger, unprepared for the swiftness of Lodbrok's attack.

OLD VIKING NARRATION: But Lodbrok could not hear him. He was beyond reason at that time. Beyond emotion.

OLD VIKING NARRATION: He became nothing more or less than the movements of his limbs, the flashing of his blades.

P4- Lodbrok's brother in FG looks at his baby brother walking away from him and toward edge of steps.

OLD VIKING NARRATION: He belonged to death in that moment. He was her finest tool.

LODBROK'S BROTHER: Lodbrok? My- my brother?

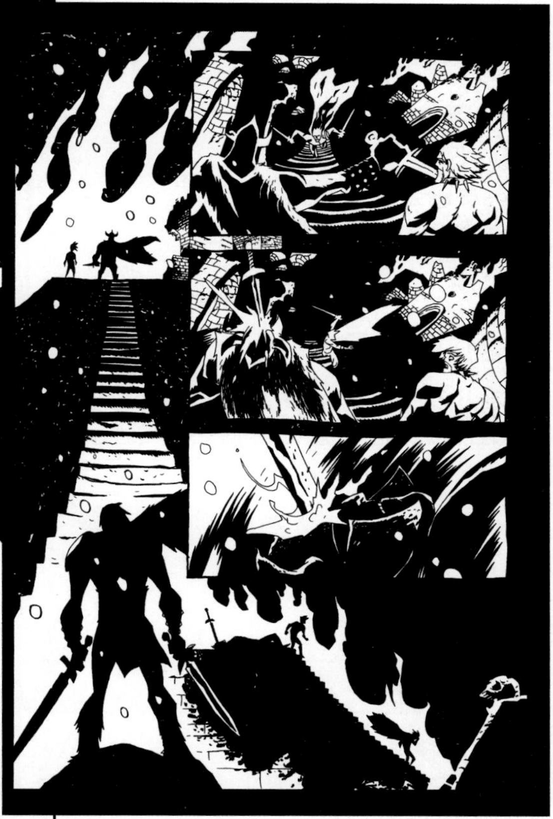

page 18, lineart

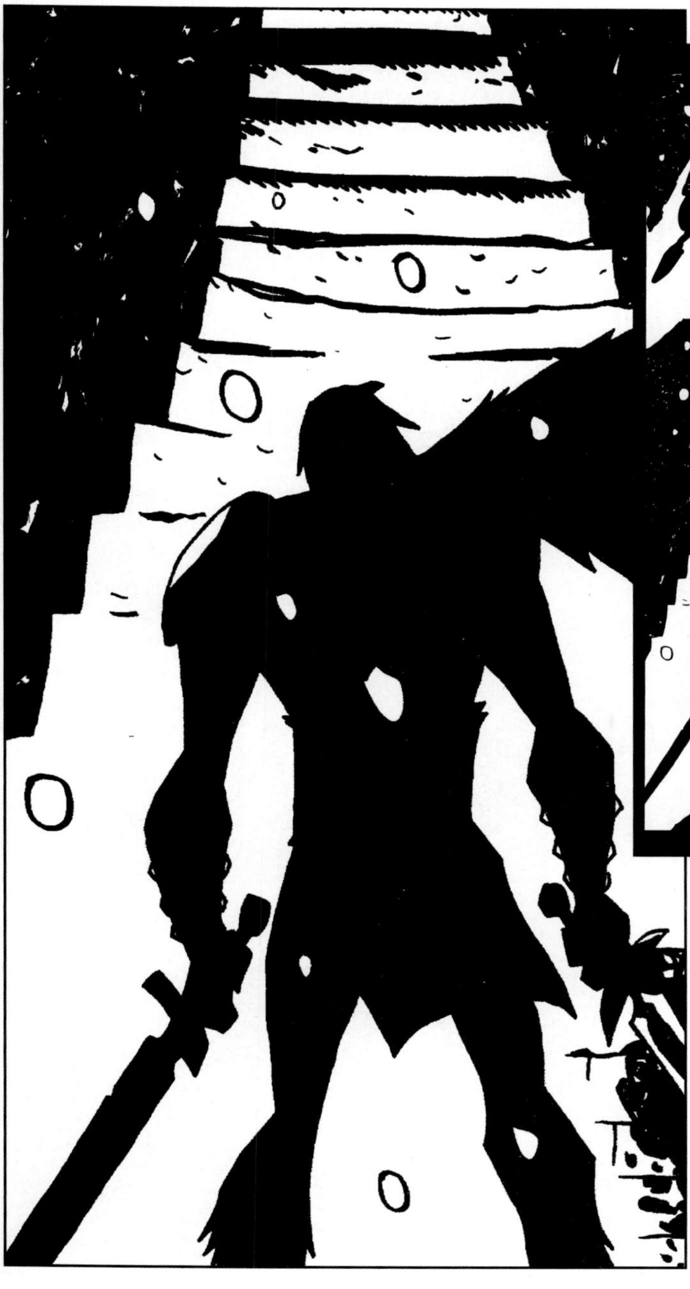

page 18, lineart detail

DARKNESS- LODBROK'S HAND, PAGE 19

P1- Nice shot of the fire dragon breaking away from the Darkness dragon and soaring away.

OLD VIKING NARRATION: And with Grimur's death the dragon he enslaved gave a scream of both anger and relief before soaring away from the battlefield.

P2- Lodbrok staggers down the steps, shellshocked. Few are left alive, and none unwounded. We see BC in FG looking out over his handiwork with some satisfaction.

BLACK CAPTAIN: War isn't what you thought it would be, is it, boy? Neither is victory.

BLACK CAPTAIN: The songs your fathers sing in the great halls aren't meant to burnish their valor, but to paint over their shame.

P3- CU tired, sad Lodbrok.

LODBROK: Let us be done.

LODBROK: Though I have already lost more than I thought I owned, I stand ready to pay your price.

P4- From above as Lodbrok falls to his knees in front of Black Captain.

LODBROK: I pledge to be your crewman.

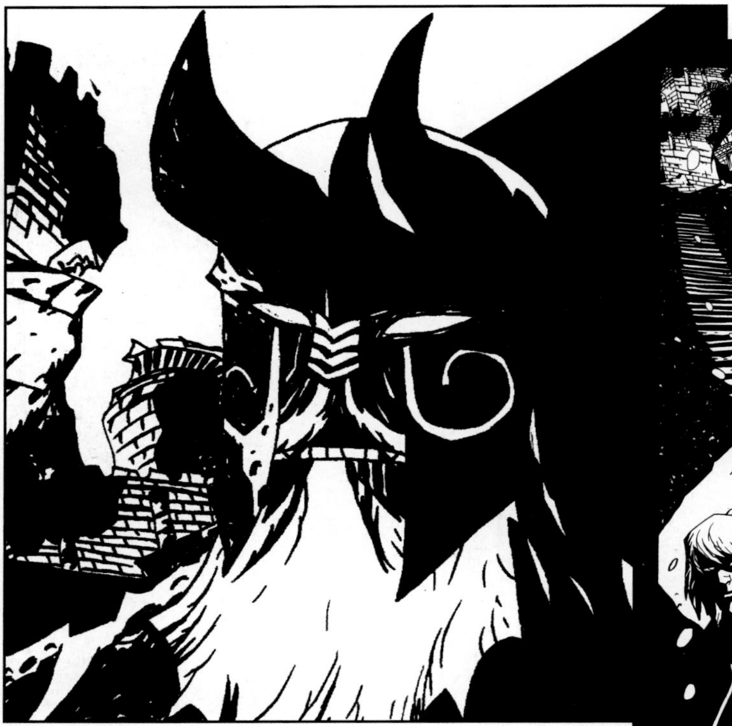

page 19, lineart detail

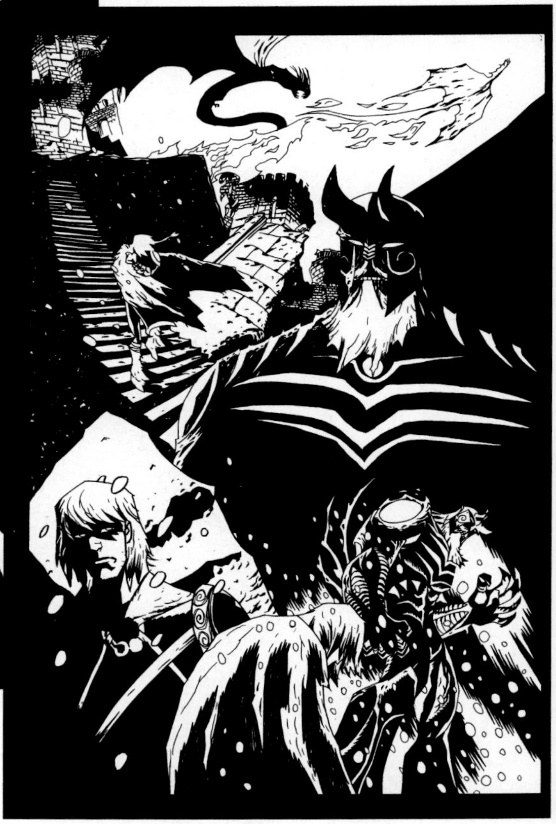

page 19, lineart

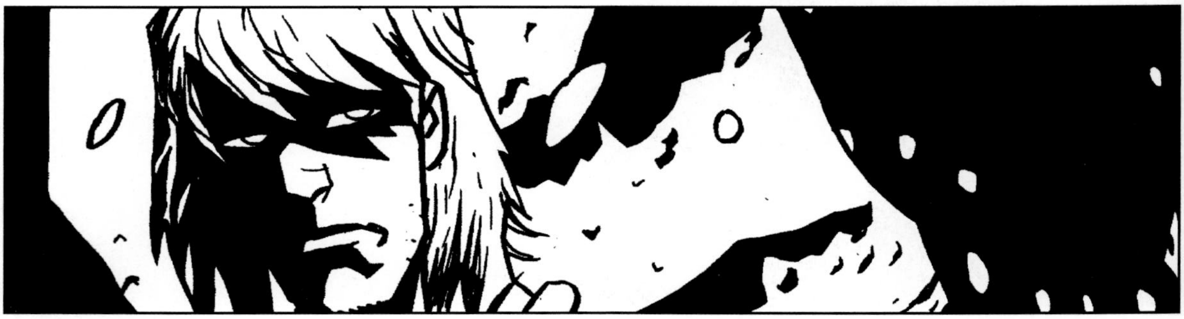

page 19, lineart detail

DARKNESS- LODBROK'S HAND, PAGE 20

P1- Upshot of BC looking down at us/Lodbrok.

OLD VIKING NARRATION: At that a smothered, gravelly rasp that could have been a laugh rose from the Black Captain's throat.

BLACK CAPTAIN: You? My crewman?

BLACK CAPTAIN: You forget our bargain. I said I would take the bravest among you.

P2- Wide shot. BC in BG panel left gestures to Freydis' body in XFG.

BLACK CAPTAIN: And there she lies.

P3- Big panel. Freydis' limp form is lifted by several Darklings. Her many wounds are now covered by Darkness formed bandages.

OLD VIKING NARRATION: Freydis rose on the shoulders of the Captain's oarsmen, her many wounds bound now by black silken bands that seemed to spin out of the night air itself.

P4- Horizontal sliver of a panel. Lodbrok reacts in horror.

LODBROK: No. Not her.

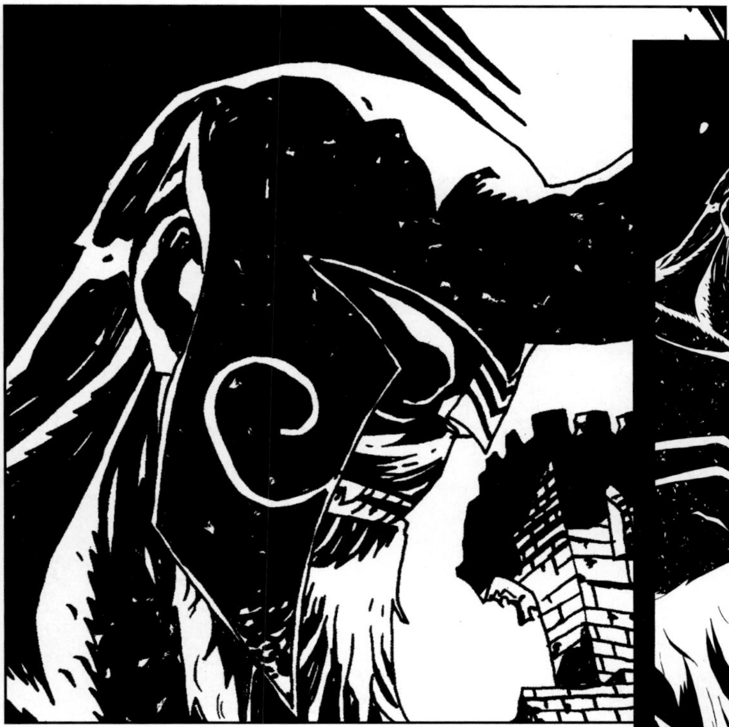

page 20, lineart detail

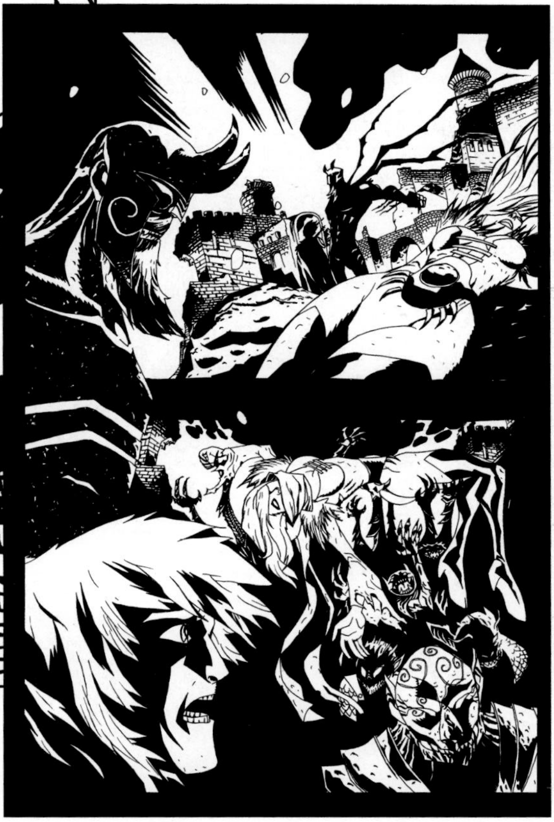

page 20, lineart

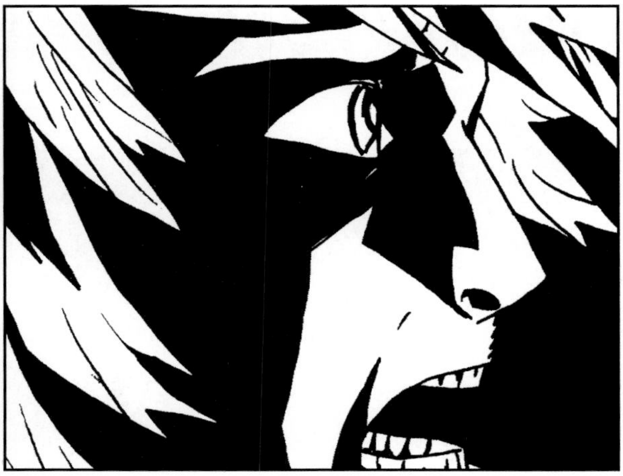

page 20, lineart detail

P1- Wide panel. The Darklings hold Freydis aloft now behind the Black Captain who faces an enraged Lodbrok, now brandishing his swords again.

BLACK CAPTAIN: She yet lives, and under my care will soon recover.

BLACK CAPTAIN: I take it you mean to fight for her freedom.

LODBROK: Freydis!

P2- Nice shot of BC easily parrying Lodbrok's attack with his black blade.

BLACK CAPTAIN: That's it, boy. But it takes more than rage to best a cursed thing like myself.

P3- More fighting. Lodbrok can't land a shot.

LODBROK: You'll never take her. I'll hunt you forever!

BLACK CAPTAIN: I admire that, child, I really do.

P4- BC lops off Lodbrok's sword hand (right, I suppose) at the wrist. Maybe Lodbrok in XFG so we see only his arm & torso?

BLACK CAPTAIN: And so, I spare you a shred of honor.

SFX: Throk!

P5- CU Lodbrok grasping his bloody stump in horror.

BLACK CAPTAIN OP: Now none can say you failed to give your full measure.

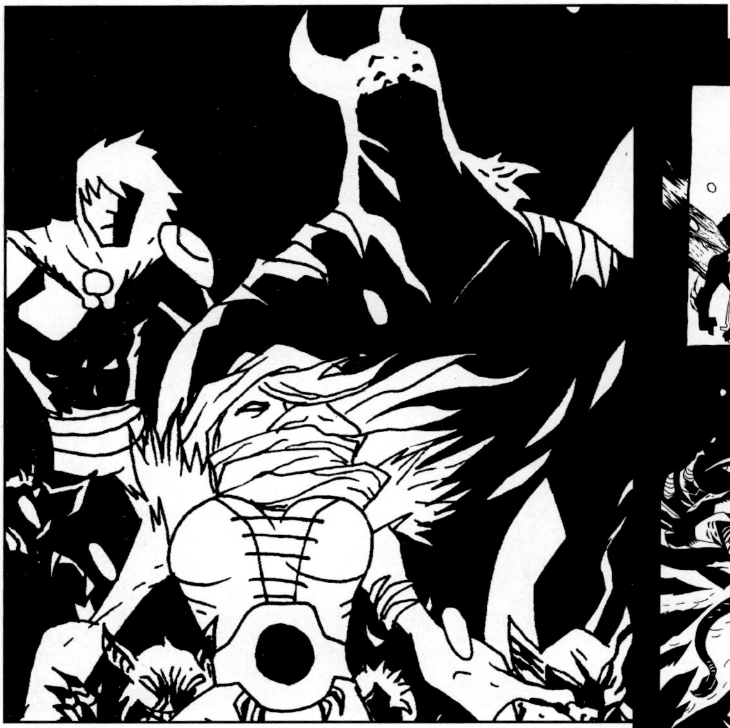

page 21, lineart detail

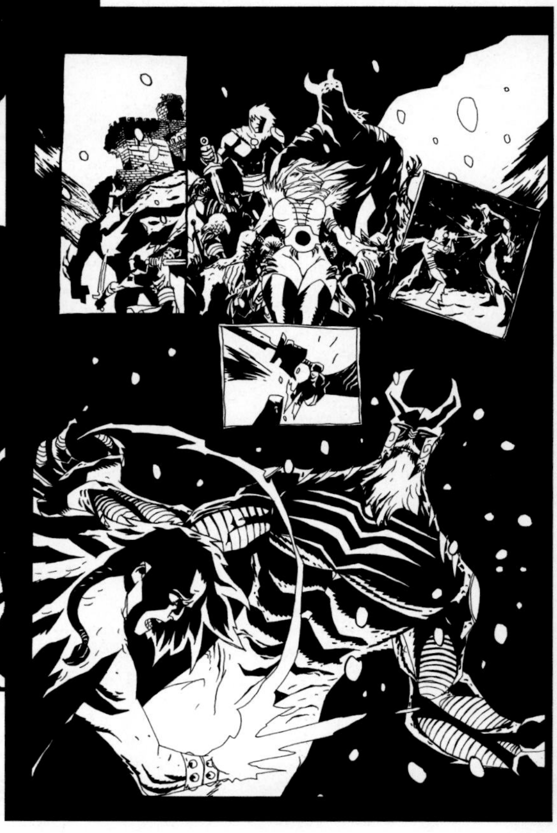

page 21, lineart

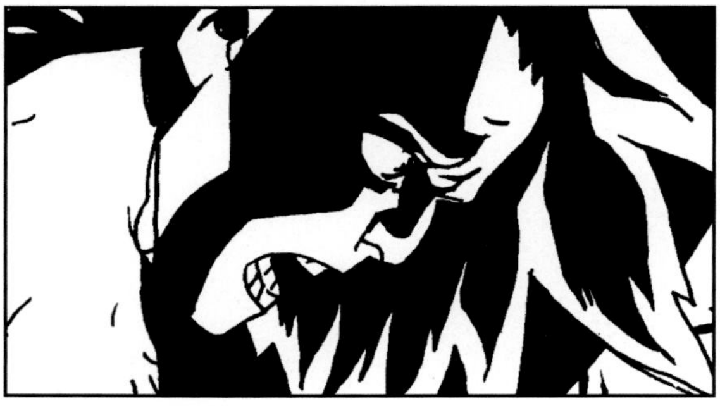

page 21, lineart detail

P1- Wide shot of the scene. BC walks away with Freydis over his shoulder and Darklings following. Lodbrok on his knees in battlefield. You could pan out and really go to town on the folly of war here, or keep it tighter and focus on Lodbrok's anguish.

OLD VIKING NARRATION: The Black Captain strode from the field, Freydis over his shoulder, while Lodbrok's screams of pain and anger chased after them into the night.

P2- Cut back to our original scene, basically a repeat of Page One- panel one, but now the young sailors stand mouth agape.

OLD VIKING: And now you know, lads, how our brave chieftain lost his sword hand.

OLD VIKING : And you also know now why he stands in the prow both day and night hoping to spy that mysterious black ship...

P3- Wide shot of the ship looking tiny on the wide open sea as dawn begins to break.

OLD VIKING NARRATION: And her even blacker captain.

TITLE: LODBROK'S HAND
Story: Phil Hester
Art: Mike Oeming
Colors: Val Staples
Letters: Troy Peteri
Edited by Rob Levin

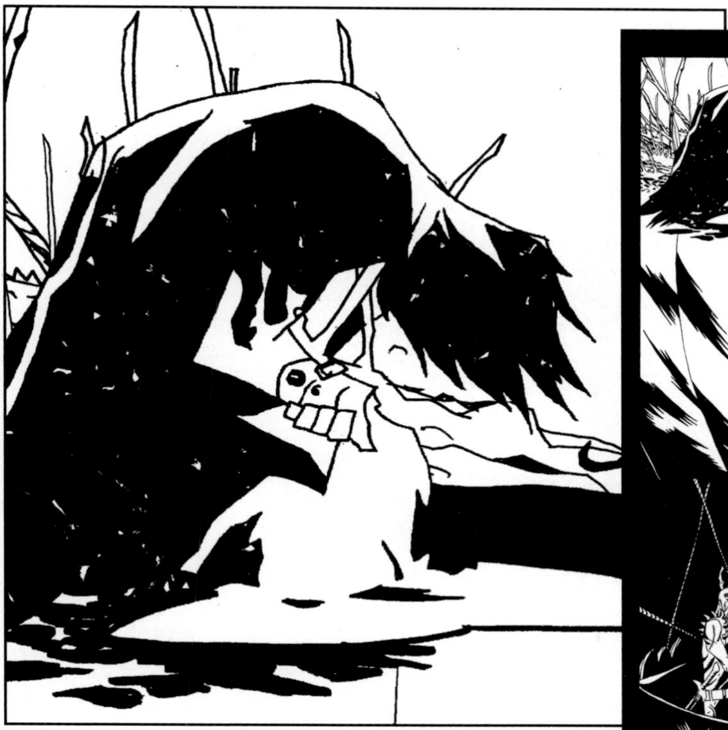

page 22, lineart detail

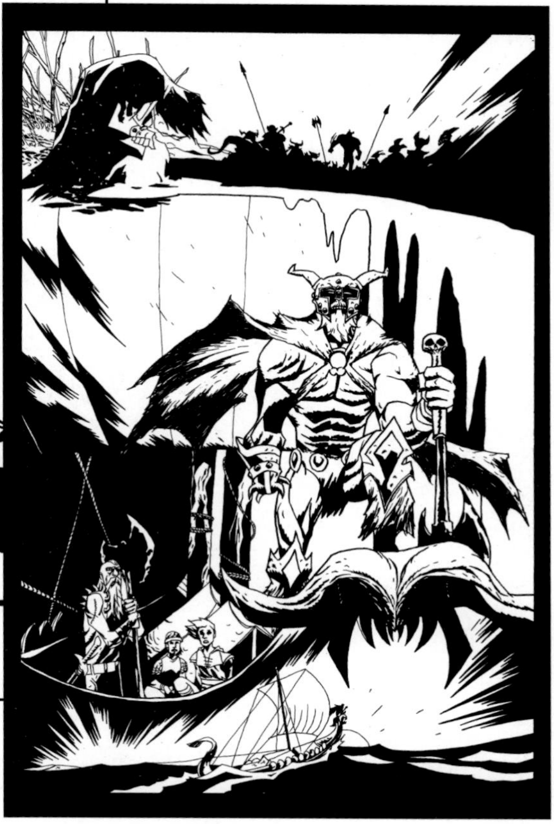

page 22, lineart

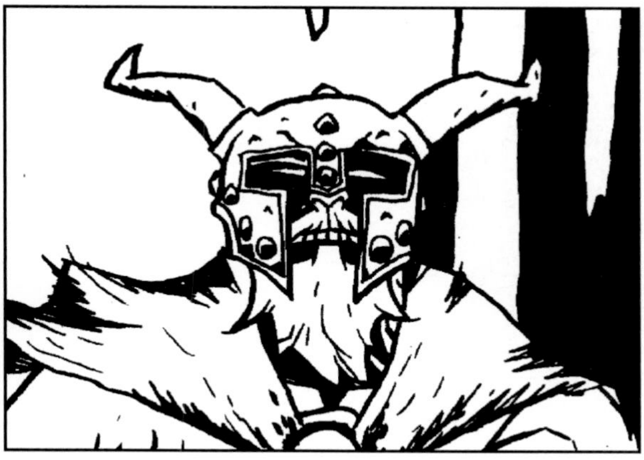

page 22, lineart detail

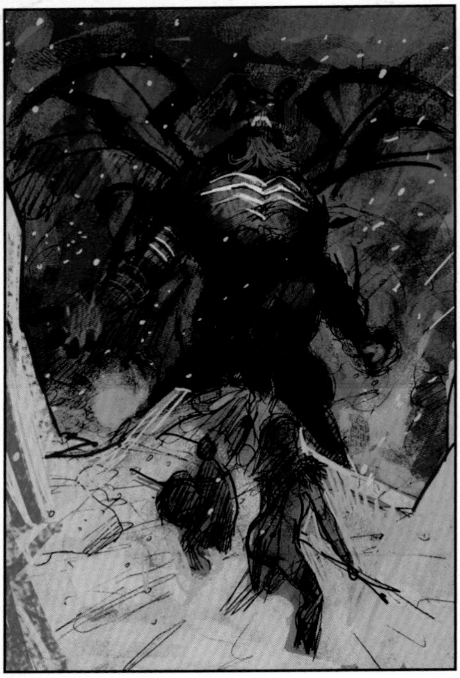

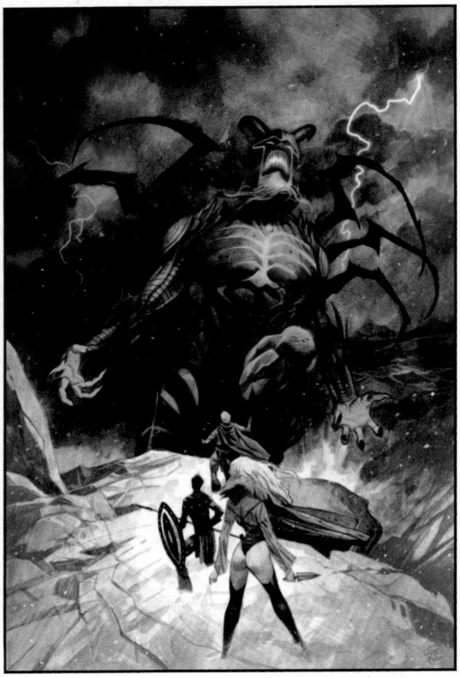

"Lodbrok's Hand"
Massimo Carnevale
left: color rough and
Final colors

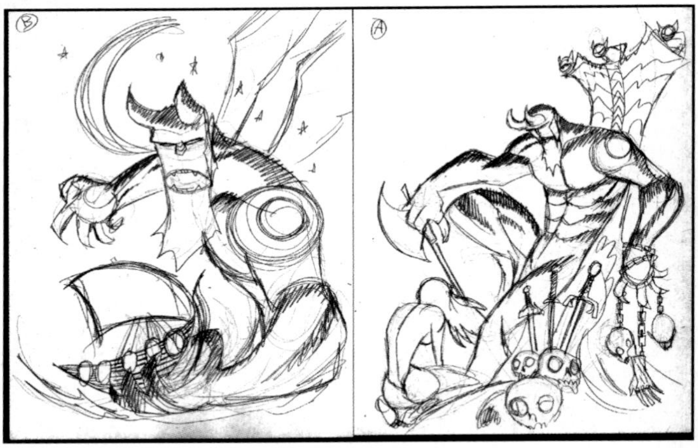

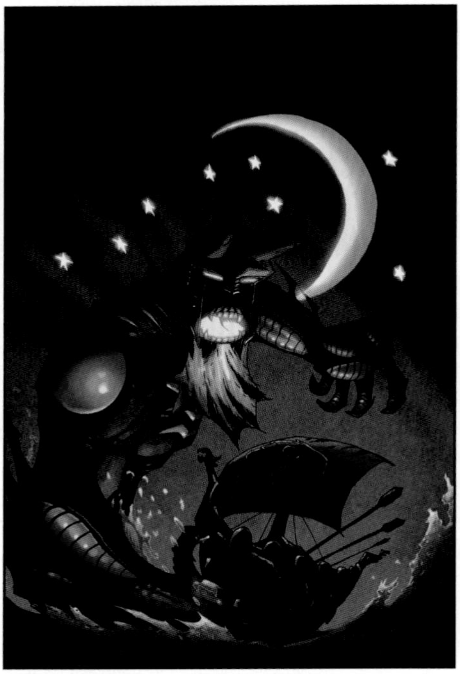

"Lodbrok's Hand"
Michael Avon Oeming
above: cover thumbnails
right: Final colors with **Val Staples**

"Lodbrok's Hand"
Michael Avon Oeming
below: character concept art

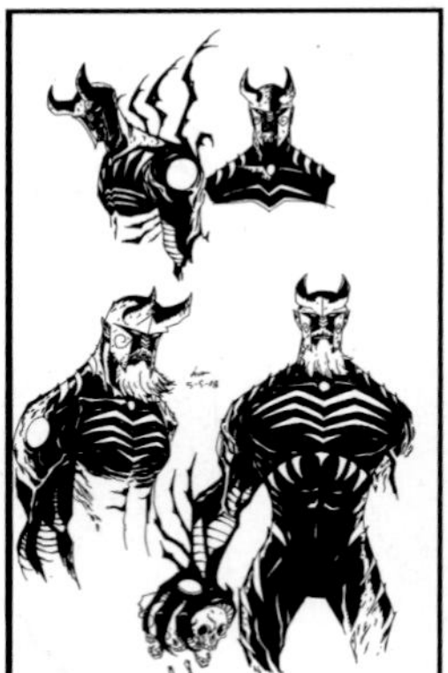

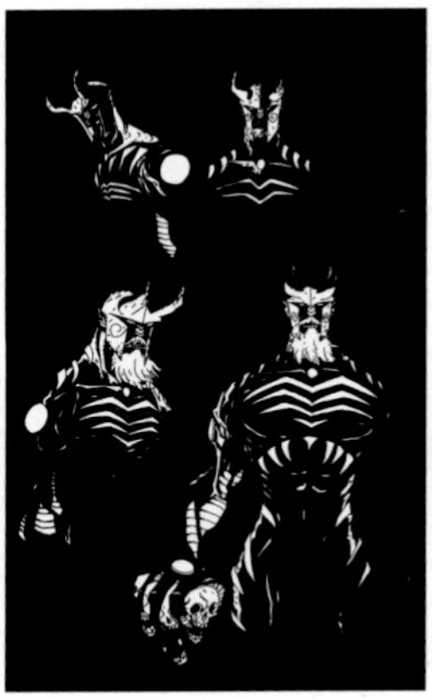

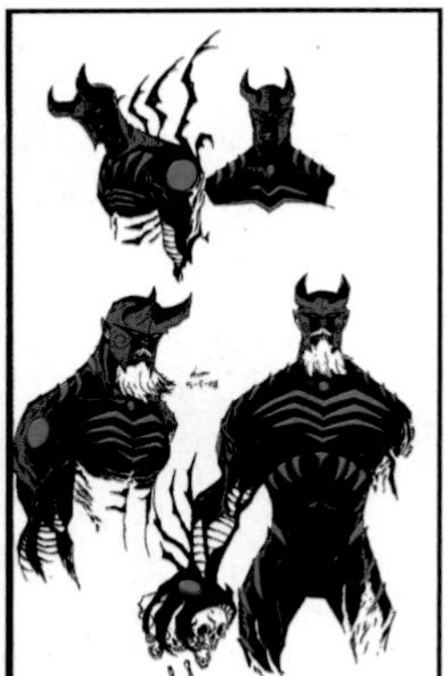

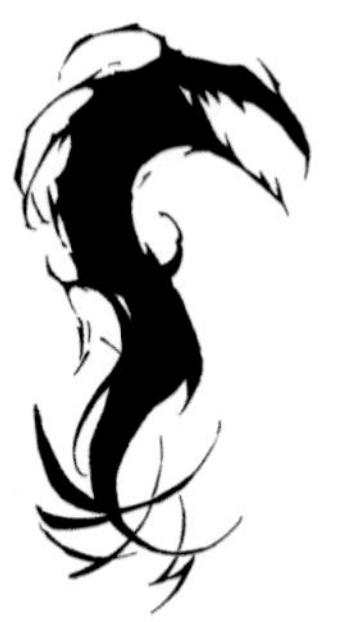

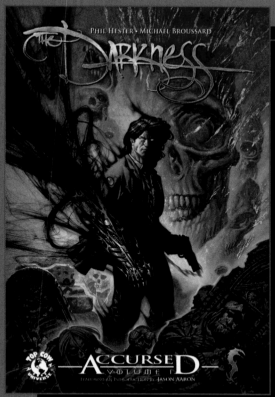
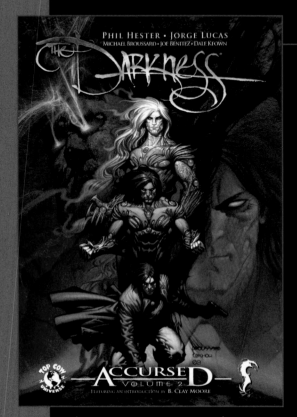

Premium collected editions

ENNIS • WOHL • CONEY • LOBDELL • JENKINS
SILVESTRI • BENITEZ • LANSANG • TAN • FINCH • KEOWN
THE DARKNESS
COMPENDIUM
VOLUME 1

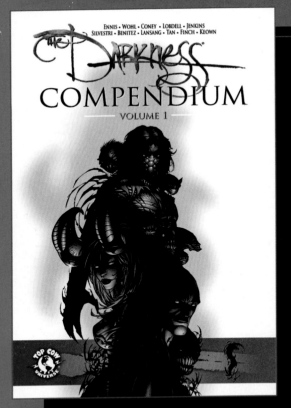

The Darkness

Compendium vol.1

written by:
Garth Ennis, Paul Jenkins, Scott Lobdell
pencils by:
Marc Silvestri, Joe Benitez and more!

On his 21st birthday, the awesome and terrible powers of the Darkness awaken within Jackie Estacado, a mafia hitman for the Franchetti crime family. There's nothing like going back to the beginning and reading it all over again-- issues #1-40, plus the complete run of the *Tales of the Darkness* series collected into one trade paperback. See how the Darkness first appeared and threw Jackie into the chaotic world of the supernatural. Get the first appearances of The Magdalena and more!

SC (ISBN 13: 978-1-58240-643-5) $59.99
HC (ISBN 13: 978-1-58240-992-7) $99.99

J. MICHAEL STRACZYNSKI'S
RISING STARS
COMPENDIUM
VOLUME 1

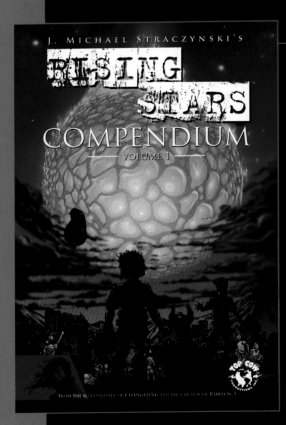

Rising Stars

Compendium vol.1

written by:
J. Michael Straczynski

pencils by:
Keu Cha, Ken Lashley
Gary Frank, Brent Anderson
and more!

The *Rising Stars* Compendium Edition collects the entire saga of the Pederson Specials, including the entire original series written by series creator **J. Michael Straczynski**, (*Supreme Power/Midnight Nation*) as well as the three limited series Bright, Voices of the Dead and Untouchable written by **Fiona Avery**, (*Amazing Fantasy/No Honor*).

Collects *Rising Stars* issues #0, #1/2, #1-24, Prelude, the short story "Initiations", the limited series *Bright* issues #1-3, *Voices of the Dead* issues #1-6 and *Untouchable* issues #1-5

SC (ISBN 13: 978-1-58240-802-6) $59.99
HC (ISBN 13: 978-1-58240-032-1) $99.99

Read more *Witchblade* in these trade paperback collections.

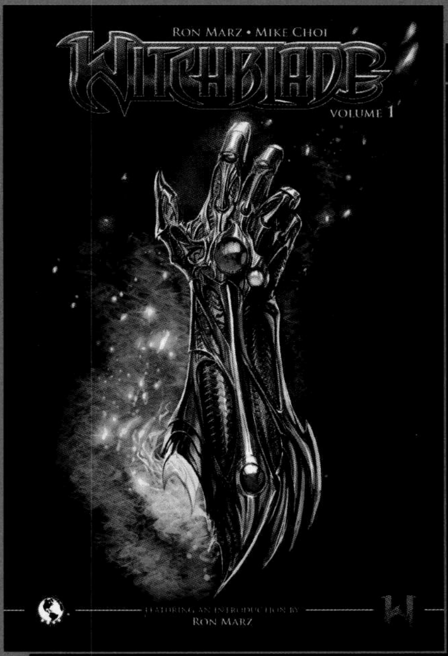

RON MARZ • MIKE CHOI
WITCHBLADE
VOLUME 1
FEATURING AN INTRODUCTION BY
RON MARZ

Witchblade

volume 1 - volume 5

written by:
Ron Marz
pencils by:
Mike Choi, Stephen Sadowski, Keu Cha, Chris Bachalo, Stjepan Sejic and more!

Get in on the ground floor of Top Cow's flagship title with these affordable trade paperback collections from Ron Marz's series-redefining run on Witchblade! Each volume collects a key story arc in the continuing adventures of Sara Pezzini and the Witchblade.

volume 1
collects issues #80-#85
(ISBN: 978-1-58240-906-1) $9.99

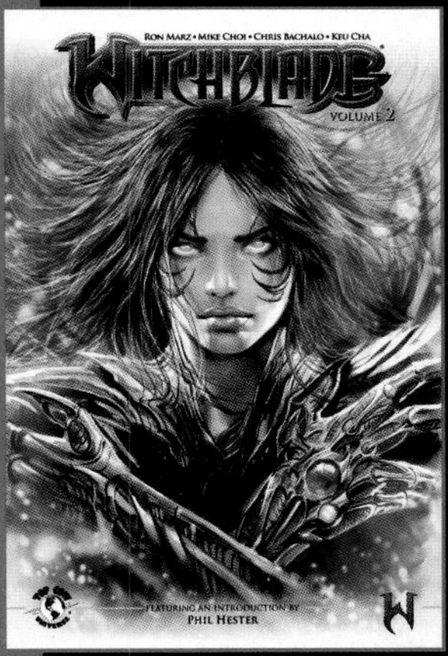

RON MARZ • MIKE CHOI • CHRIS BACHALO • KEU CHA
WITCHBLADE
VOLUME 2
FEATURING AN INTRODUCTION BY
PHIL HESTER

volume 2
collects issues #86-#92
(ISBN: 978-1-58240-886-6)
U.S.D. $14.99

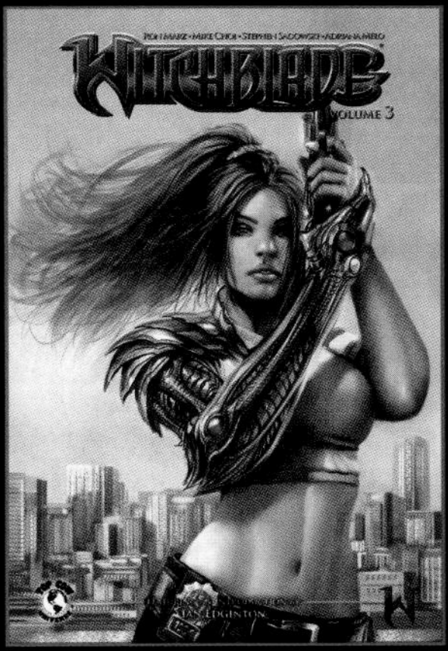

WITCHBLADE
VOLUME 3

volume 3
collects issues #93-#100
(ISBN: 978-1-58240-887-3)
U.S.D. $14.99

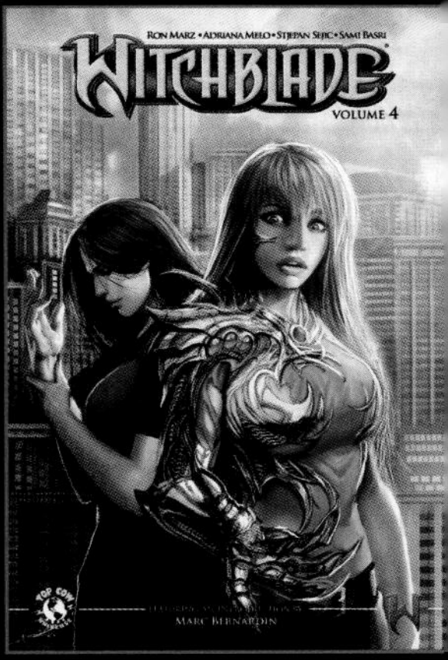

RON MARZ • ADRIANA MELO • STJEPAN SEJIC • SAMI BASRI
WITCHBLADE
VOLUME 4
MARC BERNARDIN

volume 4
collects issues #101-10
(ISBN: 978-1-58240-898-9
U.S.D. $17.99

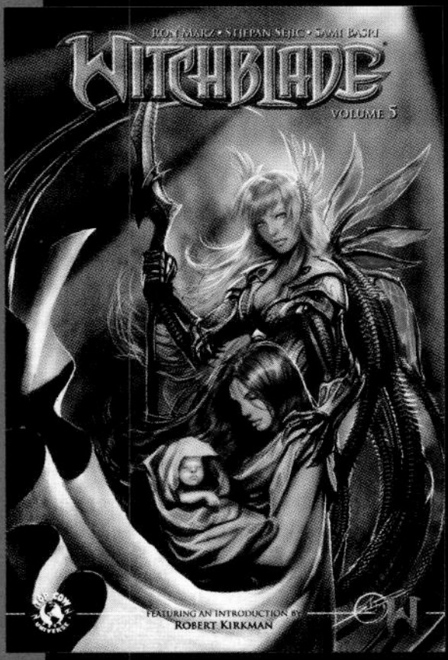

RON MARZ • STJEPAN SEJIC • SAMI BASRI
WITCHBLADE
VOLUME 5
FEATURING AN INTRODUCTION BY
ROBERT KIRKMAN

volume 5
collects issues #110-115,
First Born issues #1-3
(ISBN: 978-1-58240-899-6)
U.S.D. $17.99

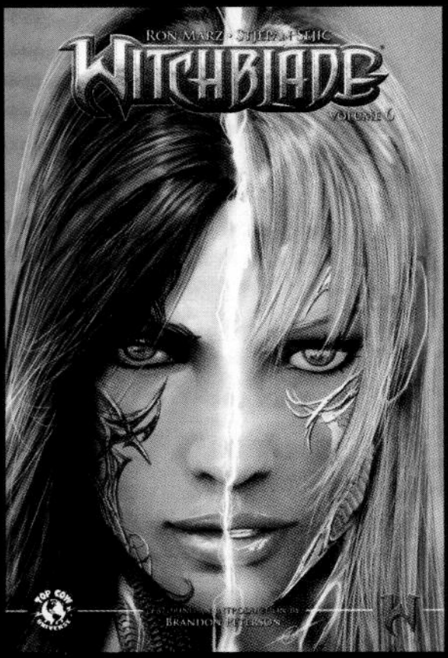

WITCHBLADE

volume 6
collects issues #116-#120
(ISBN: 978-1-60706-041-3)
U.S.D. $14.99

New York City Police De Sara Pezzini is the bea the Witchblade, a myst artifact that takes the form of a and powerful gauntlet. Now Sara try to control the Witchblade and its secrets, even as she invest the city's strangest, most superr crimes.

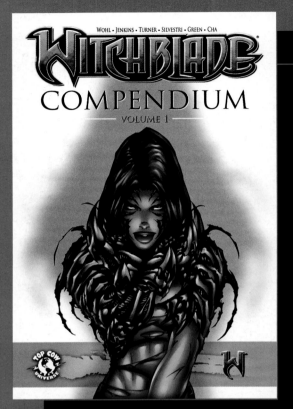

Witchblade
Compendium vol.1

written by:
David Wohl, Christina Z.,
Paul Jenkins
pencils by:
Michael Turner, Randy Green
Keu Cha and more!

From the hit live-action television series to the current Japanese anime, *Witchblade* has been Top Cow's flagship title for over a decade. There's nothing like going back to the beginning and reading it all over again. This massive collection houses issues #1-50 in a single edition for the first time. See how the Witchblade chose Sara and threw her into the chaotic world of the supernatural. Get the first appearances of Sara Pezzini, Ian Nottingham, Kenneth Irons and Jackie Estacado in one handy tome!

SC (ISBN 13: 978-1-58240-634-3) $59.99
HC (ISBN 13: 978-1-58240-798-2) $99.99

Witchblade
Compendium vol.2

written by:
David Wohl, Christina Z.,
Paul Jenkins and Ron Marz
pencils by:
Michael Turner, Randy Green
Keu Cha, Mike Choi and more!

From the "Death Pool" story arc featuring the death of a major Witchblade character to heading up the NYPD's Special Cases Unit, Witchblade bearer Sara Pezzini and her new partner Patrick Gleason find themselves with more questions than answers as their investigations lead them from haunted museums, dark alleys and forgotten tunnels beneath New York City. Meanwhile, the enigmatic Curator leaves a trails of clues for Sara, ultimately leading her to the explosive origin of the Witchblade itself!

Collects Witchblade issues #51-100

SC (ISBN 13: 978-1-58240-731-9) $59.99
HC (ISBN 13: 978-1-58240-960-3) $99.99